Feminist Interpretation

FEMINIST INTERPRETATION
The Bible in Women's Perspective

Luise Schottroff, Silvia Schroer, and Marie-Theres Wacker

Translated by
Martin and Barbara Rumscheidt

Fortress Press
Minneapolis

FEMINIST INTERPRETATION
The Bible in Women's Perspective

Cover design: Mike Mihelich
Cover graphic: Pablo Picasso, "Three Women at the Spring," Fontainebleau, summer 1921. Oil on canvas, 6'8–1/4" x 68–1/2" (203.9 x 174 cm). The Museum of Modern Art, New York. Gift of Mr. and Mrs. Allan D. Emil. Art copyright © 1998 Estate of Pablo Picasso/Artists Rights Society (ARS), New York. Photograph copyright © 1998 The Museum of Modern Art, New York. Used with permission.
Interior design: Debbie Finch

Library of Congress Cataloging-in-Publication Data
Schottroff, Luise.
    [Feministische Exegese. English]
    Feminist interpretation : the Bible in women's perspective / Luise Schottroff, Silvia Schroer, and Marie-Theres Wacker ; translated by Martin and Barbara Rumscheidt. — 1st English ed.
        p.   cm.
    Includes bibliographical references and indexes.
    ISBN 0-8006-2999-X (alk. paper)
    1. Bible—Feminist criticism.   I. Schroer, Silvia, 1958–   .
II. Wacker, Marie-Theres.   III. Title.
BS521.4.S3613   1998
220.6'082—dc21   98-11220
                                                                                                CIP

The paper used in this publication meets the minimum requirements of American National Standard for Information Sciences—Permanence of Paper for Printed Library Materials, ANSI Z329.48–1984. ♾

Manufactured in the U.S.A.   AF 1-2999
02   01   00   99   98   1   2   3   4   5   6   7   8   9   10

Contents

Part Two: Toward a Feminist Reconstruction of the History of Israel
Silvia Schroer

Part Three: Toward a Feminist Reconstruction of the History of Early Christianity
Luise Schottroff

Preface

The title *Feminist Interpretation* is meant both to signify and to guide our attempt to provide a historical context for current Christian feminist engagement with the Bible, to determine its hermeneutical location, and to elucidate its methodology. Along with diachronic tracings of their history will be synchronic soundings of the themes of both parts of the Christian Bible. Part One focuses on developments and the status of current discussions and seeks to include publications of European women scholars working within the perspective of feminism. Parts Two and Three take up in addition the literature from the United States in order to contribute to the interweaving of feminist exegetical labor. A good place to start is the now-complete ten-volume work edited by Athalya Brenner, *Feminist Companion to the Bible* (Sheffield: Sheffield Academic Press, 1993–96; a new edition is in preparation).

We call attention at the outset to two feminist commentaries on the Bible that have already appeared in the United States; we have not specifically listed their individual articles in our bibliographies. The one-volume *Women's Bible Commentary*, edited by Carol A. Newsom and Sharon Ringe, presents for every book of the Bible a self-contained, feminist commentary of relative brevity (Louisville: Westminster/John Knox Press, 1992). Elisabeth Schüssler Fiorenza has edited a two-volume commentary that looks at the New Testament and its world; it is called *Searching the Scriptures* (New York: Crossroad, 1993, 1994). Volume 1 develops historical and hermeneutical foundations; volume 2 offers short commentaries on biblical and extrabiblical writings. The purpose is to provide a multicontextual interpretation of Scripture in which women from diverse regions of the world and different cultural contexts within the United States are involved. It was precisely against this backdrop that we recognized once again how much effort is necessary so that the work of feminist theologians of other continents, as well as of Jewish women feminists, may also be taken up in our context.

Concurrent with our preparation of this work, ten feminist exegetes of the Hedwig-Jahnow research project in Marburg wrote a volume entitled *Feministische Hermeneutik und Erstes Testament* (Stuttgart: Verlag W. Kohlhammer, 1994). Along with a jointly written hermeneutical introduction and a reprint of Hedwig Jahnow's essay of 1914, "Die Frau im Alten Testament" (Woman in the Old Testament) are eight feminist "model exegeses." We gladly appropriate their linguistic pattern of referring to the Christian Old Testament as "First Testament." This calls attention to the urgent necessity of facing anew and reworking the anti-Jewish history of the Christian treatment of these sacred writings of Judaism and Christianity and what that history has wrought.

The abbreviations used in our study are those found in Siegfried M. Schwertner's "Internationales Abkürzungsverzeichnis für Theologie und Grenzgebiete," *Theologische Realenzyklopädie*, 2d ed. (Berlin: Mouton; New York: de Gruyter, 1993). In addition, we refer to Elisabeth Gossmann et al., eds., *Wörterbuch der feministischen Theologie* (Gütersloh: Gütersloher Verlagshaus/Gerd Mohn, 1991; cited as *WbfTh*), and to *Revista de Interpretación Bíblica Latino-Americana* (San José, Costa Rica: Editorial Departamento Ecuménico de Investigaciones, 1988ff.; cited as *RIBLA*). The individual articles in *WbfTh* and *Dictionary of Feminist Theologies* (ed. Letty M. Russell and J. Shannon Clarkson [Louisville: Westminster/John Knox Press, 1996]) have not been systematically incorporated into our bibliographies since they are readily accessible and constitute the basic literature, acquaintance with which is presupposed by us.

We thank many people: Ulrike Bail, Dr. Gerlinde Baumann, Corinna Clasen, Tina Hülsebus, Dr. Renate Jost, Dr. Christl Maier, Stefanie Schäfer-Bossert, Silke Schrom, Elke Seifert, and Kerstin Ulrich of the Hedwig-Jahnow Research Project, as well as the numerous women and men who in writing or by word of mouth provided us with information and literature: Ms. Monika Aumüller, Dr. Ulrike Bechmann, Ms. Eleonore Beck, Ms. Ursula Brambosch-Schaelen, Ms. Doris Brodbeck, Dr. Marga Bührig, Ms. Andrea van Dülmen, Dr. Hannelore Erhart, Ms. Beate Hofmann-Strauch, Dr. Lone Fatum, Dr. Maria Häusl, Dr. Dagmar Henze, Ms. Claudia Janssen, Dr. Else Kähler, Dr. Renate Kirchhoff, Dr. Joachim Köhler, Ms. Regene Lamb, Dr. Dagmar Mensink, Ms. Helene Möhler, Dr. Iris Müller, Dr. Annemarie Ohler, Ms. Annebelle Pithan, Ms. Veronika Prüller-Jagenteufel, Ms. Henrike Prussas, Dr. Eva Salm, Dr. Helen Schüngel-Straumann, P.D. Dr. Hannelis Schulte, Prof. Hermann Seifermann, Ms. Gabriele Swiedlik, Prof. Arie Troost, Dr. Kristin de

Troyer, Dr. Bernd Wacker. We thank also Dr. Laetitia Böhm of the University Archives, Munich, Ms. Schleicher and Dr. Real of the Federal Archive at Koblenz, and Ms. Gabriele Dress, Ms. Kathrin Fritz, and Ms. Johanna Kootz of the Central Institute for the Advancement of Women's Studies and Research at the Free University, Berlin.

What bound the three of us together in the inspiring collaboration for this book was not only joy over and sometimes anger with the Bible, but above all pride: pride in our women forebears, the women of the Bible—Israelites, Jews, Christians—pride in the women theologians who long before us searched for the traces of women's history, pride in the scholarly accomplishments of all those who in the years past, often in sickening (academic) circumstances, pursued the eros of that research which has to do with us and our lives as women. We wish that our book may set many women aflame with that eros and, in one way or another, lure them into the texts of the Bible.

Abbreviations

ANRW   W. Haase and H. Temporini, eds., *Aufstieg und Niedergang der römischen Welt* (Berlin and New York: de Gruyter, 1972–)

AOAT   Alter Orient und Altes Testament

ATD   Das Alte Testament Deutsch

ATS   Arabic Translation Series

BWANT   Beiträge zur Wissenschaft vom Alten und Neuen Testament

BWAT   Beiträge zur Wissenschaft vom Alten Testament

BZAW   Beihefte zur *Zeitschrift für die alttestamentliche Wissenschaft*

BZNW   Beihefte zur *Zeitschrift für die neutestamentliche Wissenschaft*

EvTh   *Evangelische Theologie*

FAT   Forschungen zum Alten Testament

FRLANT   Forschungen zur Religion und Literatur des Alten und Neuen Testaments

FzAT   Forschungen zum Alten Testament

FZPhTh   *Freiburger Zeitschrift für philosophie und Theologie*

HBS	Henry Bradshaw Society
HSM	Harvard Semitic Monographs
IEJ	*Israel Exploration Journal*
JAAR	*Journal of the American Academy of Religion*
JBL	*Journal of Biblical Literature*
JFSR	*Journal of Feminist Studies in Religion*
JSOT	*Journal for the Study of the Old Testament*
KatBl	*Katechetische Blätter*
MThA	Münsteraner Theologische Abhandlungen
NSK-AT	*Neuer Stuttgarter Kommentar-Altes Testament*
NTOA	Novum Testamentum et Orbis Antiquus
NTS	*New Testament Studies*
OBO	*Orbis biblicus et Orientalis*
QD	Quaestiones Disputatae
RIBLA	*Revista de Interpretación Bíblica Latino-Americana*
SBM	Stuttgarter biblische Monographien
SBS	Stuttgarter Bibelstudien
STB	Studia Biblica. Leiden
SUNT	Studien zur Umwelt des Neuen Testaments
ThB	*Theologische Beiträge*

ThQ   *Theologische Quartalschrift*

TU   Texte und Untersuchungen zur Geschichte der
         altchristlichen Literatur

UF   *Ugarit-Forschungen*

VT   *Vetus Testamentum*

WbfTh   Elisabeth Gossmann et al., eds., *Wörterbuch der*
         feministischen Theologie (Gütersloh: Gütersloher
         Verlagshaus/Gerd Mohn, 1991)

WUNT   Wissenschaftliche Untersuchungen zum Neuen
         Testament

ZAW   *Zeitschrift für die alttestamentliche Wissenschaft*

ZBK-AT   Zürcher Bibelkommentar-Altes Testament

ZDPV   *Zeitschrift des deutschen Palästina-Vereins*

ZNW   *Zeitschrift für die neutestamentliche Wissenschaft*

Part One

HISTORICAL, HERMENEUTICAL, AND METHODOLOGICAL FOUNDATIONS

Marie-Theres Wacker

Chapter One

One Hundred Years of Women and the Bible: Looking Back

For a long time, women have interposed themselves into the interpretation of the Christian Bible. One may trace this process far back into the early modern period and even beyond that. This retrospective restricts itself to the nineteenth and twentieth centuries and, to a large extent, to the world of the academy. It begins, in other words, at a time within the modern women's movement when it was no longer only individual women who raised their voices in society and church. It was a time when structural changes enabled a growing number of women to find their place also in theological scholarship and ecclesial praxis and, connected with these, in interpreting the Scriptures. Looking back on one hundred years of women dealing with the basic document of Christianity immediately provides material on which the hermeneutical and methodological reflection of the following sections may rest. But such viewing is understood to be above all a feminist labor of remembering since that labor undermines the "his-tory" of a pure history of patriarchy and its legitimating function. It is a labor that takes us back to the women of history and thereby gives their history back to women, their history of hope, suffering, resistance, failure, and accommodation, but that also opens up liberating spaces for action.

1.1 *The Woman's Bible*

In 1995, it was exactly one hundred years since *The Woman's Bible* appeared in New York, the first volume of a work that created both sensation and indignation. People who moved in the official circles of the church or who were part of the organized women's movement put distance between themselves and this project. The former greeted it as a satanic work, while the latter viewed it as a piece of sectarianism that was harmful to the effort of emancipation. For many women, however, *The Woman's Bible* was an appropriate expression of their suffering at the hands of the structures of women's oppression found in the church's congregations and the state's politics. At the same time, these women also saw reflected in that work their new self-awareness as subjects who take matters that concern them into their own hands.

The Woman's Bible came into being primarily through the labors of one woman, Elizabeth Cady Stanton, already in her seventies. It was her lifework to struggle against discrimination enshrined in the law. Together with her spouse, a lawyer by profession, she toiled as an abolitionist. In this context she also came to know women who, unlike herself, fought this fight for primarily religious reasons: in particular the sisters Angelina and Sarah Grimké, members of the Society of Friends. These women preachers quickly saw the connection between the liberation of slaves and that of women, not least because "Bible-believing" men often prevented them in their public speaking from addressing a mixed audience. ("I do not permit woman to teach!" 1 Tim. 2:12.) Already in 1837, Sarah Grimké proposed the thesis that the interpretation of Scripture by men serves the suppression of women; she called on women to learn the languages of the sacred texts and take the interpretation of them into their own hands. Attendance at an international congress of abolitionists in London in 1840 became for Elizabeth Cady Stanton a key event in bringing together the struggle for the liberation of slaves and that of women. She and the other American women were told that, because they were women, they could not be accredited as official delegates and had to take their places up in the gallery. Did that mean that the efforts of women were inferior to those of men on behalf of the human and civil rights of blacks, who were worked to death by whites in the cotton plantations of the South? Stanton now began to toil in her own context for the equality of women. She is one of the "mothers" of the gathering held July 19–20, 1848, at the Wesleyan Methodist Church in Seneca Falls, a gathering that has become part of the history of women. The convention agreed on at this gathering is seen as the spark that ignited the North American movement of women seeking the vote for women, women's education, and legal independence from their fathers' and husbands' tutelage. Black women who had been freed also realized in turn that they themselves needed to advocate for women's rights; best known among them is Sojourner Truth, who in her well-known address to a conference on women's rights at Akron, Ohio, in 1852 refuted with scriptural wisdom every biblically based argument against the equality of women before the law.

It was precisely the debate about existing laws that brought home to Elizabeth Cady Stanton to what degree the Bible was drawn on as divine authority for the religious as well as political legitimation of the injustice visited on women in the guise of the law. She was convinced that this most deeply contradicted faith in a divine being who, in wisdom and rationality, orders and rules the world and who should not be thought of in contradiction to the rationality of human rights. It was such Enlightenment thinking, which seems to have shaped her whole life, that caused her in 1887, after the death of her spouse, to initiate the project of a "woman's Bible" and to see it to its successful conclusion with the publication of its two volumes in 1895 and 1898, before she died at the age of eighty-eight in 1902. She gathered about a dozen women for the project. They were versed in literature, history, and, like herself, Greek, but there was no woman trained in theology and biblical studies, even though there were already such women, according to the membership lists of the Society of Biblical Literature. Elizabeth Cady Stanton suggested caustically that careerism and fear prevented their participation. Perhaps those few women working in the male field of exegesis just had, like their German counterparts a few decades later, a different view of the emancipation of women and felt that teaching at the newly founded colleges for women fulfilled their calling, seeing that they invested themselves there in the education of women. On the other hand, the women with Elizabeth Cady Stanton whose toil was for women's rights had no intention of interfering with the theologians' scholarly pursuits. Yet their aims were far more basic: to unmask, with the help of the educated reason of women, the church's and the state's misuse of the Bible. Or, more profoundly, to expose the propensity for misuse of the Bible that is rooted in its very own insufficiencies and to undermine thereby its divine authority. Appropriately, the first complete translation of the Bible into English by a woman, Julia Smith, became the basic text for *The Woman's Bible*.

The structure of this work follows the order of the biblical writings. Yet they are not commented on sequentially. The texts are either assessed through summary retelling (like the Book of Ruth, for example) or studied in terms of selected sections (like the Gospel of Matthew). On the one hand, such selections focus on passages that were used in the United States to legitimate the inequality of women before the law (this would explain the disproportional weight of the Pentateuch). On the other hand, they recall passages that contrariwise would permit a wholly different perception of women. A large part of the text came from Elizabeth Cady Stanton; she composed the "base text" and then coordinated the contributions of the other women with her own commentaries. Such redaction, comparable perhaps to the First Testament's "Priestly writing," let Stanton's interpretive perspective hold everything together while allowing the integration of approaches noticeably different from hers. This applies in particular to the contribution of feminist literata Lillie Devereux Blake. In her commentaries on the Books of Genesis to Numbers, Blake sees the problem less in the biblical texts themselves as in the history of their interpretation, in which they are badly distorted. The same may be said for the decisive pursuit of Ellen Batelle Dietrick to excavate a "her-story" as shown in her notes on the First and, above all, the New Testament. Finally, the perspective of Clara Colby shows such a differing approach; her notes on Genesis make it plain that for her, in keeping with what was known at the time as "new thinking," the Bible is no longer the Word of God in the sense of an authority that encounters humans "from outside." Colby seeks, rather, to discern the symbolic content of these writings and show how they correspond to the processes of human self-discovery. The issue for Elizabeth Cady Stanton was chiefly to pit enlightened reason against the historically limited men's word of the Bible and in this way to advance the public discussion of the equality of women.

For a long time, *The Woman's Bible* had no impact; shortly after its publication it seems to have vanished from public debate. A German obituary of Elizabeth Cady Stanton, published in *Die christliche Frau* (The Christian Woman) (vol. 1, no. 4 [1902/3]: 152), a recently launched journal of the time, honors her work for social issues and the women's movement but fails to say one word about *The Woman's Bible*. Through the efforts of a women's group in Seattle, the work became available again only in 1974 in the context of the new women's movement.

Elizabeth Cady Stanton, *The Woman's Bible* (New York: European Publishing Company, 1895–98), reprinted a number of times; *Eighty Years and More: Reminiscences, 1815–1897* (New York: European Publishing Company, 1898; reprint, New York: Schocken Books, 1971); Barbara Welter, "Something Remains to Dare: Introduction to *The*

Woman's Bible," in Elizabeth Cady Stanton, *The Woman's Bible: The Original Attack on the Bible* (New York: Arno Press, 1972; reprint of 1895–98 edition), v–xlii; Dale Spender, "Introduction," in Stanton, *The Woman's Bible*, abridged ed. (Edinburgh: Polygon Books, 1985), i–v; Elisabeth Schüssler Fiorenza, *In Memory of Her: A Feminist Theological Reconstruction of Christian Origins* (New York: Crossroad, 1983), 7–14; *Bread Not Stone: The Challenge of Feminist Biblical Interpretation* (Boston: Beacon Press, 1985), 52–58; Marga Bührig, "Elizabeth Cady Stanton (1815–1902) und die Woman's Bible," in Luise Schottroff and Johannes Thiele, eds., *Gotteslehrerinnen* (Stuttgart: Kreuz Verlag, 1989), 125–37; Karen Baker-Fletcher, "Anna Julia Cooper and Sojourner Truth: Two Nineteenth-Century Black Feminist Interpreters of Scripture," and Carolyn de Swarte Gifford, "Politicizing the Sacred Texts: Elizabeth Cady Stanton and the Woman's Bible," both in Elisabeth Schüssler Fiorenza, ed., *Searching the Scriptures*, vol. 1: *A Feminist Introduction* (New York: Crossroad, 1993), 41–51 and 52–63; Dorothy C. Bass, "Women's Studies and Biblical Studies: An Historical Perspective," *JSOT* 22 (1982): 6–12; *Bibel und Kirche* 50 (1995), thematic issue, "100 Jahre *Woman's Bible*."

1.2 Biblical Interpretation by Women in the Context of Feminism

1.2.1 The Beginnings of Feminist Exegesis

Since the 1970s more and more books on questions of feminist theology and scriptural interpretation appeared in the Federal Republic of Germany. At first, they were predominantly translations from English and Dutch, such as the work edited by Catharina Halkes, *Wenn Frauen ans Wort kommen* (When Women Seize the Word), which also contained contributions on biblical themes. An important contribution was made by Frank Crüsemann and Hartwig Thyen. In a work published in 1978, a scholar in First Testament and one in New Testament each develops the basic features of women's social history in biblical times. *Frauen um Jesus* (1980; Eng. trans., *The Women around Jesus*) by Elisabeth Moltmann was probably the first German-language monograph in feminist exegesis.

Moltmann places the best-known women of the New Testament at the center. She highlights their "customary" ecclesiastical (Lutheran) cooptation in the sense of what men have consistently defined as their "service." Not least through pictorial documents of Christian art, she explores alternative approaches to these biblical figures that are liberating for women. At the same time, there appeared the volume *Frauen in der Bibel* (Women in the Bible), edited by Willy Schottroff and Wolfgang Stegemann; in it are two notable contributions by women exegetes: Elisabeth Schüssler Fiorenza and Luise Schottroff. Schüssler Fiorenza's chapter was originally written for a Festschrift for the Würzburg New Testament scholar Rudolf Schnackenburg but was refused inclusion. Her chapter outlines the feminist-critical revision of the history of early Christianity, which she then fully develops in her book *In Memory of Her.* Luise Schottroff's chapter provides an outline of social history. Entitled most unpretentiously "Women as Disciples of Jesus in New Testament Times," her contribution is nothing less than the nucleus of a lifelong labor.

What was considered "women specific" in those first years was the spontaneous and predominant preoccupation with women in both the First and New Testaments. The fresh discovery and, above all, the new appropriation of those women shaped the feminist approach to the Bible to the present time. Thus, a series of monographs on the women of the Bible (see 2.1.3), written by women, came into being. Appearing as well were materials for the practice of Bible study, headed by the two-volume anthology *Feministisch gelesen* (which among others included contributions by Swiss and Austrian women). The programs of the churches' lay academies and the *Kirchentag* included the study of women in the Bible. Therefore, especially within Protestantism and its tradition of work in Scripture, women who looked on "feminist" study of the Bible with hesitation or even rejection were being addressed. This phenomenon in no small way accounted for the broad impact of this topic.

Frank Crüsemann and Hartmut Thyen, . . . *als Mann und Frau geschaffen* (Gelnhausen: Burckhardthaus Verlag, 1978); Alicia Craig Faxon, *Women and Jesus* (Philadelphia: United Church Press, 1973); Catharina Halkes and Daan Buddingh, eds., *Wenn Frauen ans Wort kommen* (Offenbach and Gelnhausen: Burckhardthaus-Laetare-Verlag, 1979); Elisabeth Moltmann-Wendel, *The Women around Jesus* (New York: Crossroad, 1982); Letty M. Russell, ed., *The Liberating Word: A Guide to Non-Sexist Interpretation of the Bible* (Philadelphia: Westminster Press, 1976); Willy Schottroff and Wolfgang Stegemann, eds., *Traditionen der Befreiung 2: Frauen in der Bibel* (Munich: Kaiser; Gelnhausen: Burckhardthaus-Laetare, 1980), including the articles by Elisabeth Schüssler Fiorenza, "Der Beitrag der Frauen zur urchristlichen Bewegung," 60–90, and Luise Schottroff, "Frauen in der Nachfolge Jesu in neutestamentlicher Zeit," 91–133—Eng. trans., "Women as Disciples of Jesus in New Testament Times," in Luise Schottroff, *Let the Oppressed Go Free* (Louisville: Westminster/John Knox Press, 1993).

1.2.2 The Challenge of Matriarchy

In the mid-1980s, Christa Mulack's studies, *The Femininity of God* and *Jesus, the Anointed of Women,* appeared, as well as Elga Sorge's *Religion and Women* and Gerda Weiler's *The Hidden Matriarchy in the First Testament.* These works deepened and sharpened feminist theological discussion and, with it, feminist-critical rereading of Scripture. For these women authors, it was no longer sufficient merely to subject the traditional forms of biblical faith to critical questions; rather, they put this foundation as such into question. Their argument did not assume the form of traditional exegesis even though their critique of Christianity was to a large extent framed in terms of critique of the Bible.

In her first monograph on the "femininity of God," the Protestant woman theologian Christa Mulack deals with the basic issue that conventional theology reveres a patriarchal God and a patriarchal image of God. She argues that in the "shadow" of that God there is still to be found, and then to be excavated, the feminine divine. Her own process of discovery and excavation is demonstrated in relation to the example she had chosen, the concept of God in Jewish *Kabbalah.* Her concluding sketch in that book, on "the way of the feminine toward the light in the consciousness of Jesus," is taken up and developed extensively in her second work, *Jesus, the Anointed of Women.* According to Mulack, Jesus was a man who had been prompted by non-Jewish women, especially the Syrophoenician woman (Matt. 15:21-28 and Mark 7:24-30) and the Samaritan woman (John 4), to recognize his "mission" and was ultimately anointed by them as the Messiah. Mulack correspondingly shows that there is a Wisdom-like, feminine imprint on Jesus' own relation to God and on certain New Testament structures of Christology. This basic dimension of the New Testament, which she identifies as "matriarchal," holds the feminine to be superior, yes, even divine. It has been thoroughly counterfeited by Christianity but is, nonetheless, accessible to feminist depth psychology and comparative cultural analysis and may be reappropriated through feminist theology and ethics. The Protestant woman theologian Elga Sorge has a similar aim; she criticizes patriarchal theologies of the cross as symbols of Christian necrophilia and stresses feminist spirituality of life- and eros-affirming forces. For this purpose she makes particular use of the Song of Songs. Gerda Weiler, a scholar in (religious) pedagogy, undertakes a comprehensive revision of the First Testament. It is based in a three-part thesis: (1) the current form of the First Testament is the product of a historicizing revision of initially cultic texts or books of worship; (2) these texts pointed to an Israelite religion of the Goddess who was worshiped together with YHWH, her son and lover; (3) this religion appropriately merits the appellation of "matriarchal," because it puts the cosmic Goddess at the center and proposes an order of society in which women set the tone. (Here Weiler relies on the cultural-historical principles developed by Heide Göttner-Abendroth.) For that reason, the monotheism confessed by Scripture is to be plainly seen as patriarchal and won at the expense of the displacement of Israel's matriarchal view of reality.

The theological concentration of feminist interpretation of Scripture could not detour around such matriarchal revision; the question of the God of the Bible had been put. If this God shows "himself" to be the product of the projection of men's will to power onto the backs of women, is there any alternative to Mary Daly's option in 1972, namely, to stage a public exodus of women from the churches? Basic questions of feminist-biblical hermeneutics arise at this point (see 2.1.4): what happens when a depth psychology hermeneutics of Scripture replaces that of history, and how is the relation of both of these issues to the interests of feminism to be determined more precisely? How critically must feminist authors deal with their scholarly (or parascholarly) male authorities, especially when it becomes known that these men did not at all, or just barely, dissociate themselves from German Fascism? What about the latent or open anti-Judaism to which feminist research in matriarchy has proven itself to be so amenable? Feminist exegesis and theology in the German-speaking world were preoccupied and formed for years by the programmatic one-sidedness of the propositions cited above and the discussion focused on them.

Heide Göttner-Abendroth, *Die Göttin und ihr Heros* (Munich: Verlag Frauenoffensive, 1980); idem, *Die tanzende Göttin* (see 2.1.2); Christa Mulack, *Die Weiblichkeit Gottes* (Stuttgart: Kreuz Verlag, 1983); idem, *Jesus, der Gesalbte der Frauen* (Stuttgart: Kreuz Verlag, 1985); Elga

Sorge, *Religion und Frau* (Stuttgart: Verlag W. Kohlhammer, 1985; 2d rev. ed., 1987); Gerda Weiler, *Ich verwerfe im Lande die Kriege: Das verborgene Matriarchat im Alten Testament* (Munich: Verlag Frauenoffensive, 1984); idem, *Das Matriarchat im Alten Israel* (Stuttgart: Verlag W. Kohlhammer, 1989); idem, *Ich brauche die Göttin* (Basel: Mond-Buch, 1990).

The literature on the critical discussion of this approach is listed in 2.1.4 and 2.4.1.

1.2.3 Most Recent Developments

In the past few years, the number of feminist women with qualifications in exegesis has grown substantially in the German-speaking world (as in Western Europe overall). Correspondingly, there is a widening differentiation in feminist exegetical work in our region, as there had been earlier in North America. Thematically that work is centered in the two foci of feminist theological research: on the one hand, the study of the present and past reality of women, and on the other, the question of an appropriate manner of speaking of God, one that corresponds to women, in which the biblically based metaphors of the feminine assume an important place.

The ongoing interest in women in the Bible is presently achieving more precise methodological and hermeneutical expression. (See also chaps. 2 and 3.)

For instance, sometimes that interest, combined with reflections in contemporary social or religious history, is focused on the literary portrayal of those women (see Ulrike Bechmann on Deborah, Maria Häusl on Abishag and Bathsheba, Christl Maier on the "foreign woman," and Ina Petermann on Ruth) and their literary-theological "placement" within the context of a biblical book (see Irmtraud Fischer on the ancient forebears of Genesis 12–26 and Monika Fander on the Gospel of Mark), as well as on the history of how these biblical texts were received (see Helen Schüngel-Straumann and Monika Leisch-Kiesl on Eve and Monika Hellmann on Judith). Next to the works just cited, there are studies of "the image of women" by biblical authors, such as in Caroline van der Stichele's analysis of 1 Corinthians 11 and Marie-Theres Wacker's book on Hosea. One needs to refer also to the "search for traces" of the presence and reality of women, such as that of the Italian exegete Carla Ricci. Working with Luke 8:1-3, Ricci endeavors to render hermeneutically productive the silence (or silencing) of the biblical text. Or there is the work of the Dutch scholar Jonneke Bekkenkamp. She interprets the Song of Songs, in comparison with medieval, Southern European love songs, as the poetry of women in a world of men. In Norway, Turid Karlsen Seim is working on a woman-related exegesis of the two-volume writing of Luke.

In yet other instances, feminist exegetes, chiefly in conjunction with their own literary analyses, focus with the eyes of social history on the world of women's lives as reflected in biblical literature and extrabiblical sources. Renate Jost has produced a systematic collection of the traces of women from Judea at the time of the Exile; Hannelis Schulte concentrated on women of the period before, and the early years after, Israel had become a state. Ivoni Richter Reimer looked at the women spoken of in Acts, Renate Kirchhoff at the reality of women in the sex trade in New Testament times in order to ground Paul's *porneia* metaphorism in terms of social history. These historical and social-historical studies of feminist women serve the larger project of an encompassing "her-story," a reconstruction of the history of Israel and of New Testament time that puts women's history at the center. An important basis of the discussion of such a project is Elisabeth Schüssler Fiorenza's work which, next to innumerable contributions to individual questions, especially offers clarification in hermeneutics. (See 2.1.5.) Next to it, the exegetical work of Luise Schottroff is of great significance. From the early 1980s onwards, her point of departure in social-historical liberation theology has sharpened increasingly in an explicitly feminist direction (see 3.4.1 and Part Three).

Recourse to the Bible's use of metaphors for femininity is of central importance for the question of feminist-biblical language of God. The biblical symbol of God as mother is of great significance here, seeing that it is readily discernible in a variety of textual configurations of the Bible. It is also an indisputable feminine symbol and, therefore, apparently suitable as a point of contact for women's experience today. Helen Schüngel-Straumann animated this discussion in the German-speaking world with her thesis that, although obscured by a patriarchal history of interpretation, the eleventh chapter of Hosea presents a purely feminine, or, more precisely, maternal image of God. Thereupon the maternal characteristics of the God of Israel are looked at more closely. (Schüngel-Straumann herself adds a study on the conception of God the creator as well as a monograph on *ruaḥ*.) This raises the hermeneutical problem of the use of ideologies of motherhood. (See Marie-Theres Wacker on Hosea 11.) The figure of (divine) Wisdom is more multifaceted and nuanced, offering fewer biologistically determined dimensions of the feminine. This figure seems to exercise a fascination, particularly on Christian feminist exegetes (Gerlinde Baumann, Silvia Schroer, Helen Schüngel-Straumann, Angelika Strotmann, and, in the United States, particularly Claudia Camp). On the one hand, this is due to the aim of establishing a genuinely biblical way toward feminine spirituality and, on the other, to the hope that, by a tradition of Wisdom still accessible in the New Testament, new ways may possibly be opened up to Christology.

In a manner more fundamental than seen thus far, feminist-biblical language of God still has to come to terms with recent findings of the history of religion with regard to the pre-monotheistic religion of Israel. To what extent female deities were worshiped in biblical Israel next to, or even in place of YHWH, and in what way women participated in or bore primary responsibility for it, requires historical clarification. Different results are to be expected, for example, when attention is focused on the diverse levels of the practice of religion, those of public state occasions (in the capital, related to kings), or those in regional or village settings or of personal, familial dimensions. What is at issue here for feminist theology is, first, what the implications are of the fact that women were being pushed out of "public" cultic events, certainly in rural regions, and restricted to the religion of the family. Second, to what extent is it a necessary correction of one-sided developments of biblical and, thus, the Christian religion, to attempt not only a historical reconstruction of pre-monotheistic and, therefore, prebiblical religion but also, at least partially, to integrate it theologically?

Finally, a biblically based, feminist theological language of God must include critical assessment of the traditional concepts of the togetherness of God and humans found in the Bible and biblical theology. These include particularly the theology of creation, the concepts of sin and guilt, and salvation and (co)responsibility. Feminist exegesis is still in its infancy here; the studies to be referred to thus far are those of Luise Schottroff (see chap. 9) and Silvia Schroer (see 6.7).

Concerning the present (institutional) church's assessment of feminist exegesis, we call attention, as far as Roman Catholicism is concerned, to the final document of the fourth Plenary Conference of the Catholic Scripture Federation, which met in Bogotá from June 27 to July 6, 1990. It desires and calls for the inclusion of women in every aspect of the apostolate of the Bible. "Biblical texts that are hostile to women or that are part of a very sexist or patriarchal tradition of interpretation, should be read only when accompanied by critical comment"

(21). There is, in addition, the document of the Pontifical Biblical Commission, published on April 23, 1994, "The Interpretation of the Bible in the Church"; in a particular paragraph (I.E.2), it specifically cites feminist exegesis and refers to it as contextual exegesis. "It is desirable, in addition, that exegesis be taught by men and women" (III.C.2). Whether such a desideratum will bear fruit remains to be seen in the German-speaking world. In terms of the Protestant Church of Germany (EKD), that is to say, the administrations of the regional churches, the establishment in 1993–94 of the Center for Women's Studies and Education at Gelnhausen and the appointment there of a woman exegete signal a not insignificant interest in incorporating feminist theology and exegesis in research, teaching, and church practice. However, the Protestant faculties of theology in Germany have thus far successfully maintained an aloofness to that desideratum.

Gerlinde Baumann, "Gottes Geist und Gottes Weisheit: Eine Verknüpfung," in Hedwig Jahnow et al., *Feministische Hermeneutik und Erstes Testament* (Stuttgart: Verlag W. Kohlhammer, 1994), 138–48; idem, *"Wer mich findet, hat Leben gefunden": Traditionsgeschichtliche und theologische Studien zur Weisheitgestalt in Prov 1–9* (Tübingen [FAT]: Mohr und Siebeck, 1996); Ulrike Bechmann, *Das Deboralied zwischen Geschichte und Fiktion: Eine exegetische Untersuchung zu Richter 5* (St. Ottilien: Eos-Verlag, 1989); Jonneke Bekkenkamp, "Het Hooglied: Een vrouwenlied in een mannentraditie," in Rita Lemaire, ed., *Ik zing mijn lied voor al wie met mij gaat: Vrouwen in de volksliteratuur* (Utrecht, 1986), 72–89; Claudia Camp, *Wisdom and the Feminine in the Book of Proverbs* (Sheffield: Sheffield Academic Press, 1985); idem, "Wisdom as Root Metaphor: A Theological Consideration," in *The Listening Heart: Festschrift for R. E. Murphy* (Sheffield: Sheffield Academic Press, 1987), 45–76; Monika Fander, *Die Stellung der Frau im Markusevangelium*, MThA 8 (Münster: Telos, 1989); Irmtraud Fischer, *Die Erzeltern Israels: Feministisch-theologische Studien zu Gen. 12–36*, BZAW 222 (Berlin: de Gruyter, 1994); Maria Häusl, *Abischag und Batscheba: Frauen am Königshof und die Thronfolge Davids im Zeugnis der Texte 1 Kön 1 und 2*, ATS 41 (Munich: Eos-Verlag, 1993); Monika Hellman, *Judit—eine Frau im Spannungsfeld von Autonomie und göttlicher Führung* (Frankfurt: Peter Lang, 1992); Renate Jost, *Frauen, Männer und die Himmelskönigin: Exegetische Studien* (Gütersloh: Gütersloher Verlagshaus Gerd Mohn, 1995); Katholische Bibelföderation, *Schlussdokument der 4. Vollversammlung, Bogotá, Colom-*

bia 27. June–6. July 1990; Othmar Keel and Christoph Uehlinger, *Göttinen, Götter und Gottessymbole,* QD 134 (Freiburg, Basel, and Vienna: Herder Verlag, 1992); Renate Kirchhoff, *Die Sünde gegen den eigenen Leib: Studien zu "porné" und "porneía" in 1 Kor 6, 12-20 und dem sozio-kulturellen Kontext der paulinischen Adressaten,* SUNT 18 (Göttingen: Vandenhoeck und Ruprecht, 1994); Monika Leisch-Kiesl, *Eva als andere: Eine exemplarische Untersuchung zu Frühchristentum und Mittelalter* (Cologne: Verlag Bohlau, 1992); Christl Maier, *Die "fremde Frau": Eine exegetische und sozialgeschichtliche Studie zu Proverbien 1–9,* OBO (Fribourg: Universitätsverlag; Göttingen: Vandenhoeck und Ruprecht, 1995); Ina Petermann, "Die Fremde und der König: Intertextuelle Studien zum Buch Ruth" (diss., Heidelberg, 1995); Pontifical Biblical Commission, "The Interpretation of the Bible in the Church," *Origins* 23, no. 29 (6 January 1994); Carla Ricci, *Mary Magdalene and Many Others: Women Who Followed Jesus* (Minneapolis: Fortress Press, 1994); Ivoni Richter Reimer, *Frauen in der Apostelgeschichte des Lukas: Eine feministisch-theologische Exegese* (Gütersloh: Gütersloher Verlagshaus Gerd Mohn, 1992); Christine Schaumberger and Luise Schottroff, *Schuld und Macht: Studien zu einer feministischen Befreiungstheologie* (Munich: Chr. Kaiser Verlag, 1988); Luise Schottroff, *Befreiungserfahrungen: Studien zur Sozialgeschichte des Neuen Testaments,* ThB 82 (Munich: Chr. Kaiser Verlag, 1990), selections in *Let the Oppressed Go Free: Feminist Perspectives on the New Testament* (Louisville: Westminster/John Knox Press, 1993); idem, *Lydia's Impatient Sisters: A Feminist Social History of Early Christianity* (Louisville: Westminster/John Knox Press, 1995); idem, "Wanderprophetinnen: Eine feministische Analyse der Logienquelle," *EvTh* 51 (1991): 332–44; Silvia Schroer, "Jesus Sophia: Beiträge der feministischen Forschung zu einer frühchristlichen Deutung der Praxis und des Schicksals Jesu von Nazareth," in Regula Strobel and Doris Strahm, eds., *Vom Verlangen nach Heilwerden: Christologie in feministisch-theologischer Sicht* (Fribourg and Lucerne: Edition Exodus, 1991), 112–28; Silvia Schroer and Helen Schüngel-Straumann, "Gott im Bild einer Frau," thematic no. of *Bibel heute* 103 (1990); Hannelis Schulte, *Dennoch gingen sie aufrecht: Frauengestalten des Alten Israel* (Neukirchen-Vluyn: Neukirchener Verlag, 1995); Helen Schüngel-Straumann, *Die Frau am Anfang: Eva und die Folgen* (Freiburg, Basel, and Vienna: Herder Verlag, 1989); idem, "Gott als Mutter in Hos 11," *ThQ* 166 (1986): 119–34; idem, *Ruaḥ bewegt die Welt: Gottes schöpferische Lebenskraft in der Krisenzeit des Exils,* SBS 151

(Stuttgart: Verlag Katholisches Bibelwerk, 1992); idem, "Weibliche Dimensionen in mesopotamischen und alttestamentlichen Schöpfungsaussagen und ihre feministische Kritik," in Wacker and Zenger, eds., *Der eine Gott und die Göttin* (see below), 49–81; Elisabeth Schüssler Fiorenza, *In Memory of Her: A Feminist Theological Reconstruction of Christian Origins* (New York: Crossroad, 1983); Turid Karlen Seim, *The Double Message: Gender in Luke-Acts* (forthcoming); Caroline van der Stichele, "Autenticiteit en integriteit van 1 Kor. 11, 2-16: Een bijdrage tot de discussie omtrent Paulus' visie op de vrouw" (diss., Leuven, 1992), edited version in Freda Dröes et al., eds., *Proeven van vrouwenstudies theologie* (Leiden and Utrecht, 1993), 271–77; Marie-Theres Wacker, *Figurationen des Weiblichen im Hoseabuch: Literarische, entstehungsgeschichtliche und religionsgeschichtliche Studien* (Freiburg, Basel, and Vienna: Herder Verlag, 1996); idem, "Frau-Sexus-Macht: Eine feministisch-theologische Relecture des Hoseabuches," in Marie-Theres Wacker, ed., *Der Gott der Männer und die Frauen* (Düsseldorf: Patmos, 1987); idem, "Gott als Mutter? Zur Bedeutung eines biblischen Gottessymbols für feministische Theologie," *Concilium* 25 (1989): 523–28; Marie-Theres Wacker and Erich Zenger, eds., *Der eine Gott und die Göttin*, QD 135 (Freiburg, Basel, and Vienna: Herder Verlag, 1991).

1.3 The German-Speaking Countries until World War II

The history of the modern women's movement in Germany has now been quite well researched, as has been that of women theologians within Protestantism. Thanks are due to Hannelore Erhart, professor of Reformed theology at Göttingen, and the "Research Project on the History of Women Theologians," initiated by her, and the dissertations and anthologies resulting from it. Except for the first explorations by Leo Karrer and Iris Müller, the history of women theologians within Roman Catholicism is still waiting to be researched. Lucie Teufl studied the history of women theologians in Austria up to the year 1971; her dissertation remains unpublished. As far as we know, the situation in Switzerland is still waiting to be researched. Therefore, the following works merely name trends and depict contours.

Elisabeth Boedeker, "25 Jahre Frauenstudium in Deutschland: Verzeichnis der Doktorarbeiten von Frauen 1908–1933," 4 vols. (Hannover, 1935–39); Frauenforschungsprojekt zur Geschichte der Theologinnen, Göttingen, ed., *"Darum wagt es, Schwestern . . .": Zur Geschichte evangelischer Theologinnen in Deutschland* (Neukirchen-Vluyn: Neukirchener Verlag, 1994); Lucie Teufl, "Das theologische Universitätsstudium der Frau in Osterreich" (diss., Vienna, 1971); Leo Karrer (see 1.4); Iris Müller, *Die Misere katholischer Theologinnen in den deutschen Universitäten* (Weinheim: Deutscher Studien-Verlag, 1987).

1.3.1 The Situation until 1918

Around the year 1848, there clearly existed a first women's movement in Germany. But a broader engagement of women on behalf of education and civil rights for women began only in Wilhelmine Germany, that is, in the 1870s.

It was around the turn of the century that the role of women in biblical Israel and in early Christianity first began to be subjected to systematic and coherent study on the part of (male) exegetes in the liberal Protestantism of German universities. In an essay published in 1900, Adolf von Harnack described the outstanding significance of women for the beginnings of Christianity. He even ventured the hypothesis that the Epistle to the Hebrews was written by a woman and that it could have been none other than Prisca. Subsequently, his pupil Leopold Zscharnack wrote about the "Service of Woman in the First Centuries of the Christian Church" (1902), and a First Testament scholar from Breslau, Max Löhr, about the "Place of Woman in the Religion and Cult of YHWH" (1908). Löhr centers his little monograph in a question that goes against the consensus of the time and appears to be crucial today for feminist reconsideration of the religion of biblical Israel. He questions "whether the religion of YHWH might have left dissatisfied the religious need of the female gender, a need that is obviously powerfully present in ancient Israel" (2). On the basis of a detailed examination of women's names in the Bible, Löhr sets out initially to show that it is untenable to claim that women have "in principle or in essence a different relation" to the religion of YHWH (32). At the same time, one must assume that the total exclusion of women from strictly priestly sacrificial functions, which was already practiced in the period before Israel's exile, caused in postexilic times a general disdain of women in ethical and spiritual perspective. Therefore, one may say in summary that "the belief . . . that YHWHism is in essence a religion for men and of much less concern to women is inappropriate for preexilic Israel but quite applicable to the cult of the Jewish congregation" (54).

However valuable Löhr's little study is for the recovery of women's history in biblical Israel, it is firmly under the spell of the construct which dominated Protestant exegesis in the nineteenth and early twentieth centuries, namely that of the history of Israel's decline into the priestly-legalistic Judaism. On the other hand, Zscharnack's work, on its very first page, makes short shrift of the Christian prejudicial belief that to this day Jewish marriage has not reached the ethical height to which Christian marriage was raised by Jesus. Written in partial fulfillment of the requirements for the licentiate, Zscharnack's study is concerned with a comprehensive documentation—valuable still for current feminist research—of the functions played, and the offices held, by women in early Christianity and patristic times. In relation to the "teaching office" of women, he believes that equality quite likely existed in the beginning (Prisca) but that soon teaching by women became restricted to women missionizing other women (Thecla). It was ultimately tolerated only as a purely domestic, nonpublic instruction that took place in the chambers of women. According to Zscharnack, the demise of Christian women prophets, the number and significance of whom can hardly be underestimated, came at the time when "the office had displaced the charism of lay men and women" (66). But, contrary to Gnosticism and Montanism, the great church never granted women sacerdotal functions, especially the right to baptize and administer the Eucharist. If, in contrast, the office of widows and the diaconate in the ancient church were a form of "legitimating the service of women and . . . employing it in the edification of the church," it was "heresy, hierarchy and monasticism which became the wicked foes that choked off the seed" (156).

This exegetical-scholarly interest in the reality of women in biblical times correlates in time with the first attempts by women, chiefly from the educated middle class, to establish themselves also in theological scholarship. Before 1900, the year when the first universities in Germany (in Baden, to be precise) gave women the right to register for study, women had access to theological lectures only as auditors, a status obtained through a complicated process of permission-seeking. Nonetheless, it was Lydia Stöcker (1877–1942), the less well known sister of the advocate for women's rights, Helen Stöcker, who already at the turn of the century studied with Adolf von Harnack in Berlin, among others, and acquired competence in exegesis. In 1907, she published a study, "Woman in the Ancient Church"; it starts from the New Testament and proceeds along interpretive lines similar to those of Zscharnack's study. In that same year, 1907, one year before Prussia granted women the full right to register for study (one of the last states of the German Reich to do so), the first woman received her licentiate in biblical studies from the University of Jena; she was Carola Barth (1879–1959). Her strong interest in history and the history of religion led her to choose as the title of her dissertation "The Reception of the New Testament in Valentinian Gnosticism." From the perspective of feminist theology today, Gnosticism seems to be an attractive research area because both the literary metaphors of femininity and the concrete reality of women are to be found there. But in Carola Barth's days that kind of preoccupation and focus was still most unbecoming. Further, it would not be obviously suggested or stimulated simply by analyzing the texts themselves. In 1908 Carola Barth became the first woman to receive from the German Archaeological Institute a one-year travel grant that allowed her to spend several months in a number of countries in the Near East. While engaged as a teacher, the only professional option open at the time to a Protestant woman theologian, she headed two high schools for women in Cologne and actively supported the education of young women. From the end of the 1920s, she was an advocate of the group known as "the women curates of Cologne," supporting them in their struggle for equal access of Protestant women theologians to the office of pastor.

Roman Catholicism at that time was still marked socially by the *Kulturkampf* and, internally, by its defense against Modernism and the *nouvelle méthode* (the beginnings of historical criticism) of biblical interpretation. Here also, however, the changed social situation of women found expression in a variety of activities of social, charitable, and educational character. Of particular note in the sphere of academe is the founding of the Association of German Catholic Women Teachers in 1885. At the beginning of the century, it launched a series of books titled Charakterbilder der katholischen Frauenwelt (Portraits of the Catholic Women's World). As author for one of the first of these volumes on women in the Bible, they were able to engage Michael Faulhaber, professor of biblical theology (subsequently bishop of Speyer and Cardinal of Munich). The first and final chapters of Faulhaber's monograph place a "royal" figure at the center: the king's mother of Proverbs 31 and Mary, the mother of the Lord. That book was published in 1912! The women of Israel are depicted in the position that their domestic, religious, social, and ethical rights assign to them but also as "heroines." The women of New Testament times are related strictly to Jesus, since they are to be found in his genealogy, his speeches, his "sphere of grace," in his service, and, also, in his subsequent community of disciples, in various "diaconates" in the apostolic congregations. However colorful and alive the picture becomes on account of this, the Old Covenant is rigidly oriented even in this disposition toward "law," over against which stands "gospel." Correspondingly, the women of the Old Covenant are presented as objects of the law. However, the women of the New Testament appear as acting subjects who, nevertheless, are limited strictly to functions of "service," of the "diaconate."

In 1903 the Catholic German Women's Alliance (KDFB) was formed. Not the least of its aims was to bring together educated women to create a new, society-shaping force based in the heart of Catholicism. In distinction from Protestantism and its direct reference to Holy Scripture, "heart of Catholicism" meant affirmation of the papacy as well as rootedness in the sacraments, particularly the Eucharist. Clearly, and wholly without dispute, the Catholic women of that time acknowledge that this form of making Christ present sacramentally was firmly bound to the hierarchical and male office of the priest. In *Die christliche Frau* (The Christian Woman), the journal of the Women's Alliance, there appeared an article in 1903/4 by Severus Raue, a Franciscan, "On the Prohibition of Public Appearance and Teaching by Women in the Epistles of St. Paul." He encouraged educated women to speak out in public since he took the Apostle's restrictions (such as that of 1 Cor. 14:34f.) to be limited solely to the priestly office for women. The Catholic women were on the whole part of the middle-class wing of the women's movement and embraced the principle of the equal worth but natural differences of the sexes. They emphasized their manifold options for action in the sense of "public motherliness" within the sphere of society and its social work and, accordingly, obtained qualifications in the areas of medicine, pedagogy, and literature.

There were some Roman Catholic women students who, on an individual basis, dared to attend lectures at faculties of Roman Catholic theology, but nothing more specific is known to date. On the whole, the association Roman Catholic women had with the Bible during the whole nineteenth and the first decades of the twentieth centuries remained limited to hearing, praying, and meditating on it in church. This included catechesis of children at home and at school and, in exceptional cases, visionary supplementation, unlocking and interpreting given biblical texts. For example, this was done in exemplary fashion by Anna Katharina Emmerick, a nun from Dülmen. But even her visions are not accessible in their authentic versions. From their first, oral presentation to their ultimate publication in print and the subsequent new editions of them, they were subjected to a series of "revisions" by men, at first and primarily by her "writer" Clemens Brentano.

In the 1870s Switzerland admitted women to its universities and to sit for examinations. In the 1880s Helene von Mülinen (1850–1924), daughter of a Bernese patrician family, took up the study of Protestant theology. Adolf Schlatter, the New Testament scholar who taught at Bern at the time, had encouraged her to do so. She enrolled as an auditor only, however, because she had not been permitted by her mother to register for regular study. Helene von Mülinen became one of the founders of the Swiss women's movement working for the vote of women. The addresses she delivered between 1897 and 1910, and once again in 1919, show that—and how—her demands for women's rights are based in biblical-exegetical reflection. In 1903, at the "Séminaire d'activité chrétienne" in Geneva, she spoke about "Woman and the Gospel." The address caused quite a stir. She openly criticized the Pauline command to women to remain silent and demonstrated how very significant women actually were in the early church. She did so in order to demand that, here and now, women be given the right to act as independent agents and that they receive professional education. For her, women's emancipation meant their growing into the full image of God.

Carola Barth, *Die Interpretation des Neuen Testaments in der valentinischen Gnosis*, TU 37.3 (Leipzig, 1911); Doris Brodbeck, "Helene von Mülinen: Frauenemanzipation als Forderung ans Christentum," *Neue Wege* 88 (1994): 356–61; *Die christliche Frau* 1 (1902/3); Michael Faulhaber, *Charakterbilder der biblischen Frauenwelt*, vol. 1, no. 1 in the series Charakterbilder der katholischen Frauenwelt, ed. Pauline Herber and Maria Grisar (Paderborn: Verlag Ferdinand Schöningh, 1912); *Frankfurter Brentano-Ausgabe*, vols. 26ff. (Stuttgart: Verlag W. Kohlhammer, 1980–), Brentano's editions of the writings of A. K. Emmerick; Adolf von Harnack, "Über die beiden Recensionen der Geschichte der Prisca und Aquila in Act. Apost. 18, 1-12," *Sitzungsberichte der Königlich-Preussischen Akademie der Wissenschaften zu Berlin*, 1900; Dagmar Henze, *Zwei Schritte vor und einen zurück: Carola Barth—eine Theologin auf dem Weg zwischen Christentum und Frauenbewegung* (Neukirchen-Vluyn: Neukirchener Verlag, 1995); Alfred

Kall, *Katholische Frauenbewegung in Deutschland: Eine Untersuchung zur Gründung katholischer Frauenvereine im 19. Jahrhundert* (Paderborn: Verlag Ferdinand Schöningh, 1983); Max Löhr, *Die Stellung des Weibes zu Jahwereligion und -kult*, BWAT 4 (Leipzig, 1908); Lydia Stöcker, *Die Frau in der alten Kirche* (Tübingen, 1907); Irmtraud Götz von Olenhusen, ed., *Wunderbare Erscheinungen: Frauen und katholische Frömmigkeit im 19. und 20. Jahrhundert* (Paderborn: Verlag Ferdinand Schöningh, 1995); Susanna Woodtli, "Helene von Mülinen: Zum 50. Todestag," *Reformatio* 23/4 (1974): 208–22; Leopold Zscharnack, *Der Dienst der Frau in den ersten Jahrhunderten der christlichen Kirche* (Göttingen: Vandenhoeck und Ruprecht, 1902).

Doris Brodbeck from Bern is currently working on a monograph on the theological dimensions of Helene von Mülinen's work.

1.3.2 Between the Wars

In 1918, after the birth of the Weimar Republic and its constitutionally enshrined declaration of the equality of women and men, the Protestant faculties of theology began to offer their women students the institutionalized possibility of sitting for the First Examination. It remained clearly set apart from the Second Examination, however, which was set by the church and required to qualify for ecclesial professions. Numerous women continued to choose the doctorate as the conclusion of their studies—among them Eva Bartschat-Gillischewski, who defended her dissertation, "The Economic Ethics of the Old Testament Prophets," at the University of Königsberg in 1921, and Selma Hirsch, whose dissertation, "The Idea of a Female *Pneuma Hagion* in the New Testament and in Ancient Christian Literature," was accepted by the University of Berlin in 1926. Hirsch's work is in history of dogma; her thesis is that the Holy Spirit is seen in the most ancient Christian perception as a "mother spirit." Hirsch then proposes ways of integrating this feminine-motherly idea of the Spirit into systematic theology.

By the mid-1920s, between fifty and eighty prospective Protestant women theologians were registered at universities in Germany. At the beginning of the thirties, the number had risen to over three hundred, not least on account of the legislation of 1926, which had created the profession of *Vikarin*. This curacy provided Protestant women theologians with an ecclesially authorized position and work in congregations, but it was clearly distinguished from the spiritual office of the (male) pastor. Pastoral care of the sick and the imprisoned as well as work among women and girls was to be the primary activity of these curates. The newsletter of the Association of Protestant Women Theologians in Germany, which began publication in 1932, again and again printed sermons by these women. They consistently focus on biblical texts or themes. Three women representing that generation are to be introduced here. They are Hedwig Jahnow, Maria Weigle, and Anna Paulsen.

Hedwig Jahnow was born in Poznan in 1879. She first attended a school for women teachers in Berlin and then enrolled at the university there to complete examinations for senior-level teaching. In 1907 she was appointed senior teacher at a school in Marburg; there she renewed her contact with the university and attended in particular the lectures of Hermann Gunkel in nearby Giessen. In 1932 she published her monograph "The Funeral Dirge within the Poetry of Nations" for which she was awarded an honorary doctorate. A pupil of Gunkel's, she focused on the history of genre, that is, she described the funeral dirge as a type of text, placing it into the comparative literary and cultural framework of social-historical material. Such a procedure will by necessity bring characteristic dimensions of women's life repeatedly into view: the death of many young women during or shortly after giving birth is reflected in the texts of dirges as mourning for one who died much too early or, more generally, as fear of death, which does not spare even little children. The institution of the funeral dirge itself is interculturally maintained chiefly by women. Hedwig Jahnow discussed such women-specific dimensions with scholarly thoroughness, but did not address them specifically as such. On the other hand, she wrote a small series of articles as early as 1913–14 on the topic "Women in the Old Testament." In the context of religious instruction at school, she devoted herself to the education of young women. As the daughter of a Jewish father who had converted to Protestant Christianity, she fell victim to the Nuremberg Racial Laws and was deported to Terezin on September 6, 1942, where she died two years later. In memory of her and her work, a number of women founded a working group of feminist exegetes at Marburg in 1991.

Maria Weigle (1893–1979) was a child of the manse from the western central German region of Bergisches Land. From 1919 to 1924, she studied Protestant theology at Bonn, Tübingen, and Berlin and successfully passed the examinations for high-school teachers as well as the First Examination in theology. Initially, she taught for two years at an urban middle-level school for young women. Then she moved to the head office of a Protestant charity for women in Potsdam, where she edited a journal for women and ran the travel service that assisted in the continuing education of women volunteers in congregational Bible study. In 1929 she completed the Second Examination in theology and worked part-time as a curate until 1933. Then she developed a program of courses in biblical studies that in 1936 she was able to consolidate into a nationally accredited Bible school. In the course of this work, she designed her own blueprint for teaching biblical studies with women. After the war, when she became director of the School for the Church's Community Work at Stein near Nuremberg, she integrated this blueprint into the educational program for women parish workers. Her most important goal was to teach women to see things for themselves and to express themselves. Methodologically this resulted in her initially choosing New Testament texts (she did not dare tackle the First Testament!) that were simple and close to the experience of women. She did not interpret those texts herself but provided questions to the text that gave structure to its study, so that genuine conversation with the Bible could arise. Choosing for discussion with untrained women the passage of Mark 10:13-16, about the blessing of children, Maria Weigle directs attention to those who "were bringing children." She facilitates the realization that they must surely have been women with their babies. In this way, the women who participate in such conversations with the Bible are addressed deeply within their own experience as women. They become ready to relate to themselves that God's reign has been given to them already without any of their doing, as it has to their babies.

Anna Paulsen (1893–1981) came from a pastor's family in the region of the German-Danish border. She studied theology from 1916 to 1921 at Kiel, Tübingen, and Münster and obtained the licentiate in 1923 at Kiel with a dissertation about dogmatic and historical interpretation of Scripture. She was called in 1926 to the principalship of the newly founded Training Center for Bible Studies and Youth Leadership and The School for Women's Service in the Church at the Burckhardthaus in Berlin. She worked there until the end of the war, developing and implementing a two-year program for women parish workers. In 1951 she was appointed to the chancery of the Evangelische Kirche Deutschlands at Hannover; her portfolio there was chiefly women's work in the church. In addition to this work, Anna Paulsen continued to write and publish. In addition to biblical exegesis, she wrote about how women in ministry understood themselves and their work and how their positions could be secured legally. Finally, she worked on the interpretation of Søren Kierkegaard. Her monograph, with the unpretentious title "Mother and Maid-Servant: Biblical Language about Women," is a noteworthy piece of biblical exegesis from the perspective of women. It is a historical portrayal and evaluation based on biblical theology of the entire textual material of both testaments on the subject of "woman." Having enjoyed two prewar printings, in 1960 this work appeared in a revised edition as *Geschlecht und Person* (Gender and Person). This title depicts more clearly the basic theological-biblical thesis of the book. Paulsen maintains dispassionately that the conditions of patriarchy must be taken as determinative of both First and New Testament times. And yet the Holy Scriptures may be drawn on in the labor for women's equality. For in it is a theological thread that calls on women to become God's partners in dialogue and to develop their own personalities in faith. Women are seen here as clearly having the same place as men in the I-You relation between humans and God. Anna Paulsen calls this thread of biblical tradition "prophetic" but understands it less as genre-related and more as a theological qualification that applies especially to the *imago Dei* assertion of Gen. 1:26f. On first glance it appears as if she were pursuing a dialogical process with the entire Bible. Closer reading, however, shows something else. She divides, as it were, the First Testament into the prophetic thread, which was brought to its fulfillment in Christ, and the basic law-related feature, which then comes into its own in postexilic Judaism. It is to the latter that the now fully accomplished exclusion of women from all cultic offices corresponds. As this early example already demonstrates, even such an attempt to give contour to a women's history of the biblical faith is not invulnerable to anti-Jewish clichés. In this instance, it is the stereotype of Jesus following in the prophetic line while Judaism entrenched itself in the law. Anna Paulsen invokes this latter cliché, calling it "rabbinical" or "Pharisaic," every time a disagreeable tradition in the New Testament is to be disposed of, such as 1 Cor. 11:3ff. or 1 Tim. 2:12f.

What Romano Guardini called "the awakening of the church in the soul" is also a subject of discussion among Roman Catholic women in the Weimar period. In those years there were isolated cases of women attending courses at theological faculties. Stirred by the spirit of the liturgical movement, such women initially wished to complete the entire program of studies without looking toward eventual employment. Franziska Werfer (1906–85) was the first woman to be officially registered in Germany and able to complete these studies with both episcopal and governmental approval. In 1929, she passed the theological examination at the Catholic faculty of theology in Tübingen. Following her studies, she held a diocesan appointment as a teacher of religion in primary schools and, at the junior-year level, in an educational institution for women. The advanced instruction of religion remained in the hands of priests. According to official statistics, between 1924 and 1932–33 there was only one other woman registered at a Roman Catholic theological faculty. By 1938, however, ten women completed theological studies at Tübingen alone. Among them were Rosa Feifel and Magdalena Prato, who were hired in 1936 and 1939 respectively by the Catholic Women's Association of Stuttgart. At the beginning of the Third Reich, the association had urged the creation of programs of adult education and catechesis in connection with which Franziska Werfer was given a number of tasks to do. She and Magdalena Prato belonged to the so-called Circle of St. Mark, which was directed by a priest from Stuttgart named Breucha. For years, both in public education events and within the circle, he trained people in ongoing reading of Scripture.

In the 1930s, the four Roman Catholic faculties of Austria (Vienna, Innsbruck, Salzburg, and Graz) also counted only one woman among their students. It was Charlotte Leitmaier, LL.D., who had obtained special archiepiscopal permission to register as a regular student. In 1937 the Austrian Conference of Bishops prohibited the presence of women students in theological faculties. This prohibition was occasionally ignored but was lifted only in 1945. In Vienna, the single Protestant theological faculty in the country became incorporated into the university in 1922 and admitted women to the study of theology. In 1940, Irmgard Schmalenburg was the first woman to be granted the doctorate. She had written on a biblical theme, "The Interpretation and Use of the Old Testament in the Epistles of Paul." The records indicate that up to the year 1970 no other woman followed in her steps.

For a number of women during those years, turning toward the church as the "mystical body of Christ" became the reason to begin studying theology (and, in 1926, for the author Gertrud von le Fort, who had studied Protestant theology, to convert to Roman Catholicism). Many of those women were of the upper middle class, for which reason such a turn was viewed critically by other Roman Catholic women, who were more closely associated with the political movement of women. In 1922, an article on the question of female pastoral caregivers made for some public commotion. It had been published not by a Roman Catholic journal but in *Die Frau*, a journal of the bourgeois women's movement. The writer was Dr. Margarete Adam, a Roman Catholic philosopher. She complained about the growing lack of interest in politics and society, especially among younger Catholic women. She had in mind a twofold structure of the priestly office: while keeping the "sacrificial priesthood" restricted to men, she would urge the admission of women to a priestly office of pastoral care, especially in relation to the specific problem of women created by industrialization. In the same year, the Roman Catholic historian Gerta Krabbel—who became the director of the Catholic German Women's Alliance in 1926—made a contribution to the association's journal *Die christliche Frau*. It reads like a confirmation of Adam's critical analysis. Krabbel confirms the spiritual hardship of women, particularly in the present time. She rejects the demand for women's priesthood, because it is "alien to the Roman Catholic woman" and takes away from the particular religious internal gifts of woman.

But when one looks at the literary work of Catholic women of the time, it becomes apparent that this diagnosis does not depict "the" Roman Catholic woman. Emanuele Meyer, a woman physician, published a work called *Amboss meiner Seele*, a collection of aphorisms forged on "the anvil of her soul." The aphorisms, many of which have a remarkably matriarchal-feminist air, seek to combine both the emphasis on the particular religious gifts of women and the downright satirical mocking of the still-dominant "scholastic undervaluation" of women in the church (p. 130 and elsewhere). She takes it for granted that such was envisaged "neither in the old nor the new covenant as being the will of God" (131). This she demonstrates in relation to the First Testament in terms of an interpretation of the creation account according to which woman is the crown and fulfillment of creation (126f.). In relation to the New Testament, she demonstrates her case among other interpretations in connection with Mary Magdalene as the first witness to the resurrection (133). Meyer believes that today the Apostle Paul would have given his first epistle to the Corinthians a different form, especially in relation to matters concerning women (141ff. and 163f.), and she asserts that for women of her day "emancipation is God's will" (171).

Hochland, the leading Roman Catholic cultural journal, published more traditional writers like Gertrude von le Fort or Ruth Schaumann but it did not close its pages to "radical" ones. Ilse von Stach's "The Women of Corinth," published in 1928/9, takes St. Paul to task in unusually sharp fashion. She portrays a group of women on the market square of that town. They discuss the Apostle's recently arrived first letter with its injunction about having to wear veils (11:2f.) and the commandment to remain silent (14:34f.). In the heroine of the piece, who has the telling name of Elephteria (Freedom), von Stach expresses unmistakably her own indignation at the allegedly divinely ordained subordination of women.

Margarete Adam, "Weibliche Seelsorge," *Die Frau* 29, no. 7 (1922): 198–207 and 365–72; Andrea Bieler, *Konstruktionen des Weiblichen zwischen Zwang und Widerspruch: Eine feministisch-befreiungstheologische Analyse des Werkes der Theologin Anna Paulsen im Kontext der bürgerlichen Frauenbewegung der Weimarer Republik und verschiedener nationalsozialistischer Positionen* (Gütersloh: Gütersloher Verlagshaus Gerd Mohn, 1994); *Die christliche Frau* 18 (1919/20), and following issues; *Frauenbefreiung und Theologie*, 1st, 2d, and 3d editions (Mainz: Grünewald; Munich: Kaiser, 1978–82); Eva Gillischewski, "Die Wirtschaftsethik der Propheten" (diss., Königsberg, 1921); Selma Hirsch, "Die Vorstellung von einem weiblichen *pneuma hagion* im Neuen Testament und in der altesten christlichen Literatur: Ein Beitrag zur Lehre vom Heiligen Geist" (diss., Berlin, 1926); Hedwig Jahnow, *Das Leichenlied im Rahmen der Völkerdichtung* (Giessen: A. Töpelmann, 1923); idem, "Die Frau im Alten Testament," *Die Frau* 21 (1913/4): 352–58 and 417–26, reprinted in Hedwig Jahnow et al., *Feministische Hermeneutik und Erstes Testament* (Stuttgart: Verlag W. Kohlhammer, 1994), 26–47; Doris Kaufmann, "Vom Vaterland zum Mutterland: Frauen im katholischen Milieu der Weimarer Republik," in Karin Hausen, ed., *Frauen suchen ihre Geschichte* (Munich: C. H. Beck, 1983), 250–75; Joachim Köhler, "Ein bedeutender Schritt: Vor 50 Jahren legte Franziska Werfer als erste Frau Deutschlands ein theologisches Examen ab," *Katholisches Sonntagsblatt* (Mainz) 10 (1979): 26; Gerta Krabbel, "Zur Frage des weiblichen Priestertums," *Die christliche Frau* 20, no. 6 (1922): 83–88; Emanuele L. Meyer, *Vom Amboss meiner Seele: Splitter und Funken* (Heilbronn, 1921); *Mitteilungen des Verbandes Evangelischer Theologinnen in Deutschland* 1 (1932), called as of 1941 *Die Theologin* (publication was interrupted from 1943 until 1953 and ceased altogether in 1967); Elisabeth Moltmann-Wendel, ed., *Frau und Religion: Gotteserfahrung im Patriarchat* (Frankfurt: Fischer Taschenbuch Verlag, 1983); Anna Paulsen, *Mutter und Magd: Das biblische Wort über die Frau* (Hamburg, 1935; 2d. ed., 1938; 3d revised ed., entitled *Geschlecht und Person*, 1960); Ilse Ueckert, ed., *Maria Weigle—Bibelarbeit mit Frauen* (Gelnhausen: Burckhardthaus-Laetare Verlag, 1979); idem, *Mit der Bibel leben: Maria Weigle und die Frauen*, Laetare Pamphlets 295 (Gelnhausen: Burckhardthaus-Laetare Verlag, 1980); Ilse von Stach, "Die Frauen von Korinth," *Hochland* 26, no. 2 (1928/9): 141–63 (published as a book in Breslau, 1929); Maria Weigle, *Bibelarbeit—Methodik der Bibelarbeit mit Frauen* (Potsdam, 1938); Wirtschaftshilfe der Deutschen Studentenschaft, e.V., vol. 175 (Federal Archive, Koblenz, file R.149/175), especially the statistics about how the number of female students grew between 1924 and 1933.

Beate Hofmann-Strauch is working on her dissertation in Munich on Maria Weigle in the context of the Bavarian service of care for mothers.

1.4 From the Postwar Years to the Beginning of the "New Women's Movement"

The one and only habilitation-dissertation of a woman theologian produced in the time of National Socialism was that of the Protestant Hanna Jursch at the University of Jena. Her work was in the field of Christian archaeology and bore the title "The Images of Judas Iscariot in the Ancient Church." The Nazi state never granted the dissertation the required official recognition. Only in 1952 did another Protestant woman submit a habilitation-dissertation. It was Marie-Louise Henry, born in 1911, whose work on the so-called Apocalypse of Isaiah (chaps. 24–27) was accepted at the then—East German University of Rostock. To date, not too many women have followed her example. To the best of our knowledge, the following have successfully completed their habilitation in the field of exegesis: Eva Osswald (First Testament) at Jena in 1956; Luise Schottroff (New Testament) at Mainz in 1969; Eta Linnemann (New Testament) at Marburg in 1970; Barbara Aland (textual research in New Testament) at Münster in 1972; Hannelis Schulte (First Testament) at Heidelberg in 1982; Anneli Aejmelaeus (First Testament/Septuagint) at Göttingen in 1983; Ingrid Riesener (First Testament) at Berlin in 1985; Brigitte Kahl (New Testament/ecumenics) at Berlin in 1986; Ina Willi-Plein (First Testament) at Basel in 1974/88; Julia Männchen (New Testament) at Greifswald in 1991; Christa Schäfer-Lichtenberger (First Testament) at Heidelberg in 1992; Jutta Hausmann (First Testament) at Neuendettelsau in 1992; Oda Wischmeyer (ancient Judaism/New Testament) at Heidelberg in 1992; Beate Ego (First Testament/Judaism) at Tübingen in 1993. To date, only three women have succeeded in their habilitation in this field of study in the German-speaking Roman Catholic academy. They are: Silvia Schroer (First Testament) at Fribourg in 1989; Irmtraud Fischer (First Testament) at Graz in 1993, and Marie-Theres Wacker (First Testament) at Münster in 1995.

The 1950s and 1960s saw Protestant women theologians in Germany once again drawn into vehement discussions about their admission to the office of pastor in its full scope. In these discussions, the controversy about the Bible was very far-reaching. It was in those years that the dissertations of Else Kähler on Paul's concept of "subordination" and Ilse Bertinetti on the question of the office were written. Only then did the first regional churches venture to establish procedures for equality that continued, nonetheless, to include next to the often-mentioned "financial considerations" the so-called celibacy clause for women clergy. It was not until the early 1990s that the clause was finally abandoned.

The papal encyclical *Divino afflante spiritu* of 1943 was an important step for biblical exegesis within Roman Catholicism. It affirmed for the first time historical-critical research, especially the two components of form-critical study and *Gattungsgeschichte*. It became authorized for use in the education of theologians. After the war, the Catholic faculties in Germany and Austria formally offered the opportunity to laity—and therefore to women—to register. In this newly won chance to study theology, these persons were also able to experience the first baby steps of critical-historical exegesis of Scripture in the world of Catholicism.

In 1949, when Eleonore Beck had completed theological studies, she applied to the University of Tübingen to pursue doctoral studies in First Testament. She was reminded of the existing regulation that only persons ordained to the subdiaconate could be admitted to such studies, a regulation which excluded women from the start simply because of their sex. Undaunted by that information, and without academic or episcopal "ordering," she began to translate works of French theologians and exegetes into German. She became coeditor of Die Welt der Bibel, the series of mini-commentaries published by Patmos Verlag beginning in 1960. In 1951, she took over the editorial secretariat of the newly founded *Internationale Zeitschriftenschau für Bibelwissenschaft und Grenzgebiete* (*IZBG*) and is now known as the author of numerous biblical monographs and articles for both scholars and nonspecialist readers. On the other hand, Katharina Neulinger, registered at the University of Tübingen from 1941 to 1945, moved to Vienna after the final examinations. There she received the doctorate in 1952 with a thesis on "Female Characters in the New Testament" (the university having awarded its first doctorate to a woman in Catholic theology in 1946). For many years she then worked both full- and part-time for the Catholic Bible Institute in Stuttgart. Maria Richter (1915–93) had studied history and Catholic theology, among other subjects, at Munich in the 1930s; with no chance of pursuing doctoral studies, she switched to the faculty of philosophy. In 1946, she obtained the doctorate in history with one of her minor subjects being Catholic dogmatics. This testifies to the support afforded her by Michael Schmaus, professor of Catholic dogmatics at Munich. Richter then taught at various levels in the school system. She continued to deepen her exegetical knowledge, lectured in adult continuing education, and established a Bible-study circle in a parish in Munich. After she retired, Professor Hermann Seifermann, who teaches First Testament exegesis in the department of religious pedagogy of the Catholic University Eichstatt in Munich, involved her in many ways in his scholarly and pedagogical work.

Munich was the first German faculty of theology to drop the subdiaconate clause, thus enabling women to study for the theological doctorate. After Gertrud Reidick had obtained her doctorate in canon law in 1953, Elisabeth Gössmann and Uta (Ranke) Heinemann in 1954 completed doctorates in dogmatics (once again under the direction of Michael Schmaus). It was not until nearly two decades later that the first women completed doctoral studies in exegesis: Hannelore Steichele (New Testament) in 1971 and Hildegard (Hagia) Witzenrath (First Testament) in 1973. The first woman doctoral graduate at Freiburg was Johanna Kopp (practical theology) in 1958; in exegesis it was Annemarie Ohler (First Testament) in 1966. Hildegard Gollinger and Ingrid Maisch (both New Testament) followed in 1968 and 1970, respectively. Münster followed in 1962 with its first woman doctorate: Helga Voss was awarded the degree for her studies in liturgical history. Adelheid Stecker and Iris Müller were the first women to complete doctorates in exegesis, the former in 1968 (New Testament) and the latter in 1970 (First Testament). The Catholic faculty of theology at Bonn awarded its first doctorate to a woman—and a layperson—to Helen Schüngel-Straumann in 1969. She had worked on a thesis on the Decalogue.

At the time of the Second Vatican Council, Elisabeth Schüssler obtained the licentiate of theology degree from the University of Würzburg with a study on "The Forgotten Partner" in the church, referring to "the professional collaboration by women." (This work anticipated her subsequent and explicit feminist engagement.) At the same time, two women theologians from Münster were to be found among the cosigners of a petition to the Vatican Council on changes to Canon 968 CIC, which excludes women from ordination to the priesthood; they were Iris Müller (First Testament) and Ida Raming (canon law). But at Tübingen, the attempt of a woman to complete theological studies with a doctorate failed once again. In 1966, Andrea von Dülmen submitted her thesis on the theological position of the law in Paul. She had already been confronted by the fact that the then-professor of New Testament at Munich had invited her, a talented (unmarried) prospective doctoral student, to work with him only to be "dismissed" by him when she became married. Despite the solid support of her *Doktorvater,* Karl-Herrmann Schelkle, she had to endure the objections which prevailed over her in the Tübingen faculty, namely that she was a "layperson" (i.e., not a priest!) as well as a scholar who went her own ways. Disenchanted, she withdrew her work. Schelkle tried in vain to reopen the process, particularly in light of the good reviews of the by then published work. It was only in 1972 that a woman, Dorothy Irwin of the United States, was awarded the doctorate in First Testament exegesis. Linda Maloney, also from the United States, was the first woman scholar in New Testament studies to obtain a doctorate at that faculty with a thesis directed by Schelkle's successor, Gerhard Lohfink; she was awarded the degree in 1989. It was also not until 1972 that a woman was awarded the doctorate by the Catholic faculty of theology at the University of Würzburg; Ruthild Geiger wrote her thesis on Luke's end-time discourses.

Helga Rusche is a New Testament scholar who by 1943 had already obtained a doctorate at Heidelberg; at that time she was still Protestant, but subsequently converted to Roman Catholicism. She became known through her writings, especially in the 1950s; *Töchter des Glaubens* (Daughters of Faith), her book based on a series of articles in the journal *Frau und Beruf* (Woman and Vocation) (1956), is most likely the first monograph on women in the Bible from the pen of a German-speaking Catholic woman theologian. Her presentation profiles individual women and women's roles from both Testaments. The title signals her twofold purpose. First, Helga Rusche seeks to present a panorama of women, both those known by name as well as the unnamed, who show their faith in that they heeded the call of God. Second, she speaks of "daughters of faith" because they are placed in line with the faith of Abraham, the "father of faith," whose turning to the God of Israel remained the foundation also of Christianity. For its time, the little book was exceptional in that it revealed a sensitive depiction of the meaning of the "old covenant" without, in the manner of Christian presumptuousness, denigrating it as antiquated and superseded by the new covenant.

In the winter of 1969–70 Elisabeth Schüssler Fiorenza graduated from the University of Münster with a doctorate on the Apocalypse of John. When her thesis was published in 1972, she was already living in the United States. There, the discussion about feminist theology was already in full swing. In 1968 Mary Daly had published her *The Church and the Second Sex* in which, adopting Simone de Beauvoir's analysis and conceptuality, she charged the Catholic church with androcentrism in its teaching and practice. In 1973, in the book *Beyond God the Father*, she broke with Christianity. A year later, Rosemary Radford Ruether edited a volume on *Religion and Sexism*; in the same year, 1974, Letty Russell published the first book on feminist theology. Phyllis Trible had begun in 1973 to publish exegetical-feminist studies on the Hebrew Bible; Rachel Conrad Wahlberg's *Jesus according to a Woman* appeared in 1975. These were the years during which, at universities in the Federal Republic of Germany and Switzerland, young women also took up the study of Catholic theology as a principal subject. For the first time, the church offered them and their male lay colleagues a vocational opportunity other than in the school system, namely that of pastoral agent. The presence of a great number of women studying theology was most likely a necessary "institutional" precondition for the fact that feminist theology and its feminist exegetical work could develop in German-speaking countries. Likewise, within Protestantism, we may speak of an approach to the Bible oriented by feminism only since the time when the "new women's movement" began to make its case in public. It demonstrated that the ongoing failure to institutionalize equal rights for women was an expression of a deeper crisis, namely that of the worldwide and historically all-embracing patriarchy which has to be resisted and toppled by an equally all-embracing solidarity of women.

Ilse Bertinetti, *Frauen im geistlichen Amt: Die theologische Problematik in evangelisch-lutherischer Sicht* (Berlin: Evangelische Verlagsanstalt, 1963); Elisabeth Boedeker and Maria Meyer-Plath: *50 Jahre Habilitation von Frauen in Deutschland* (Göttingen: O. Schwartz, 1974); Mary Daly, *The Church and the Second Sex* (New York: Harper and Row, 1968); idem, *Beyond God the Father* (London: Women's Press, 1973);

Andrea von Dülmen, *Die Theologie des Gesetzes bei Paulus,* SBM 5 (Stuttgart: Echter, 1968); Rachel Conrad Wahlberg, *Jesus according to a Woman* (New York: Paulist Press, 1975); Hannelore Erhart, "Theologin und Universität—Das Beispiel Hanna Jursch," *Jahrbuch der Gesellschaft für niedersächsische Kirchengeschichte* 89 (1991): 385–98; idem, "Die Theologin im Kontext von Universität und Kirche zur Zeit der Weimarer Republik und des Nationalsozialismus," in Leonore Siegele-Wenschkewitz and Carsten Nicolaisen, *Theologische Fakultäten im Nationalsozialismus* (Göttingen: Vandenhoeck und Ruprecht, 1993), 223–49; Ruthild Geiger, *Die lukanischen Endzeitreden: Studien zur Eschatologie des Lukas-Evangeliums* (Frankfurt: Peter Lang, 1973); Hildegard Gollinger, *Das "grosse Zeichen" von Apokalypse 12,* SBM 11 (Würzburg and Stuttgart: Echter, 1971); Dorothy Irwin, *Mytharion: The Comparison of Tales from the Old Testament and the Ancient Near East,* AOAT 32 (Kevelaer: Butzon und Berker; Neukirchen-Vluyn: Neukirchener Verlag, 1978); Else Kähler, *Die Frau in den paulinischen Briefen unter besonderer Berücksichtigung des Begriffs der Unterordnung* (Zurich: Gotthelf-Verlag, 1960); Leo Karrer, *Von Beruf Laientheologe?* (Vienna, Freiburg, and Basel: Herder, 1970); Ingrid Maisch, *Die Heilung des Gelähmten: Eine exegetisch-traditionsgeschichtliche Untersuchung zu Mark 2:1-12,* SBS 52 (Stuttgart: KBW-Verlag, 1971); Iris Müller, "Die Wertung der Nachbarvölker Israels, Edom, Moab, Ammon, Philistäa und Tyros/Sidon nach den gegen sie gerichteten Drohsprüchen der Propheten" (diss., Münster, 1970); Josefa Theresia Münch, "Welche Dienstmöglichkeiten findet die katholische Frau heute in ihrer Kirche?" *Die Theologin* 24, no. 1 (1965): 14–25; Annemarie Ohler, *Mythologische Elemente im Alten Testament* (Düsseldorf, 1969); Rosemary Radford Ruether, ed., *Religion and Sexism* (New York: Simon and Schuster, 1974); Helga Rusche, *Töchter des Glaubens* (Mainz, 1959); Letty Russell, *Human Liberation in a Feminist Perspective: A Theology* (Philadelphia: Westminster Press, 1974); Helen Schüngel-Straumann, "Tod und Leben in der Gesetzesliteratur des Pentateuch unter besonderer Berücksichtigung der Terminologie von 'toten'" (diss., Bonn, 1969); Elisabeth Schüssler, *Der vergessene Partner: Grundlagen, Tatsachen und Möglichkeiten der beruflichen Mitarbeit der Frau in der Heilssorge der Kirche* (Düsseldorf: Patmos Verlag, 1964); Elisabeth Schüssler Fiorenza, *Priester für Gott: Studien zum Herrschafts und Priestermotiv in der Apokalypse* (Münster: Aschendorff, 1972); Adelheid Stecker, *Formen und Formeln in den paulin.: Hauptbriefen und in den Pastoralbriefen* (diss., Münster, 1967); Hannelore Steichele, "Vergleich der Apostelgeschichte mit der antiken Geschichtsschreibung: Eine Studie zur Erzählkunst in der Apostelgeschichte" (diss., Munich, 1971); Phyllis Trible, *God and the Rhetoric of Sexuality* (Philadelphia: Fortress Press, 1978); Hagia Witzenrath, *Das Buch Jona: Eine literaturwissenschaftliche Untersuchung*, ATS 6 (St. Ottilien: Eos Verlag, 1978).

Chapter Two

Feminist Exegetical Hermeneutics

According to its self-understanding, feminist exegesis of the Christian Bible of the First and New Testaments situates itself where exegesis and feminism intersect. *Biblical exegesis* here means the historical and literary, scholarly interpretation of the Bible within the overall framework of Christian theology. Authenticated in scholarly responsibility and related to the experiences of "the people of God," it means the account that Christian theology on its part gives about that faith of which the Bible is seen to be the witness to the (self-)revelation of God. "Feminism" here refers to the determined movement in recent times of women seeking to come free from the judicial and economic predominance of "fathers" and also from the psychic and ideological tutelage of men. (See 2.2.1.) Dorothee Sölle puts it as follows: "Feminism is women's breaking away from tutelage—whether imposed by others or self-inflicted." This depiction of feminism as a "movement" must be placed alongside the understanding of feminist scholarship as a scholarly occupation by women that does not lose sight of the (ethical-pragmatic) goal of every woman becoming a subject. Because of this understanding, feminist scholarship does its work in a "biased" state when it seeks to uncover unexamined sexual dualisms and stereotypes of femininity in all scholarly disciplines of the *universitas scientiarum* and to develop approaches that are of a different nature and do justice to women.

Christian theology has been hitherto de facto reserved for men and the office of priest is de jure reserved in the Roman Catholic church to the (unmarried) male. Finally, the philosophical-theological explication of God-talk is caught in diverse, unenlightened clichés of masculinity and femininity which thwart women's coming and being of age. For these reasons, the relation between feminism and feminist scholarship, on one side, and Christian theology and the existing ecclesiastical-congregational practice, on the other, cannot be an uncritical-affirmative one. Which hermeneutical principles are then determinative for Christian women exegetes?

2.1 Types of Theologically Informed Approaches of Women to Scripture and Its Hermeneutics

In 1985, Carolyn Osiek, an American feminist exegete and member of a Roman Catholic religious community, proposed a typification of feminist study of the Bible. It is oriented by how women responded to the realization that in the history of Christianity, the Bible was a primary instrument in the establishment and consolidation of the patriarchal exercise of power. She gives *feminism* a broadly encompassing meaning to include consciously every effort toward the dignity and advancement of woman in every domain of society. In what follows, and in accordance with her suggestion, we will discuss the German-language feminist literature with a view to its theological-hermeneutical options. Relying on selected examples, the typification attempted here will make use of the differentiation or the characterization of feminist theological positions. This is done in terms of different levels of reference that go beyond those of Osiek and are in line with those of Hedwig Meyer-Wilmes, a feminist theologian teaching at Nijmegen and Louvain Universities.

Hedwig Meyer-Wilmes, *Rebellion auf der Grenze* (Freiburg, Basel, and Vienna: Herder Verlag, 1990), pt. 2; Carolyn Osiek, "The Feminist and the Bible: Hermeneutical Alternatives," in Adela Yarbro Collins, ed., *Feminist Perspectives on Biblical Scholarship*, SBL Cent. Publ. 10 (Chico, Calif.: Scholars Press, 1985), 93–105; Marie-Theres Wacker, "Gefährliche Erinnerungen: Feministische Blicke auf die hebräische Bibel," in Marie-Theres Wacker, ed., *Theologie-feministisch* (Düsseldorf: Patmos, 1988), 14–58.

2.1.1 The Hermeneutics of Loyalty

The first type, which Osiek calls "the hermeneutics of loyalty," sees the problem of biblically legitimated discrimination against women not in the Bible itself but solely in its interpretation. It sees how the Bible, albeit in a form bound and "accommodated" to the people of its time, tells of the order of creation and redemption that God willed. In this order a place is assigned to men and women that is specific to them but not of a different qualitative level. Passages in Scripture that appear to be objectionable to women today are either only seemingly problematic in appearance, since their depth has not been grasped, or are strictly limited in their application. In terms of German material, reference is to be made once again to Michael Faulhaber's work *Charakterbilder der biblischen Frauenwelt* (see 1.3.1), which sought to support and empower Catholic women teachers in their calling to educate young women. It may be called a "feminist" work in the wider sense of Osiek's definition. In keeping with the traditional treatment of the Old Testament, Faulhaber refers to the limited and preliminary nature of the possibilities available to the guiding "hand of God" in the moral code of Israel, particularly in relation to the protection of "the honor of women." In contrast, Jesus manifests himself as God's son who overcomes these limitations, liberating women for their true service. The injunction of Paul against women teaching is restricted to specific women—and to them only—whose unauthorized arrogation to themselves of an official teaching activity in the church, related to one of its offices, "had made the ruling necessary" (230).

The strength of this hermeneutic is its attention to the whole Bible; its chief problem is the supranaturalistic conception of Jesus Christ's activity and that of the apostles. In these conceptions the unchanging, divine ordinances for church and world are made manifest and soon thereafter faithfully recorded in Scripture. Within such a view, there are only two possible reactions to the discrimination of women: either one explains it away, or one sees it as an accidental departure from a good and timelessly valid order. What seems not possible is a consistent feminist analysis of patriarchy. This would pay heed to the human, or, more accurately, the male mediation of both the revelations testified to in Scripture and of the official institutional agencies which interpret them. For that very reason, it is not appropriate to designate this hermeneutic "feminist." Even though in its point of departure it is biblical, it is paternalistic.

2.1.2 The Hermeneutic of Rejection

Another type of approach to the Bible, the polar opposite of the one just discussed, is characterized by a decisive "hermeneutic of rejection." In this approach, what is rejected is not a possibly defective interpretation here and there but traditional Christian interpretation as a whole, together with the document to be interpreted. In this perspective, the Bible can have no authority for women anymore, because the history of what the Bible has led to has to be seen throughout as a history of patriarchy. This is because the revelation of God, asserted by and in the Bible, has—precisely on account of that patriarchy—finally disqualified itself as irretrievably sexist. The required withdrawal from the tradition of biblical faith as a whole, which is concomitant with such a conviction, is undertaken with recourse to different religious-theological positions. Elizabeth Cady Stanton (see 1.1) did so on the basis of a deistic principle of reason beyond the antagonisms of gender. This provided motivation and foundation for politically enlightened activity. Mary Daly went on her way after "bidding God the Father farewell" in the name of a speculatively and existentially grasped primordial ground of all being called "God/ess." Finally, Heide Göttner-Abendroth proposed to withdraw in the name of the Goddess, the cosmic Great Feminine, whose efficaciousness is experienced in ritual and liturgies and requires no mediation anymore by a sacred scripture.

The strength of this hermeneutic is that it relentlessly confronts with its factual particularity the biblical-Christian tradition's claim to universality and thereby forces it into reconsideration. However, the alternatives cited are in their own way not themselves free of dilemma. Mary Daly's vision of a gynocentric counterworld at the edges of the world-embracing patriarchy remains dependent ideologically and economically on the dominant structures. Elizabeth Cady Stanton's optimism of reason lies on the other side of this century's two world wars and the terrors of fascism and Stalinism. In their shadow, one may speak in the best-case scenarios of "the dialectics of the Enlightenment," if one does not already have to speak of "deadly progress." Recourse to Heide Göttner-Abendroth's cosmic-divine (see 2.1.4) offers a counterconcept, namely, that of a spirituality which is critical of reason and puts greater weight on nature, sensuousness, and femaleness. She claims that this will do away with the patriarchal myth which burdens woman with the fall in the Garden of Eden. Yet her counterconcept and its basic *thealogoumenon* of the fusion of the feminine-divine and the world cannot do without a Fall—of the male—while also tending to be far too uncritical of human thinking and doing.

Elizabeth Cady Canton, *The Woman's Bible* (see 1.1); Mary Daly, *Gyn-Ecology* (Boston: Beacon Press, 1979); Heide Göttner-Abendroth, *Die*

Göttin und ihr Heros: Die matriarchalen Religionen in Mythos, Mär-chen und Dichtung (Munich: Verlag Frauenoffensive, 1980); idem, *Die tanzende Göttin: Prinzipien einer matriarchalen Aesthetik* (Munich: Verlag Frauenoffensive, 1982; enlarged ed., 1984), Eng. trans.: *The Dancing Goddess: Principles of a Matriarchal Aesthetic* (Boston: Beacon Press, 1991).

2.1.3 The Hermeneutic of Revision

Since it follows a critical-historical approach, "revisionistic" hermeneutics takes note throughout of the historically conditioned refractions of God's Word in the human word, including in the New Testament, and does so more clearly than the hermeneutic of loyalty. It sees the existing patriarchal form of the Bible as a *husk* (the human word) that is distinguishable from the nonpatriarchal *kernel* (the divine word) of the biblical revelation. In order to demonstrate the legitimacy of this distinction and, if need be, combine it with a call for the required change in traditional habits of interpretation and in the praxis of the church, it has to be shown also that the biblical world is not utterly determined by patriarchy. The feminist exegetical approach now described achieves this, first by historical research and, in particular, by "gender research" (see 2.2.3) that brings to light the diverse reality of women in biblical times. It demonstrates that women did have space for freedom of action and self-determination and possessed, within a context undeniably patriarchal, status and dignity. In other words, in the midst of the androcentrism of life's order that ruled women's reality, it was an androcentrism that was not a priori and utterly sexist-misogynist. The second way this approach makes its point is in developing literary-feminist modes of reading the biblical text. Not least, it probes the text's God-language for "structures of the feminine." This not only methodically leads into a new perspective of reception but also seeks to imbue textual content that is affirming of women with theological significance (as a "word of Scripture").

The publications of Methodist exegete Phyllis Trible are an example of this approach; it is she who coined the phrase "the nonpatriarchal principle" of the Bible (see 3.2.3). In her work, this principle remains more or less formal, while other feminist women provide it with material content. Letty Russell, for example, recalls the Scripture's foundational notion of "the healing of creation" as a feminist-biblical principle; Rosemary Radford Ruether holds up the critique of domination, as it is found especially in the prophets, as the (Hebrew) Bible's basic message for feminist women. A unique and interesting development is Klara Butting's proposal (see 3.4.1).

A further differentiation of this feminist-biblical hermeneutic within the German-speaking world is useful at this point. Represented in this phenomenon are women exegetes who, either before the emergence of the feminist movement or at a certain distance from it, worked at a revised interpretation of Scripture while clearly articulating that their interest was in theological practice. These women exegetes, however, made no strict distinction between interpretation of a text and historical reconstruction and, moreover, favored an individualizing formulation of the nonpatriarchal principle. For example, one can already see this in Anna Paulsen (see 1.3.2), who presupposed, and was herself engaged in, historical-exegetical work. Whatever affirmed that women, too, are in the image and likeness of God, she had called the "prophetic" thread of the Bible. She understood this to be the nonpatriarchal dimension of tradition as described above. It is against this that she measures passages of Scripture problematic to women. In a manner similar to Anna Paulsen, Maria Sybilla Heister, a now-retired Protestant minister, names the central theological-anthropological assertion in the Bible, the First Testament to be precise, against which the history of Israel and the New Testament is to be tested. It is also the statement against which theology and ecclesiastical practice today must let themselves be tested: man and woman are in the image of God (Gen. 1:26f.). In their respectively different being, man and woman are in a dialogical relation to God and to one another. Wherever the dialogical principle was disregarded in relation to women, it was done to the detriment of everybody. Thus, the women of ancient Israel, who had to put up with severe restrictions in cult and society, did not accidentally become the opening for foreign, idolatrous cults that offered them room to move. Heister interprets historical factors directly in terms of biblical theology (regarding the biblical portrayal of history as the faithful mirror of historical events). The Catholic exegete and longtime teacher of women and men pastoral associates in Freiburg, Annemarie Ohler, focuses more directly and soberly on the actual patriarchal context of the biblical world. She published two monographs, *Women in the Bible* and *Motherhood;* she argued that at the heart of Scripture was not the male, but God's free saving activity which is made manifest in and also through women. Both of these women intend to show that women may find a deepened, spiritual rootedness in the Bible's traditions of redemptive history. Naturally and without fanfare, the engagement of women in church and society is to grow, as if to be taken for granted, from this insight. Here, one does not speak of "the rights of Christians" or of "women's rights" as these would be foreign notions.

There are women exegetes who represent the "hermeneutic of revision" and yet explicitly understand themselves to be feminist theologians. In other words, they do not shy away from combining the conclusions they established exegetically with a critique of existing social and ecclesial conditions and from taking up the "cause of women." But they also maintain that embedded in the androcentric perspective of the texts are to be found elements of understanding the world or the reality of life that are relevant to and even specific to women. These may be used as elements of current feminist-biblical theology without becoming in their substance part of a guiding principle. Helen Schüngel-Straumann, the Roman Catholic professor of biblical theology at Kassel, is one of these exegetes. While attentive to how the history of interpretation of a text and the consequences of the text itself have often yielded that text to misogyny, she also consciously seeks to bring into awareness (again) biblical traditions that had been supplanted or forgotten. Her monograph *Die Frau am Anfang* (Woman at the Beginning) shows very well how these two aims are combined; her studies on the Spirit as creative life force and on "God as Mother in Hosea 11" highlight the recollection of biblical images of God determined by the reality of women, so that use can be made of them in theology—and not only in feminist theology (see 1.2.3). A similar aim is followed, albeit in a more narrative manner, by Virginia Mollenkott's study on forgotten images of God, *The Divine Feminine: The Biblical Image of God as Female*, and by Eva Schirmer in *Müttergeschichten* (Stories of Mothers).

Klara Butting (see 3.4.1); Maria Sybilla Heister, *Frauen in der biblischen Glaubensgeschichte* (Göttingen: Vandenhoeck und Ruprecht, 1984); Marie-Louise Henry, *Hüte Dein Denken und Wollen: Alttestamentliche Studien, mit einem Beitrag zur feministischen Theologie*, ed. Bernd Jankowski (Neukirchen-Vluyn: Neukirchener Verlag, 1992); Virginia Ramey Mollenkott, *The Divine Feminine: The Biblical Imagery of God as Female* (New York: Crossroad, 1983); Annemarie Ohler, *Frauengestalten in der Bibel* (Würzburg: Echter Verlag, 1987); idem, *Mutterschaft in der Bibel* (Würzburg: Echter Verlag, 1992); Rosemary Radford Ruether, "Feminist Interpretation: A Method of Correlation," in Letty M. Russell, ed., *Feminist Interpretation of the Bible* (Philadelphia: Westminster Press, 1985), 111–24; Letty M. Russell, "Authority and the Challenge of Feminist Interpretation," in Russell, ed., *Feminist Interpretation of the Bible*, 137–46; Helen Schüngel-Straumann (see 1.2.3); Eva Schirmer, *Müttergeschichten: Frauen aus dem Alten Testament erzählen aus ihrem Leben* (Offenbach, 1986); Phyllis Trible, "Depatriarchalizing in Biblical Interpretation," *JAAR* 41 (1973): 30–48.

2.1.4 The Hermeneutic of the "Eternal Feminine"

The hermeneutic of revision insists that a divine reality is to be found in the Bible even though it is admittedly steeped in androcentrism and sexism. This reality transcends such historically factual deformations and has revealed itself as enabling both men's and women's full humanness. This is not enough, however, for the fourth type of feminist-biblical hermeneutics. The Bible may continue to claim validity for today only if the divinity to which it points is essentially comprehended in symbols of the Great Feminine. This can happen only if the Great Goddess, whom the history of humankind and the individual psyche set forth as the primal source and who alone can be the ground of a thea-logy and spirituality that respond to the challenges of today, also defines the God of the Bible. Osiek calls this hermeneutic "sublimationist." The existence of corresponding structures in the world of biblical Israel, the New Testament, and in the history of Christianity (and Judaism) serves in this "hermeneutic of the eternal feminine" as evidence in support of the universal validity of a "matriarchal" *Weltanschauung*, one which sees the Goddess and the cosmos as fused into one another.

Clara Colby of the team around *The Woman's Bible* (see 1.1) is a representative of the "new," that is, symbolic, thinking. As such, she may be regarded as an example of this type of hermeneutics, as may the contemporary feminist reader of Scripture, Gerda Weiler (see also Christa Mulack, 1.2.2). In Weiler's view, the original matriarchal religion of Israel has the Goddess-hero structure and is pervaded by the symbol of the cosmic Goddess and her son-lover who dies and must be given new birth every year. The return to such a religion, its powerful cultic-liturgical shape, its repudiation of an ethic of good and evil, its orientation toward protecting and advancing life, and its cyclical understanding of time will pave the way toward a spirituality of women as well as men. For Weiler, it is a spirituality that, especially at the present time, will help overcome divisions of every kind.

Matriarchal-feminist hermeneutics claims to offer a rigorously woman-centered perspective that not only brings together material "about" women but also interprets it specific to women. The suggestive power of this hermeneutic resides in its conception of a cosmic web of women of all times and continents, brought forward methodologically by a depth-psychological reading of Scripture on the one hand and ritual or aesthetic appropriation on the other. This is meant to bridge the "nasty ditch," so much lamented in theology, between the world of the Bible and ours and to give women today the feeling of an encompassing sisterhood. The newly won security in the bottomless mechanics of critique (including feminist critique) ultimately derives from the female body as that which signals the utmost communality of women. That focus brings to view clearly the story of how the Bible was passed on from one generation of Christians to the next as the thrice-woven story of exploitation and domination of nature, enmity to the body and sexuality, and oppression of women on grounds of gender only. However necessary it is critically to confront matriarchal-feminist hermeneutics, for example, for its quite uncritical embrace of expert men, such as Robert Ranke Graves or Carl Gustav Jung, its anti-Judaism (see 2.4.1), or its fundamental melding of Goddess and cosmos, this particular perspective remains a constant and critical "thorn" of the Christian feminist endeavor.

Doris Brockmann, *Ganze Menschen—ganze Götter: Kritik der Jung-Rezeption im Kontext feministisch-theologischer Theoriebildung* (Paderborn: F. Schöningh, 1991); *Schlangenbrut,* issues no. 42 (1993), "Erfundene Wirklichkeit? Matriarchatsforschung," and no. 44 (1994), "Göttin—kein abgeschlossenes Kapitel"; Marie-Theres Wacker, "Die Göttin kehrt zurück: Kritische Sichtung neuerer Entwürfe," in Marie-Theres Wacker, ed., *Der Gott der Männer und die Frauen* (Düsseldorf: Patmos, 1987), 11–37; idem, "Göttinnen," in *Neues Handbuch theologischer Grundbegriffe,* 2d ed., vol. 4 (Munich: Kösel Verlag, 1991), 266–72; Gerda Weiler (see 1.2.2).

2.1.5 The Hermeneutic of Liberation

The fifth type is the approach of feminist liberation theology; its notable mark is that it locates itself decidedly in the modern women's movement. For this reason, the hermeneutic of liberation sets out from theologies for which the heart of biblical revelation is that, in God's sight, every human being becomes a subject (as political theologies like Johann Baptist Metz's maintain). Yet those theologies are found to be an insufficient foundation under prevailing conditions. The hermeneutic of liberation demands that the litmus test be how women are seen to become subjects. In distinction from "revisionist" hermeneutics, it seeks to do exegesis and to be about liberating praxis, not merely side by side, but actually to hold them together in one comprehensive hermeneutical conception. Engagement on behalf of women becoming subjects, as an option of theological practice for a woman exegete, charts the feminist and critical path for her historical-exegetical labor; in turn, her exegetical-scholarly labor remains connected to the feminist movement. This hermeneutic is close to the fourth type mentioned earlier, because it holds scholarship and praxis together. It insists just as resolutely that all scholarship is inseparable from its location, thereby exposing that, rather than being universal or objective, much of prevalent discourse is actually androcentric. (See 2.2.2 and 2.2.3.) It follows from this statement that the existing women's community of interpretation must be regarded as the hermeneutical center of both the hermeneutic of "liberation" and of the "eternal feminine." This is because only with that community can the androcentric perspective of the Bible, how it was received in history and what it brought about, be truly broken. In the absence of such community, "revisionist" hermeneutics is in danger of uncritically identifying androcentric philanthropy and women-centered visions. But feminist liberation-theology hermeneutics, unlike that of the fourth type, does not lean to a feminism of the "natural-feminine." It leans toward a feminism of justice or of toil for equality. Its understanding of the community of interpretation, among other things, makes that quite clear. The feminism of the "eternal feminine" views this community as a cosmic-natural, as it were, organic community of women of "one substance" with the Goddess. It seeks to actualize it in mystical-spiritual fashion. The hermeneutic of liberation sees this community as one of ethical decision making and political engagement on behalf of all (women) becoming subjects.

Elisabeth Schüssler Fiorenza's work, which was groundbreaking for the German-speaking context as well, represents this type. Her reconstruction of Christian origins, as found in numerous articles and, above all, in her monograph *In Memory of Her*, serves to give Christian women today a feminist theological foundation for their liberation-seeking faith and action. According to the hermeneutical system, which she has depicted above all in her *Bread Not Stone*, feminist exegesis must set out from a "hermeneutic of suspicion," not only against the patriarchal monopolizing of Scripture throughout the history of interpretation, but also against the androcentrism of Scripture itself. A text that seems to speak positively about women is not therefore directly applicable to feminist purposes but must first be analyzed for the "systemic androcentrism" which pervades Scripture. But whenever there are tensions and contradictions in New Testament descriptions and judgments about women, a "hermeneutic of remembrance" may infer an early Christian movement in which women and men committed to Jesus were part of a "discipleship of equals." What constitutes the movement is an encompassing well-being which Jesus himself lived and taught and which was subsequently taken up by his followers and passed on, a well-being that becomes concrete in the economy and politics, in ethics and theology. For this reason, it has a direct and critical impact on patriarchy. It is essential for Elisabeth Schüssler Fiorenza that the step from the text to the historical context be taken, because such a step alone allows one to move forward from a mere cultural critique of the text to a critique of structures of power dominant in the past and the present, and to the requisite transformation. In like manner, such a step brings out more clearly the actual part of women in the shaping of early Christianity. At the same time, it stimulates critical opposition to the marginalization of women that is already apparent in the sacred writings and, more so still, in the history of Christianity. Christian women today, who understand themselves to be followers of Jesus and who wish to live out this "discipleship of equals" are, as an "ecclesia of women" in the very heart of the church itself, a critical challenge to the existing structures of the church which, being patriarchal, are not appropriate to the gospel.

Schüssler Fiorenza's proposal of a "hermeneutic of liberation" has been criticized, among others, by the feminist New Testament women scholars Lone Fatum (Denmark) and Carolyn Osiek (United States). Although differing in their emphases, both are concerned that historical study that is bound to a biased feminist option cannot adequately discern conditions in antiquity. Such study will only confuse historical-exegetical reconstructions with systematic-theological legitimation of what today's feminist theologians are demanding. This critique is grounded in some of Elisabeth Schüssler Fiorenza's own formulations, which are at times open to misunderstanding. Such critique may point to different basic decisions in feminist hermeneutics that need to become subject to discussions in critical solidarity beyond the domain of feminist exegesis.

A feminist exegetical "hermeneutic of liberation" within the German-speaking context will have to be attentive to the specific location of feminist exegesis in three of the world's richest countries. Because of such privilege, it will also need to make every effort to listen and to make known the voices of women from the context of the so-called Two-Thirds World. The least that can be done at this point is to declare this desideratum and to name some of the women who, in their various contexts, work for an interpretation of the Bible by and for women that is oriented by liberation theology: Teresa Okure (Nigeria), Elisabeth Dominguez (Philippines), Elsa Tamez (Costa Rica), and Ivoni Richter Reimer, Alicia Winters, and Tania Mara Vieira Sampaio (all Brazil). The first feminist-liberation theological reading of Scripture from Japan is that of Hisako Kinukawa. A valuable source of information from Latin America is the annual publication *Bibliografía Bíblica Latino-Americana*, edited by Milton Schwantes (São Paulo: Programa Ecuménico de Pos-Graduação em Ciencias da Religião, 1988–).

Elisabeth Dominguez, "New Testament Reflections on Political Power," in John S. Pobee et al., eds., *New Eyes for Reading: Biblical and Theological Reflections by Women from the Third World* (Geneva: WCC, 1986), 45–49; Lone Fatum, "Image of God and Glory of Men: Women in Pauline Congregations," in Kari E. Børresen, ed., *Image of God and Gender Models in Judaeo-Christian Tradition* (Oslo: Solum Forlag, 1991), 56–136; idem, "Women, Symbolic Universe, and Structures of Silence: Challenges and Possibilities in Androcentric Texts," *Studia Theologia* 43 (1989): 61–80; Hisako Kinukawa, *Women and Jesus in Mark* (Maryknoll, N.Y.: Orbis Books, 1994); Teresa Okure, "Feminist Interpretations in Africa," in Elisabeth Schüssler Fiorenza, ed., *Searching the Scriptures*, vol. 1 (New York: Crossroad, 1993), 76–85; idem, "The Johannine Approach to Mission: A Contextual Study of John 4:1-42," WUNT, 2d ser., vol. 31 (Tübingen: J. C. B. Mohr, 1988); idem, "Women in the Bible," in Virginia Fabella and Mercy Amba Oduyoye, eds., *With Passion and Compassion: Third World Women Doing Theology* (Maryknoll, N.Y.: Orbis Books, 1988), 47–59; Carolyn Osiek (see 2.1); Ivoni Richter Reimer, *Frauen in der Apostelgeschichte des Lukas* (see 1.2.3); idem, "Widerstand und Hoffnung," in Dorothee Sölle et al., eds., *Für Gerechtigkeit streiten* (Gütersloh: Chr. Kaiser and Gütersloher Verlagshaus, 1994), 66–70; Tania Mara Vieira Sampaio, "El cuerpo excluido de su dignidad: Una propuesta de lectura feminista de Oseas 4," *RIBLA* 15 (1993): 35–46; idem, "Die Entmilitarisierung und die Befreiung zu einem Leben in Würde bei Hosea," *Texte und Kontexte* 16, no. 57 (1993): 44–55—see also *RIBLA* 8 (1991): 70–81; idem, *Mulher uma prioridade profética em Oseias* (São Paulo: Instituto Metodista de Ensino Superior, São Bernardo do Campo, 1990); Helen Schüngel-Straumann and Christine Schaumberger, "Bibel," in *WbfTh*, 49–58; Elisabeth Schüssler Fiorenza, *Bread Not Stone* (see 1.1); idem, *In Memory of Her* (see 1.1), chap. 1; Elsa Tamez, *The Amnesty of Grace: Justification by Faith from a Latin American Perspective* (Nashville: Abingdon Press, 1993); idem, "The Woman Who Complicated the History of Salvation," in Pobee et al., eds., *New Eyes for Reading*, 5–17; idem, "Women's Rereading the Bible," in Fabella and Oduyoye, eds., *With Passion and Compassion*, 173–180; Alicia Winters, "La memoria subversiva de una mujer: II Samuel 21, 1-14," *RIBLA* 13 (1993): 77–86; idem, "La mujer en el Israel premonárquico," *RIBLA* 15 (1993): 19–34.

2.2 Basic Categories of Feminist Exegesis

There are certain determinative concepts in feminist praxis and scholarly literature that have also become part of feminist exegesis. The following list of definitions and brief annotations are not to be taken as a final lexicon but as an invitation to further discussion and clarification.

2.2.1 Patriarchy/Matriarchy

The primary concern of the feminist movement (and, correspondingly, of feminist scholarship) is to trace the mechanisms of women's suppression, functioning in society and in individual lives. It is developing alternative plans of action or perspectives that enables women to achieve their full humanity. In this connection, the term *patriarchy* is frequently used to give a name to the complex of all those forces that oppose this aim. Therefore, patriarchy is foremost a concept of struggle. Its analytical meaning is brought into view best by its historical location. Since Aristotle, patriarchy has been a concept of law or politics referring to the concrete dominance exercised by the *pater familias* over his household, that is, his physical family (spouse and children) as well as his male and female wage earners and slaves. This view of patriarchy also signals the economic component of the concept or the social reality it embodied. In such an economic-social structure of domestic life, legal and political power was restricted to the *pater familias* (or at least to the extensive rights accorded him). The entire organism of state was guided by the terms of patriarchy. Since such structures were not restricted to Greece and Rome, the term is suitable for the general characterization of the "rule of the fathers" and its concrete result in the juridical, political, and economic dependency of women, children, and serfs.

There is a shift in the meaning of *patriarchy* whenever it is used as a counterconcept to *matriarchy*. The latter, too, was originally a concept of law and politics, signifying certain forms of social organization that were defined not in terms of the father but the mother (maternal right of succession, use of the mother's surname, matrilocality of marriage, and so forth). "Matriarchal" traces in this sense may, indeed, be found in the Hebrew Bible; they are listed, for example, in the work of Werner Plautz. But since the concept of matriarchy was introduced to the German-speaking world in connection with Swiss legal historian Johann Jakob Bachofen's thesis of a primordial gynaikocracy in world history, it has taken on a meaning that reaches far beyond that. According to Bachofen, patriarchy as it currently exists was preceded in the history of development by an age of women, the foundation of which is laid in "the nature of women," namely motherhood, which is also a profoundly religious mysterium and which elevates woman to the level of religious being per se. The early gynaikocracies were in every aspect shaped by religion; faith in the oneness of essence of woman, earth, cosmos, and nature guided all of life. Such basic Bachofenian concepts have been positively appropriated and expanded even by women and have left their imprint on the approach to matriarchal feminism. *Matriarchy* refers here to that form of society that includes the religion of the cosmic Goddess and her son-lover, a religion aligned with the cycles of nature and seen to be the source and basis of the orders of society. Its opposite is *patriarchy*, referring to that order of society which is determined by a religion or ideology of male monotheism. It is a religion also which seeks to eliminate the divine-feminine and aspires to dominate the whole cosmos. In its soil grow contempt of woman and of nature; in such a religion, it is inevitable that the law and ethics of its society develop from rules and orders that were not derived from the natural-internal but from what is external.

Feminist exegesis also encounters the term *patriarchy* in the sense of referring to the "primal father." In traditional translations of the Bible, Abraham, Isaac, and Jacob are called "the patriarchs," and the New Testament already speaks of David (Acts 7:8), the twelve sons of Jacob (Acts 2:29), and Abraham (Heb. 7:4) as "patriarchs." An additional meaning is applied to the term in scholarly exegesis, namely that of the concrete family structure found in biblical Israel, including the age of Jesus. Two interpreters of the New Testament, Elisabeth Schüssler Fiorenza and Luise Schottroff, have made very poignant use of the concept and its concomitant juridical-political-sociological perspective. In harmony with their liberation theology approach, they intend to call attention to the need for feminist labor to "keep its feet firmly on the ground" and to devote its energies on concrete political and social structures if the liberation of women is truly to succeed. Because of the danger of being interpreted too narrowly, it has been proposed by Elisabeth Schüssler Fiorenza that *patriarchy* might be replaced by *kyriarchy*.

Donate Pahnke, "Matriarchat," in *Wbf Th*, 283–85; Werner Plautz, "Zur Frage des Mutterrechts im AT," *ZAW* 74 (1962): 9–30; Christine Schaumberger and Luise Schottroff, "Patriarchat," in *Wbf Th*, 319–22; Luise Schottroff, *Lydia's Impatient Sisters* (see 1.2.3), 17–42; Elisabeth Schüssler Fiorenza, *But She Said* (Boston: Beacon Press, 1992); Beate Wagner-Hasel, ed., *Matriarchatstheorien der Altertumswissenschaften*, Wege der Forschung 651 (Darmstadt: Wissenschaftliche Buchgesellschaft, 1992).

2.2.2 Patriarchy—Androcentrism—Sexism

In appropriating the concept *patriarchy*, feminist (exegetical) analysis has opted for a theory of feminism in which attention to concretely existing women, including the class and age they belong to, has priority over speculations about "the feminine." It is a choice for a theory which depicts the domination of women as an aspect of the domination by the man who, on the basis of his procreation of sons, lays claim to authority over nonfathers. Since for that very reason the "analysis of patriarchy" is first and foremost analysis of social conditions, the category of *androcentrism* fits more readily into the feminist exegetical task of reading texts. The term refers to conceptions, patterns of ideas, and thought structures and gives a name to the fact that cultural expressions of patriarchal societies present themselves entirely as man-centered. Often, language sees the male human being (*Mann*) and human being (*Mensch*) as identical. Philosophy ranks the male attributes of what is immaterial and rational before the female ones of what is connected with the body and the sensual. Religion is about a father-god, whom the spiritual fathers represent on earth. The orientation of ethics is in terms of norms rather than relations, and so forth. In short, woman is seen as the man's "other." With very few exceptions, such as the Song of Songs, the Bible may be spoken of in its entirety as an androcentric literature. Such androcentrism becomes *sexist* when it turns into the ideological basis for the exclusion of women, solely as women, from certain activities that it seeks to safeguard for men, solely as men. In the nineteenth and early twentieth centuries, the arguments against women's rights to vote were strongly sexist. They were intended to keep women bound to home and family because of their "nature." The argumentation the official teaching of Rome presents against the admission of women to the office of priest bears features of sexism because the biological dissimilarity of women to the man Jesus of Nazareth represents for it a decisive criterion for exclusion. And finally, the argument of 1 Tim. 2:12-15 is sexist because it dispossesses women of ecclesiastical authorization to teach and counsels them instead that their way to salvation lies in giving birth to children.

Ina Praetorius, "Androzentrismus," in *WbfTh*, 14–16.

2.2.3 Femininity—Gender Difference— Gender Complicity

Feminist theory formation must address the basic issue of whether it is possible to specify the category of *femininity* in order to provide grounding, both epistemologically as well as in terms of "subject areas," for a discourse of feminist science. Definitions of *femininity* cover a broad range, beginning with citing natural or quasi-invariable factors like the ability to give birth to and nurse children. Or, they cite the cultural factor seen to be nearly universal, namely, that mothers and women are charged with raising small children. Such definitions draw on cultural studies and conceive of "femininity" as a conglomerate of specific roles which may well prove constant in history and geography but are in principle open to being changed. The process of defining *femininity* extends all the way to the refusal of substantive determination and to the willing movement toward an open, utopian understanding of femininity. In relation to feminist exegesis and its historiographical work, the first two of these "definitions" of femininity come more readily to hand in describing the biblical picture, whereas experimenting with the utopian understanding is hermeneutically more fascinating. That is because this latter understanding looks less at "similarities" between then and now. It focuses more on "falsifications" and the overturning of gender identities that are occasionally hinted at in the Bible. (For example, in 1 Samuel

1-2, Hannah is loved by her marriage partner "in spite" of her childlessness, and she does not keep the longed-for son but gives him away.) The distinction between *sex* and *gender*, between biological and (culturally) attributed sex, cuts across the categorization of *femininity*. Even though this distinction may be viewed as the result of feminist scholarly reflection, it is nonetheless "neutral" for feminism because it simply stipulates that not only time, space/location, and class and race, but also people's sex deeply shapes their history and that characteristics attributed to sex constitute an important element of cultural values and norms. Increasingly, the perspective of "gender research" finds acceptance also in the established sciences. Within the feminist agenda, an important contribution to biblical gender research is the joint work of the Israeli biblical scholar Athalya Brenner and the Dutch woman exegete Fokkelien van Dijk-Hemmes. They explore the conditions and possibilities for tracing texts back to male or female "origins" and what meaning and usefulness such an undertaking has. (See 3.1.3.) The Danish New Testament scholar Lone Fatum also understands her feminist exegetical work as "gender orientated" and combines this approach with an explicit critique of "biased" feminist hermeneutics (see 2.1.5).

In its beginning, feminism tended to perceive women one-sidedly in the role of victims, and/or equally one-sidedly, it advocated an exodus to a gynocentric counterworld. By contrast, current feminist scholarship seeks to discern the ever-existing entanglement of women in the history of patriarchy. It was Christina Thürmer-Rohr who introduced the concept *Mittäterschaft*, complicity, and set the tone for the discussion in the German-speaking world. Paying attention to the complicity of women may protect one against reconstructing something like an intact time of origin in history; it urges, instead, the development of historical models that are less concerned with showing how things evolved. Such models are more interested in women's experiences of oppression and their liberating struggles but also in their accommodative practices, all of which are present and must be made visible for every epoch. (See 9.1.)

On femininity: Doris Brockmann (see 2.1.4), 35–44.

On gender: Athalya Brenner and Fokkelien van Dijk-Hemmes, *On Gendering Texts: Female and Male Voices in the Hebrew Bible* (Leiden: Brill, 1993); Peggy L. Day, ed., *Gender and Difference in Ancient Israel* (Minneapolis: Fortress Press, 1989); Lone Fatum (see 2.1.5).

On complicity: Christine Schaumberger and Luise Schottroff, *Schuld und Macht* (see 1.2.3); Studienschwerpunkt "Frauenforschung" and Technical University Berlin, eds., *Mittäterschaft und Entdeckungslust* (Berlin: Orlanda-Verlag, 1989); Christiana Thürmer-Rohr, *Vagabonding: Feminist Thinking Cut Loose* (Boston: Beacon Press, 1991).

2.2.4 Objectivity—Partiality

For all intents and purposes, the ground has disappeared from under the scholarly ideal of striving for the "pure" cognition of an object to be known. Its disappearance is a result of the insistence of the sociology of knowledge that everyone seeking knowledge is bound to her and his context. Even the determination of one's object of study is not independent of the studying subject; the scholarly methods of researching "objects" contain what is by no means a universal but all too often a very particularistic hermeneutic. The history of research has its own gravity which retards or prevents necessary paradigm shifts. Sciences said to be only and wholly "interested in their objects of study" are involved by institutional or economic ties in a web of presuppositions, predeterminations, and dependencies. The impact of these on scholarship should be worked out rather than denied or ignored. It is from this point of view that feminist science criticizes the current business of scholarship which, in actual fact, is still almost exclusively a male domain shaped by ideological androcentrism and robust patriarchal structures. Feminist scholarship is fully conscious of its partiality in that, in relation both to the "object" of its research and the purpose and application of it, it consciously places women at the center. Feminist research focuses single-mindedly (but by no means in a narrow sense) on the reality of women. It looks for ways that assist women in particular to achieve subjecthood. This does not imply that proven methodologies will be abandoned or that communication with male scholarship will cease; what it does mean is that dominant structures will be subjected to critical scrutiny and undergo feminist transformation. (See 2.1.5.)

Hedwig Meyer-Wilmes, *Rebellion auf der Grenze* (Freiburg, Basel, and Vienna: Herder Verlag, 1990), pt. 3; Ulrike Müller-Markus, "Parteilichkeit," in *WbfTh*, 315–17; Luise Schottroff, *Lydia's Impatient Sisters* (Louisville: Westminster/John Knox Press, 1995), pt. 1.2.3.

2.3   The Question of the Biblical Canon

Feminist Christian exegesis cannot avoid taking up the fact that the canon of Scripture is fixed, that the Bible is a given and determined corpus. For exegetical-historical work in the narrower sense of reconstructing historical connections, this givenness of the canon seems to be a minor problem. On this level it can be readily admitted that a "patriarchal selection" (Elisabeth Schüssler Fiorenza) of the sources did indeed take place. It resulted in a minimal basis for resources in women's history. For this reason, historical-exegetical work must go beyond the writings in the biblical canon for its exploration of the sources. The apocryphal and pseudepigraphical writings of both the First and New Testaments need to be included as well as the contemporary literature of the political/cultural superpowers (Egypt, Assyria, Babylonia, Persia, Greece, and Rome). Finally, the numerous, but mostly brief, epigraphical sources of Israel's/Palestine's neighbors need to be included. However, one must also include nonwritten "sources," above all iconography and archaeologically produced materials such as remains of buildings, contents of tombs, bones, and even seeds of grain, all of which yield valuable clues to everyday life, not least to the lives of women in biblical times (see 3.4.1 and 3.4.2).

The givenness of the biblical canon raises sharper problems for a theology which in a feminist mode seeks to discern its foundation in Scripture. Elisabeth Schüssler Fiorenza has suggested that the process of formation of the New Testament canon paralleled the increasing exclusion of women from ecclesiastical offices. If this is so, it raises the problem, certainly in relation to the question of office, that only such texts that seemed congenial to excluding women from those offices were deemed inspired by those whose aim it was to exclude women. In relation to the First Testament, feminist exegetes from the churches of the Reformation must deal with the fact that important wisdom writings (Sirach, Wisdom, as well as Baruch) are not counted among their sacred writings. Therefore, little canonical material is available to them in developing a biblical theology of Wisdom bridging the two testaments. That is why the community of interpretation of critical women is essential. While not reversing the patriarchal selection, it nonetheless makes the canon, understood as a fixed selection of sacred writings claiming authority, the subject of critical discussion. Elisabeth Schüssler Fiorenza proposes to distinguish between the Bible as "archetype" and the Bible as "prototype." Understood as archetype, it is as if the Bible had fallen from the sky as God's universally valid Word, independent of time and context. A prototypical understanding holds that the Bible not only became historical but that it must be brought into relation with new situations as they arise. Notwithstanding the fact that Christian identity is unthinkable without recourse to the Bible, in communities of faith the Bible must be ratified ever anew as Holy Scripture.

Claudia Camp, an American feminist exegete unassociated with a mainline church, has sketched three models of dealing with Scripture as authority in feminist-Christian hermeneutics: (1) The *dialogical authority model:* it proceeds from the words to persons (especially women) and stresses the community of believers from biblical Israel up to the present. (2) The *metaphor model:* it begins with the word of Scripture and views the Bible as "poetic classic"; "classic" in terms of its capability of calling forth new appropriations right into our own time, and "poetic" in that it unveils what the Word declares. (3) The *liminal model:* it reads Scripture from the margins, taking seriously the demarcations and rejections found in biblical writings, applying them to itself and then taking them back to the texts in a critically creative way. This is "reading as a foreign woman," against the text, subversively.

Claudia Camp, "Feminist Theological Hermeneutics: Canon and Christian Identity," in Elisabeth Schüssler Fiorenza, ed., *Searching the Scriptures,* vol. 1 (New York: Crossroad, 1993), 154–91; Elisabeth Schüssler Fiorenza, *Bread Not Stone* (see 1.1), 12ff. and 36ff.; idem, *In Memory of Her* (see 1.1), chap. 8.

2.4   Christian Feminist Anti-Judaism?

The history of Christian exegesis of both the First and New Testaments is accompanied by and entangled in anti-Judaism. Reference has already been made to the model of interpretation developed in nineteenth-century Protestant exegesis of the decline of Israel into the legalistic Judaism of postexilic times and the related theory of the "prophetic connection." This model not only turned Jesus into a non-Jew who, as a true believer in YHWH, embraced only what was genuinely Israelite. Such interpretation also repudiated the Judaism of Jesus' time, and its subsequent history until now, as petrified and ultimately alien to God.

Until well after World War II, that is, long after the Shoah, at both university and parish-practice levels, Protestant and Catholic interpretations worked on the basis of premises in biblical and systematic theology that held the Christian interpretation of the First Testament to be the only truly valid one. Judaism was, in a manner of speaking, dispossessed of its Scripture since it was held to be a false road, or worse still, a deliberate repudiation of revelation in Jesus Christ. Even though it is not yet generally accepted, it is now at least possible within Christianity to speak of God's first and never abrogated covenant, which Judaism continues to this day. Next to it, there is a second covenant—or better, a second step in that first covenant—that rendered God's revelation accessible to "heathen" women and men, so that in the perspective of Christians and in gratitude for the establishment of this new covenant, both ways are to be acknowledged as genuine ways to God.

For a long time, feminist rereading of Scripture did not detect this deeply rooted and widespread Christian anti-Judaism. Not until the late 1970s, when Jewish feminists in the United States began to speak and write openly about anti-Jewish trends in Christian feminist theology, did the discussion begin. In Germany, it began on a broader basis only in the second half of the 1980s; it was the time of the *Historikerstreit* (the feud of the historians) when in broad sectors of society Germany's anti-Semitic past and how it could be overcome historically was bitterly debated. At this time, it had also just begun to be possible within feminism to move on from a phase of "sisterhood," in which all differences were subordinated, to a more differentiated and self-critical (re)formulation of feminist postulates and utopias.

Charlotte Klein—"Pionierin der Verständigung" (Bendorf: Hedwig-Dransfeld-Haus, 1992); Charlotte Klein, *Anti-Judaism in Christian Theology* (Philadelphia: Fortress Press, 1978); Johanna Kohn, *Haschoah: Christlich-jüdische Verständigung nach Auschwitz* (Munich: Chr. Kaiser; Mainz: Grünewald Verlag, 1986); Rosemary Radford Ruether, *Faith and Fratricide* (New York: Seabury Press, 1974); Leonore Siegele-Wenschkewitz, "Antijudaismus," in *WbfTh*, 22–24; Erich Zenger, *Am Fuss des Sinai: Gottesbilder des Ersten Testaments* (Düsseldorf: Patmos, 1993); idem, *Das Erste Testament: Die jüdische Bibel und die Christen* (Düsseldorf: Patmos, 1991); idem, *Ein Gott der Rache?* (Freiburg, Basel, and Vienna: Herder Verlag, 1994).

2.4.1 The Issues at the Heart of the Debate

In the eyes of Christian feminist women who study New Testament traditions of patriarchy, the narratives about Jesus' dealings with women appear to be a suitable point of departure for a biblically based feminist critique of patriarchy. For those accounts are about women disciples who followed Jesus, about ill and, for that reason, marginalized women to whom Jesus gives back their human dignity. They are also about the theological disputes between Jesus and women and may indeed function as thorns in the flesh for the church's domestication and marginalization of women. But whenever Jesus, the friend of women, or even Jesus, the "feminist" (see still Leonard Swidler, *Yeshua: A Model for Moderns* [1988]), is set against a bleak foil of the allegedly thoroughly misogynist Judaism of his time, the historical reality of Judaism is disfigured in anti-Jewish terms. Here, the figure of Jesus himself is elevated to a woman-positive "liveried divinity" (Karl Rahner coined the phrase *Gott in Livree*) as well as being deprived of his concrete humanity as a Jew of his particular time. In the language of dogmatics, this is anti-Judaism as the flip side of Monophysitism. In relation to Paul, who did indeed manifest a fairly ambivalent position toward women, the framework of interpretation that offers itself even to feminists seems to be what has already been referred to above in connection with Anna Paulsen. She had suggested that either Paul was split between Jewish tradition and Christian conversion or else that the basic impulse of early Christianity was in the process of being re-Judaized. This, too, is anti-Jewish insofar as what is Jewish is charged, both in terms of individuals and structures, with obscuring what is genuinely Christian.

Feminist critique of the Hebrew Bible, that is, the Christian Old Testament, fell victim to anti-Judaism especially where it sought to bring to light or revitalize buried traditions of the Goddess. One the one hand, this applies specifically to language and the adoption of the anti-Semitic jargon of the Nazis in some feminist presentations. On the other hand, it applies to the uncritical reception of literature (from the pen of "expert men") which not infrequently was itself the bearer of anti-Jewish clichés. The basic pattern of feminist revision of the history of biblical Israel is also subject to anti-Judaism. Truly, it is no longer a matter of dispute that the veneration of one or more goddesses was no merely marginal matter in ancient Israel, and one must surely speak of goddess worship being pushed back and decried as heresy in postexilic Israel. But when early Jewish groups, to whom the Goddess was a thorn in the side, are identified simply with *the* Jews, without any kind of time reference, the result is a limited historical focus that cuts out the real multisidedness of 2,500 years of Judaism and finally becomes anti-Jewish. First, Christians accused Jews of killing God by crucifying Jesus; now, as critical Jewish feminists put it, feminists accuse Jews of killing the Goddess. What is more, relatively simplistic lines are drawn from the effects of the opposition of early Judaism to the Goddess to the male-instrumental rationality that rules today, as well as to the destruction of nature and the enmity toward eroticism and sensuousness. Such connections once again put Jews in the role of scapegoats for false developments or detours. But these may be explained seriously only through differentiated, historical analysis in which Christianity's history of guilt is taken as seriously as the specific problems of modernity (the roots of which are in Western Europe).

Charlotte Kohn-Ley and Ilse Korotin, eds., *Der feministische "Sündenfall?" Antisemitische Vorurteile in der Frauenbewegung* (Vienna: Picus, 1994), with articles by Susanne Heine, Hannelore Schröder, Ilse Korotin, Johanna Gehmacher, Susannah Heschel, Anita Nassmenig, Charlotte Kohn-Ley, and Maria Wölflingseder; Christine Schaumberger, ed., *. . . weil wir nicht vergessen wollen: Zu einer feministischen Theologie im deutschen Kontext* (Münster: Morgana-Frauenbuchverlag, 1987), with articles by Christine Schaumberger, Rita Burrichter, Johanna Kohn, and Anette Kliewer; Luise Schottroff, "Antijudaismus im Neuen Testament" in *Befreiungserfahrungen* (see 1.2.3), 217–28; idem, "Die 'Schuld der Juden' und die Entschuldung des Pilatus in der deutschen neutestamentlichen Wissenschaft seit 1945," in *Befreiungserfahrungen*, 324–57; Leonore Siegele-Wenschkewitz, ed., *Verdrängte Vergangenheit, die uns bedrängt* (Munich: Chr. Kaiser Verlag, 1988), with articles by Susannah Heschel, Eveline Goodman-Thau, Leonore Siegele-Wenschkewitz, Jutta Flatters, Marie-Theres Wacker, Bernd Wacker, Luise Schottroff, and Dieter Georgi; Katharina von Kellenbach, *Anti-Judaism in Christian-Rooted Feminist Writings: An Analysis of Major U.S. American and West German Feminist Theologians* (Atlanta: Scholars Press, 1994).

See the journal *Kirche und Israel*, vol. 5, nos. 1 and 2, with articles by Judith Plaskow, Asphodel P. Long, Leonore Siegele-Wenschkewitz, Fokkelien van Dijk-Hemmes, and Marie-Theres Wacker; see also *Schlangenbrut*, vols. 16–18 (1987), and the debate there on feminist anti-Judaism.

2.4.2　How to Meet Anti-Judaism

Feminist exegetes and theologians may counter anti-Judaism in two ways: negatively, with a precise knowledge of its manifestations and, positively, with as thorough an acquaintance as possible of the history of Judaism and the self-awareness of contemporary Jewish women and men. The first way includes Germans allowing the specifically German history of Christian anti-Judaism and racist anti-Semitism to encounter them as their own negative history and working hard to deal with it. It also includes the very critical examining of the literature of scholarly exegesis for anti-Jewish stereotypes. This means scrutinizing language not only for expressions of sexism and androcentrism but, parallel to it, also for those of anti-Judaism. It is important to keep in mind that the Jesus movement was initially a movement within Judaism. It must be understood in the context of contemporary Judaism rather than in an aprioristic separation from it. In addition, the question of the worship and disappearance of female deities in biblical Israel needs to be taken up in conjunction with a particularly sensitive hermeneutic of suspicion about one's own patterns of reconstruction. The second and positive way of countering anti-Judaism includes especially coming to know how Jewish people understand themselves and honoring their understanding of themselves. Seeking out occasions for dialogue and conversation with Jewish women and men (and not only in the German-speaking world) is, therefore, essential.

Luise Schottroff and Marie-Theres Wacker, eds., *Von der Wurzel getragen: Deutschsprachige christlich-feministische Exegese in Auseinandersetzung mit Antijudaismus* (Leiden: Brill, 1995), with articles by Eveline Valtink, Geburgis Feld, Brigitte Kahl, Johanne Petermann, Ilse Müllner, Christl Maier, Marlene Crüsemann, Renate Jost, Martina Gnadt, Gerlinde Baumann, Angelika Strotmann, Luise Schottroff, and Marie-Theres Wacker.

2.4.3　Jewish Feminist Ways of Dealing with the Bible

The largest number of Jewish feminists live and work primarily in the United States; there are some in Israel as well as in European countries such as England, the Netherlands, and Switzerland. The specific shape of their feminism, the kinds of questions and problems they address, depends, among other things, on what movement of Judaism they feel they belong to. Women who associate themselves with Orthodox Judaism focus their feminist interests most readily on an interpretation and application of the halakah that is friendly to women, especially the rules governing synagogue worship and family life. Hanna Safrai (Jerusalem and Amsterdam) is a specialist working on rabbinic methodology and theology of women from the period of the Second Temple. Because a German-speaking audience needs to become familiar first with Jewish traditions of interpretation, German-speaking Jewish women like Eveline Goodman-Thau (Halle and Jerusalem, modern orthodox) and Pnina Navè Levinson (for a long time in Heidelberg, now in Jerusalem and Mallorca, liberal Judaism) devote their time speaking and writing explicitly on texts of the Hebrew Bible.

Feminists in the traditions of Reform Judaism have ventured upon the task of questioning the system of the halakah as such, because its androcentrism is amenable to change from within. For example, for Judith Plaskow (New York), going back to the Hebrew Bible is a way of verifying her Jewish history of women, which can or must be recalled or created in the first place by means of feminist *midrashim* (Lilith!). Surely, Judith Plaskow is the one who, to an extent larger than other Jewish feminists, engages in a movement of thought comparable to that of Christian theology, reflecting in that manner her Jewish feminism. It is no coincidence that she and Elisabeth Schüssler Fiorenza worked closely together, for example as coeditors of the *Journal of Feminist Studies in Religion* (1985–). Other Jewish feminists draw on the methods of interpretation of modern historical scholarship or of recent secular literary science. Of note in this context is Adele Reinhartz (Hamilton, Ontario) whose work focuses on texts of the New Testament, especially the Gospel of John, as well as on gender-specific issues, and Ross Kraemer (Philadelphia) and Amy-Jill Levine (Vanderbilt University, Nashville), who study the history and literature of early Judaism and Christianity. T. Drorah Setel (New York) has examined the Book of Hosea in particular against the background of feminist analyses of pornographic literature; Athalya Brenner (Haifa and Amsterdam) has published a literary-sociological study of woman in ancient Israel, as well as numerous articles on the Hebrew Bible in a feminist-literary perspective. She also edits the monograph series A Feminist Companion to the Bible, published by Sheffield Academic Press.

Finally, there are feminists with a Jewish background who consciously take up traditions of magic, matriarchy, and goddesses, pleading in the name of women that Jewish life be transparent to these displaced traditions. Such a feminist is Asphodel Long (England), whose subject is biblical and postbiblical traditions of wisdom. For her, the figure of Wisdom in Jewish literature is a reflection of the archaic and once universally venerated Great Goddess Nature. Savina Teubal, an Argentinean now residing in California, has provided interpretations of biblical texts on the primordial mothers, especially Sarah; according to Teubal, such texts are relics of nonpatriarchal forms of society and religion in early Israel. She wishes to inspire women today to appropriate this inheritance in a creative fashion for themselves.

Athalya Brenner, *The Israelite Woman: Social Role and Literary Type in Biblical Narrative* (Sheffield: Sheffield Academic Press, 1985); Athalya Brenner, ed., A Feminist Companion to the Bible (series) (Sheffield: Sheffield Academic Press, 1993–); Eveline Goodman-Thau, "Auf der Suche nach Identität—orthodoxe Frauen in Israel," in Renate Jost and Ursula Kubera, eds., *Befreiung hat viele Farben* (Gütersloh: Gütersloher Verlagshaus Gerd Mohn, 1991), 121–37; idem, "5. Mose 6, 4-10: Höre ihre Stimme," in Eva-Renate Schmidt et al., eds., *Feministisch gelesen*, vol. 2 (Stuttgart: Kreuz Verlag, 1989), 63–73; idem, *"Zeitbruch"—Zur messianischen Grunderfahrung in jüdischer Tradition* (Berlin: Akademie Verlag, 1995), of which pt. 1 is on the Book of Ruth; Ross Kraemer, *Her Share of the Blessings: Women's Religions among Pagans, Jews, and Christians in the Greco-Roman World* (New York: Oxford University Press, 1992); Amy-Jill Levine, ed., *"Women Like This": New Perspectives on Jewish Women in the Greco-Roman World* (Atlanta: Scholars Press, 1991), containing, inter alia, an article by Adele Reinhartz on Mary and Martha; Pnina Navè Levinson, *Eva und ihre Schwestern: Perspektiven einer jüdisch-feministischen Theologie* (Gütersloh: Gütersloher Verlagshaus Gerd Mohn, 1992); idem, *Was wurde aus Saras Töchtern? Frauen im Judentum* (Gütersloh: Gütersloher Verlagshaus Gerd Mohn, 1989); Asphodel P. Long, *In a Chariot Drawn by Lions* (London: The Woman's Press, 1992); Judith Plaskow, "The Coming of Lilith: Toward a Feminist Theology," in Carol P. Christ and Judith Plaskow, eds., *Womanspirit Rising: A Feminist Reader in Religion* (San Francisco: Harper and Row, 1979), 198–209; idem, *Standing Again at Sinai* (San Francisco: Harper and Row, 1990); Adele Reinhartz, "The New Testament and Anti-Judaism: A Literary-Critical Approach," *Journal of Ecumenical Studies* 25 (1988): 524–37; Hanna Safrai, *Women and Temple: The Status and Role of*

Women in the Second Temple in Jerusalem, Studia Judaica 12 (Berlin: Walter de Gruyter, 1995); T. Drorah Setel, "Prophets and Pornography: Female Sexual Imagery in Hosea," in Letty M. Russell, ed., *Feminist Interpretation of the Bible* (Philadelphia: Westminster Press, 1985), 86–95; Savina Teubal, *Sarah the Priestess: The First Matriarch of Genesis* (Athens, Ohio: Swallow Press, 1984); Marianne Wallach-Faller, "Zwanzig Jahre jüdische feministische Theologie," *Neue Wege: Organ der religiös-sozialistischen Vereinigung der Deutschschweiz* 90 (1996): 3–11.

Chapter Three

Methods of Feminist Exegesis

Feminist exegesis does not develop new methods as such. It is methodologically innovative in organizing the steps taken by a method and in testing them critically. It makes use of existing methods to uncover findings relevant to women or to supplement them with specific ways of asking questions. In doing so, it also examines methods for stated or unstated premises inasmuch as they may block cognition relevant to feminism.

In the last two decades, the tools utilized in methods of scholarly exegesis were supplemented beyond those of classic historical-critical methods by the numerous new approaches in linguistics, literary science, history, ethnology, sociology, religious studies, and psychology. As a result, the already existing multileveled composition of exegetical labor has become even more differentiated in its literary, historical, religious-theological, and existential dimensions. This manifold spectrum is not taught or widely used to its full extent at German-speaking universities and has (still) not been widely received in feminism. The following survey is limited essentially to German-language feminist exegesis; it will refer also to literature from neighboring countries in Europe and, wherever it serves clarification, from the United States.

3.1 Historical Criticism in Feminist Revision

In the German-speaking world, the methods brought together in historical criticism continue as ever to be the most widely used, particularly because a series of newer methods has emerged that has extended both the questions and approaches of historical criticism. For feminist exegetes in Germany, the historical-critical method and its diverse foci are normally the bases on which they do their work with the Bible. In what follows, the customary steps found in this method are set into a feminist context. They are examined in terms of what results relevant to feminism they (may) yield when applied in the traditional manner and, more fundamentally, how or where, from the point of view of feminism, each step in the method has its limitations. Since the more precise delineation of those individual steps in Old and New Testament exegesis is approached differently in each case and is not even consistent within each of these two exegetical areas, the following descriptions are by necessity selective and subjective.

Monika Fander, "Historical-Critical Methods," in Elisabeth Schüssler Fiorenza, ed., *Searching the Scriptures*, vol. 1 (New York: Crossroad, 1993), 205–24.

3.1.1 Textual Criticism and Translation

In sorting out what the ancient traditions of the manuscripts of the Hebrew and Greek Bible were and in comparing the early translations of the Bible, textual criticism discovers variations in ancient texts. This in turn promises what in feminist perspective are interesting insights. Textual variations in the Book of Acts are a well-known example, partly because of their impact on the question of ecclesiastical office. Variations in the "Western" text of Acts, which is based on Codex Bezae ("D"), relegate Paul's companion Prisca to the background in favor of her marriage partner Aquila, indeed, causing her to disappear altogether (Harnack). Kristin de Troyer is preparing a feminist textual criticism which compares the versions of the Book of Esther. She has already written a number of articles on this subject. Angela Standhartinger has made a comparison of the various (Greek) manuscripts of the Jewish-Hellenistic book Joseph and Asenath. She shows that they differ in distinctive features, including in how women are imaged.

Comparing texts in various translations of the Bible is a form of textual criticism that can be undertaken even without acquaintance with ancient languages. Monika Fander demonstrates this in comparing translations of Hosea 11. A further example are the much-disputed translations of the Greek word *diakonos,* which Paul uses in his concluding greeting in Romans 16 to address Phoebe from Cenchreae.

The aim of textual criticism is to reconstruct the Hebrew or Greek "original text" of a biblical writing by comparing its manuscripts and versions; this aim need not be a high priority for feminists' own work since text critics themselves subject it to critical evaluation. However, it would be salutary if the history of a text's copies were researched in conjunction with the social-historical contexts of those copies and if the history of women in particular were attended to in the process. One thinks here of the woman prophet Huldah who, according to 2 Kings 22:14ff., was shown a copy of the book of the law of Moses. She would, therefore, be able to read. This raises the question as to whether women had any part in copying the scrolls discovered in and near Qumran. How fascinating it would be were this method to be applied also to illustrations in medieval manuscripts and printed versions of Holy Scripture so that their iconography could be examined with special attention to the deposition of women's reality.

Mention must be made in this context of the efforts, especially by women, to provide translations of the Bible in a language that does justice to women. (See 4.3.1.) A new translation of Genesis was prepared in Belgium by Mary Phil. Korsak which, comparable to the translations of Fridolin Stier or André Chouraqui, seeks to capture the flow of language and the atmosphere of the original text.

Elizabeth A. Castelli, "*Les belles infidèles*/Fidelity or Feminism? The Meanings of Feminist Biblical Translation," in Elisabeth Schüssler Fiorenza, ed., *Searching the Scriptures,* vol. 1 (New York: Crossroad, 1993), 189–204; Kristin de Troyer, *An Eastern Beauty Parlour: An Analysis of the Hebrew and the Two Greek Texts of Esther 2:8-18,* in Athalya Brenner, ed., *A Feminist Companion to Esther, Judith, and Susannah* (Sheffield: Sheffield Academic Press, 1995), 47–70; Monika Fander (see 3.1); Mary Phil.. Korsak, *At the Start . . . Genesis Made New* (Louvain: Leuvense Schrijversaktie, 1992); Angela Standhartinger, *Das Frauenbild in jüdisch-hellenistischer Zeit: Ein Beitrag anhand von "Joseph und Aseneth"* (Leiden: E. J. Brill, 1995); Adolf von Harnack (see 1.3.1).

3.1.2 Methods in the History of Origins

For a feminist exegesis with an interest in history, the analysis of how the biblical writings came into being is utterly unavoidable. That is because the text as it exists now tells in the first instance only of the situation of the community in which the text received its present form; it informs us, in other words, about the late postexilic time of Israel or the "post-Easter" period of early Christianity but not about the royal period of Israel, for example, or the beginnings of the Jesus movement. Studies in the history of origins today presume a great diversity of materials and how they were worked with. No longer is it taken for granted (as it had been in "classical" literary criticism) that the writings as they exist now are based on "sources." Extant written fragments or orally transmitted units, such as hymns, may have been fused into new units. (This is how the approaches of the "history of tradition" or composition criticism state the case.) A text may have had brief glosses or longer commentaries on specific points (supplemented writings: *Fortschreibung*) added to it or may have become a preliminary step in a new, interconnected editing phase (redaction).

A *diachronic* look at a biblical text notices shifts in the perception of women's reality. For example, one would conclude from the literary-critical observations arising from a study of Greek and Hebrew texts of Jeremiah 44 that, in verses 15-19 and verses 24 and following, there has to be a fragment that has been worked into the existing longer text. In the fragment, it is not the whole people, represented by its men, that confronts Jeremiah, but rather women who are in conflict with him because they raise their voices on behalf of the Goddess. To be sure, one may not infer that this fragment also reflects faithfully a presumed reality of religious history, for this fragment, too, is a literary entity with its own structure. It clearly manifests a "YHWH-centric" orientation: while YHWH speaks through the mouth of Jeremiah, the women raise their voices on their own authority and rise up against the true God in the name of their "Queen of Heaven" who is a dumb idol, after all. It requires other material from this text and from elsewhere to demonstrate that the gender-specific alignment of women to the heavenly queen is not a purely literary-polemical construct but corresponds to the practice of religion in Judea before and during the Exile. In this case, the process of redaction incorporated the fragment of Jer. 44:15-19 and verses 24 and following and its argument in terms of gender-specific opposition. But by including men in the picture it has exonerated women in a way in that the whole people is said to be guilty. Or in relation to the Book of Hosea, there is considerable discussion among scholars about the second verse in the first chapter and its multiple layers, which has far-reaching implications for the perception of the book's theology. Hosea's marriage partner became a "wanton" woman only in a subsequent redaction of the text in which she represents Israel. At first, the accent of that first chapter lay on the symbolic names of the children and, concomitantly, on the announcement that the motherly-compassionate (*Lo-Ruchama*) and the fatherly-congenial (*Lo-Ammi*) affection of YHWH would be withheld. The theology of the Book of Hosea is not reflective of the tragic marriage of the prophet but, rather, is the reflection on the part of several generations about YHWH's relationship with Israel and its correspondence to the relationship between man and woman. Finally, the Australian exegete Elaine Wainwright has shown that the redaction of the Gospel of Matthew was based on a positive-inclusive outlook, since it worked numerous texts concerning traditions of women into important places.

Renate Jost (see 1.2.3), esp. sec. 6.2; Marie-Theres Wacker, *Figurationen des Weiblichen* (see 1.2.3); Elaine Wainwright, *Toward a Feminist Critical Reading of the Gospel according to Matthew*, BZNW 60 (Berlin: de Gruyter, 1991).

3.1.3 Form and Genre Criticism

Form and genre criticism is held to be the "classic" method that holds together text and social setting. The small and smallest forms contained in a biblical book and established initially at the literary level refer to concrete happenings in life (*Sitz im Leben*). For example, a victory hymn refers to the celebration which was prepared for the warriors returning after a victorious battle; a dirge refers to a village's responding to a death, or to a people's song of mourning, or to common liturgies of mourning. Since many of these small genres had their origin in oral discourse, and since it is to be assumed that in ancient Israel women took part in far smaller numbers than men in the process of writing, it is precisely the discovery of oral forms that uncovers a possible source of women's literature (in the widest sense). In her monograph *On Gendering Texts*, written with Athalya Brenner, Fokkelien van Dijk-Hemmes has brought together all those forms or genres of the Hebrew Bible that are said to belong to such "women's literature." She particularly addresses the question whether, in light of the fact that all the songs of women are transmitted in contexts authored by men or are reflective of an androcentric perspective, women may be seen at all as authors of such songs. She decided not to speak, therefore, of women authorship but of "female voices" in the androcentric discourse of the Bible.

Monika Fander supplies a beautiful example from the New Testament for the feminist options offered by *Formgeschichte*. She interprets the short reference of Mark 1:29-31 to the healing of Peter's mother-in-law as a miracle narrative, the purpose of which is to call attention to a woman having founded the congregation of Capernaum. Luise Schottroff consistently analyzes form and genre criticism particularly with a critical eye for aprioristic deflections (resulting from androcentrism, anti-Judaism, racism, and the like) that have to be challenged and neutralized by means of different understandings. (See Part Three on this point.)

Form and genre criticism have become the point of contact for newer methods of literary science; it is here where text-centered perspectives have entered into traditional exegesis and, as a result of their ultimate conclusions, have transformed it.

Monika Fander (see 3.1); Fokkelien van Dijk-Hemmes, "Traces of Women's Texts in the Hebrew Bible," in Brenner and van Dijk-Hemmes (see 2.2.3), 17–109.

3.1.4   History of Tradition

The method of history of tradition fastens onto how the substance of biblical culture is formed, from literary motifs and themes on one end, to perceptual complexes and interpretive patterns, on the other. In feminist perspective, the traditions with women as their subject merit first consideration. The tradition of Miriam comes to mind. It is composed of different elements: the motif of the woman prophet who is a singer and an ecstatic (Exod. 15:20f.) and someone who receives revelation (Num. 12:1ff.), and the motif of a woman coleader of the Exodus (Micah 6:4). Another element is the tradition of her grave (Num. 20:1). This bundle of motifs points to a tradition of Miriam, confirming the great significance of this woman (Schüngel-Straumann). Another example is the tradition of Magdalene in the New Testament. The Magdalene woman is not only cited in all four Gospels as one of the first witnesses of the resurrection, but is portrayed in the Gospel of John as one whose great faith equals, if not measures greater than, that of John and Peter. In the apocryphal writings of the second or third century, especially in *Pistis Sophia* and the *Gospel of Mary*, she appears as an outright antagonist of Peter, suggesting that there existed genuine power struggles between Christian groups who individually appealed to different "authorities" (Schüssler Fiorenza). In terms of the history-of-tradition method, the question that is central for feminist research is one which relates to social history, namely whether groups of women in particular can be identified as bearers of tradition.

Helen Schüngel-Straumann, "Wie Miriam ausgeschaltet wurde," in *Schlangenlinien* (Bonn: AGG-Frauenbroschüre, 1984), 211–21; Elisabeth Schüssler Fiorenza, *In Memory of Her* (see 1.2.3), 285ff., esp. 304–6.

3.2 Feminist Revisions of Methods of Literary Studies

As a result of the study of new developments in linguistic and literary studies, new methods of biblical exegesis came into existence, especially in Anglo-Saxon North America and in France. Only some of them saw themselves as a continuation of genuine historical exploration. Examples of this are the studies on the style and poetry of Hebrew literature or the method of rhetorical criticism. But even they share the perspective of "literary studies," for they do not regard the biblical text in the first instance as a source of information "for" real history but as a web of texts, as texture which, it is true, is still said to be understood and interpreted historically. Other methods consciously switch over to a perspective that orients itself by generalizable structures. This is described in the terms of linguistics, semiotics, structuralism, psychoanalysis, or mythology. In the German-speaking world, there has been no extensive echo to these approaches. For this reason, the following, brief description also focuses on the work of feminist exegetes from other European countries.

3.2.1 Textual Linguistics

The Roman Catholic Old Testament scholar Wolfgang Richter and his school at Munich University have developed a method of analyzing texts of the Hebrew Bible that pursues a twofold goal, which is to base the exegesis of the First Testament on the most exact possible linguistic grasp of the original biblical texts and to work toward creating a Hebrew grammar founded on linguistics. Specifically feminist concerns may benefit from this area of linguistic studies, especially in its comprehensive linguistic description of the grammatical and the semantic "place" which the feminine occupies in the Hebrew (and by analogy the Aramaic and Greek) language.

In a lexical study, Maria Häusl has shown that throughout the Hebrew Bible the feminine designations of persons are supplied morphologically with a special feminine ending, so that the grammatical-syntactical gender was obviously fitted to the natural one. There are three exceptions: the term for "mother" ('*emm*), "the woman-spouse of the king" (*egal*), and "concubine" (*pilaga*); in other words, three terms that could not be any more "feminine." How is one to explain this phenomenon? A different kind of example is provided by the verb form *t^edabber* which is found at the opening of the section of Num. 12:1 and following. According to conventional interpretation, it is a form of the third-person singular feminine and can only refer to the subject identified by name, which is Miriam. From the point of view of literary criticism, Aaron, who is also mentioned in that sentence, is accordingly of secondary significance. That the predicate of the sentence was not changed when the supposed addition of the name Aaron took place may cause one to conclude that this literary-critical argument is actually circular. For is it not possible to believe that the grammatically feminine form of the verb in question could have been understood as semantically inclusive, that is, as including a female and a male subject? Psalm 42:1 leads to such a conclusion as well; the Hebrew text there leaves a masculine subject "deer" and a feminine predicate next to each other without correction. Observations and questions like these (see the intimations here of G. Vanoni) call for further exploration in a feminist linguistics that will surely not ignore relevant aspects of other disciplines such as those of the history of language, developmental psychology, and social history.

Maria Häusl (see 1.2.3); Gottfried Vanoni, "Göttliche Weisheit und nachexilischer Monotheismus," in Marie-Theres Wacker and Erich Zenger, eds., *Der eine Gott und die Göttin* (Freiburg, Basel, and Vienna: Herder, 1991), 183–90.

3.2.2   The Study of Narrative Guided by Structuralism

A narratological approach to biblical texts seeks to interpret them in terms of the basic categories of narrative analysis. On the level of the "story," this analysis pays particular attention to characters, actions, and modifications in space and time; it distinguishes between the material of a narrative and its concrete realization and, on the level of this concretely realized narrative, it differentiates between the perspective of the narrator and that of the actors. Finally, it also differentiates between the intended and actual readers of the text and, correspondingly, the implied and the actual author. Narrative analysis is by nature suited particularly to the story texts of the Bible, the Gospels, Acts, and the so-called historical books of the First Testament, but can discern narrative structures in other text genres as well.

Drawing on the narratological concepts of French structuralism, the Dutch scholar of literary studies Mieke Bal has sought to state the question of the "subject" with more precision. It is in this work that she has established herself as a feminist. When women engage in narrative analysis and become thereby a narratological subject themselves, they may become particularly aware that in the narration the various characters may very well appear as actual subjects, whereas on the level of the concrete realization of the narrated material, they are not necessarily the subjects of their own actions and perceptions. Rather, they are organized and colored in every instance by the perspective of the narrator and, beyond that, might be presented or "focalized" through the perspective of another character in the narrative. For that reason, Mieke Bal distinguishes between the one/those who narrate(s) (*narrator*), the one and those who determine(s) the perspective of narration (*focalizer*), and the one/those who act(s) (*actor*). A distinction like this from literary studies may be regarded as a precise methodological transposition of the suspicion of androcentrism: in paying heed to who it is that creates form narratively, and when and how and from what perspective, one will finally also come to see gender-specific modifications. The impetus at the core of Mieke Bal's work may be said to be one of pursuing the notion of "becoming a subject" or "hindrance to becoming a subject" all the way to "the death of the subject" in literary texts, particularly for female characters. She brings to light literary plans of action (often through recourse to psychoanalytical patterns of interpretation) and exposes them as political in nature.

In dialogue with the exegete Fokkelien van Dijk-Hemmes, Mieke Bal has given concrete demonstrations of her feminist narratology in relation to a number of diverse texts of the First Testament, especially the Book of Judges. Another example that may serve as a model of feminist methodology is the analysis of Hosea 2:4-25, provided by Fokkelien van Dijk-Hemmes herself. Both "narrator" and "focalizer" of the dispute that this text dramatizes, namely between the "actors" husband and wife, is the I of the male-divine speaker, from the perspective of whom the seemingly direct speech of the "woman" also is presented. In order to obtain a genuinely woman-centered version of the dispute, Fokkelien van Dijk-Hemmes introduces the contrast reading by means of an intertext which, in this instance, is the Song of Songs. The latter has a number of literary points of contact with Hosea 2. To a high degree it presents the theme of love between woman and man from the perspective of the loving woman. In her monograph on the Book of Hosea, Marie-Theres Wacker has endeavored to combine the method developed by Mieke Bal with more traditional elements of rhetorical criticism. She has analyzed in detail the three opening chapters of Hosea, as well as chapters 4 and 9. With an eye on biblical-feminist theology, she is attentive to the possibility that within the unquestionably patriarchal texts themselves traditions critical of patriarchy were incorporated.

Mieke Bal's and Fokkelien van Dijk-Hemmes's methodology became the stimulus for Arie Troost of Utrecht to develop further the aspect of intertextuality. Along with a hitherto unpublished study, which places Genesis 21 into a critical dialogue with the seventh homily of Origen, he has worked on the two "lost sons" of Genesis 21 and Luke 15:11 and following and on the two pairings of women Elizabeth/Mary and Naomi/Ruth.

The American scripture and literature scholar Cheryl Exum, currently at the University of Sheffield, has also developed a form of feminist narratology and presented it in relation to numerous blocks of biblical texts. One of her primary topics is violence perpetrated against women in writing—the form of violence done to women on account of the viewpoint or literary perspective of men. Cheryl Exum also includes in her feminist perception the depiction of the male in (biblical) texts and, like Mieke Bal, draws in her analysis on pictorial material from the history of art, also including contemporary films and videos.

Mieke Bal, *Anti-Covenant: Counter-Reading Women's Lives in the Hebrew Bible* (Sheffield: Sheffield Academic Press, 1989); idem, *Death and Dissymmetry: The Politics of Coherence in the Book of Judges* (Chicago: University of Chicago Press, 1988); idem, *Femmes imaginaires* (Utrecht: HES, 1986); idem, *Lethal Love* (Bloomington: Indiana University Press, 1987), rev. ed. of *Femmes imaginaires;* idem, *Murder and Difference: Gender, Genre, and Scholarship on Sisera's Death* (Bloomington: Indiana University Press, 1988); idem, *Narratologie* (Paris: Klincksieck, 1977); Mieke Bal, with Fokkelien van Dijk-Hemmes and Grietje van Ginneken, *En Sara in haar tent lachte—pa-*

triarchaat en verzet in bijbelverhalen (Utrecht: HES, 1984); Cheryl Exum, *Fragmented Women: Feminist (Sub)versions of Biblical Narratives, JSOT* Supplement 163 (Sheffield: Sheffield Academic Press, 1993); idem, *Plotted, Shot, and Painted* (Sheffield: Sheffield Academic Press, 1996); idem, *Still amid the Corn? Feminist and Cultural Studies in the Biblical Field* (Sheffield: Sheffield Academic Press, 1996); idem, *Tragedy and Biblical Narrative: Arrows of the Almighty* (Cambridge: Cambridge University Press, 1992; Sheffield: Sheffield Academic Press, 1996); Arie Troost, "Elizabeth and Mary—Naomi and Ruth: Gender Response Criticism in Luke 1–2," in Athalya Brenner, ed., *A Feminist Companion to the Bible: The Hebrew Bible in the New Testament* (Sheffield: Sheffield Academic Press, 1996), 159–96; idem, "Reading for the Author's Signature: Gen. 21:1-21 and Luke 15:11-32 as Intertexts," in Athalya Brenner, ed., *A Feminist Companion to the Bible*, vol. 2: *Genesis* (Sheffield: Sheffield Academic Press, 1993), 251–72; Fokkelien van Dijk-Hemmes, "The Imagination of Power and the Power of Imagination", *JSOT* 44 (1989): 75–88; Marie-Theres Wacker, *Figurationen des Weiblichen* (see 1.2.3).

3.2.3   Literary Criticism

The designation "the new literary criticism" refers to the large palette of Anglo-American studies on texts in the orientation of literary studies. It is above all the studies of Phyllis Trible that have made literary criticism oriented by feminism accessible to the German-speaking world. According to her own testimony, what she presents is often no more than a close reading of biblical texts in their present form while paying attention to linguistic-rhetorical figures in the text. This is close to the work of rhetorical criticism. In addition, she depicts the courses of action and the characters involved, especially women. Her first monograph focuses on texts that support her theological option for a "nonpatriarchal principle" of Scripture, such as Genesis 2–3, the Book of Ruth, and the Song of Songs. In her second book she takes up "texts of terror" (Judges 17–19; 2 Samuel 13; Genesis 34; Genesis 16 and 21) and places them in the context of the passion story of the New Testament.

Barbara A. Bozak, a Canadian nun who teaches in Ottawa, represents the version of literary criticism as exercised at the Pontifical Biblical Institute in Rome. She examines style in combination with a description of the major themes of a text. Her minute analysis of the poetic and thematic structures of Jeremiah's "Consolations" in chapters 30 and 31 shows the high degree to which metaphors of the feminine have entered into this text and in what forms. Angela Bauer made it her task to work through the entire Book of Jeremiah and to determine its gender-specific metaphors; in an impressive manner, she shows how this prophetic writing may be appropriated when read with the eyes of a woman. Elaine Wainwright's *Toward a Feminist Critical Reading of the Gospel according to Matthew* was published in Germany; it is an explicitly feminist rereading of Matthew that methodically combines literary criticism and redaction criticism.

Angela Bauer, "Tracking Her Traces: A Literary-Theological Investigation of Gender in the Book of Jeremiah" (diss., New York, 1993); Barbara A. Bozak, *Life "Anew": A Literary-Theological Study of Jeremiah 30–31*, Analecta Biblica (Rome: Editrice Pontifico Instituto Biblico, 1991); Elizabeth Struthers Malbon and Janice Capel Anderson, "Literary Critical Methods," in Elisabeth Schüssler Fiorenza, ed., *Searching the Scriptures*, vol. 1: *A Feminist Introduction* (New York: Crossroad, 1993), 241–54; Phyllis Trible, *God and the Rhetoric of Sexuality* (Philadelphia: Fortress Press, 1978); idem, *Texts of Terror—Literary-Feminist Readings of Biblical Narratives* (Philadelphia: Fortress Press, 1984); Elaine Wainwright (see 3.1.2).

3.2.4 Reader-Response Criticism

This section brings together diverse methodologies which do not differ strictly from the approaches discussed in sections 3.2.2 and 3.2.3. They seek to provide interpretations whose point of orientation is the reader (the recipient) of the text, be it by focusing attention chiefly on the implied reader and, consequently, doing more strictly historical work (see Elaine Wainwright on Matthew), or by consciously thematizing the present situation of how women receive biblical texts and then confronting that situation with biblical texts (see Renita Weems on Hosea 2). In the German-speaking world, the elaboration of this approach as an exegetical method has only just begun. Elke Seifert approaches the story of Lot and his daughters suspecting that it is a text in which there is buried material that has to do with men and fathers having to face that they sexually assaulted their own daughters. She therefore confronts Gen. 19:30-38 line by line and motif by motif with the declarations of sexually assaulted daughters and their fathers. Ulrike Bail interprets the psalms of lament as prayers that may be uttered by women. Using Psalm 55 as an example, she shows how women's experience of violence may draw on the psalm's motifs and themes for clarity and thus transform the psalm into a woman's prayer.

Ulrike Bail, "Vernimm, Gott, mein Gebet: Psalm 55 und Gewalt gegen Frauen," in Hedwig Jahnow et al., eds., *Feministische Hermeneutik und Erstes Testament* (Stuttgart: W. Kohlhammer Verlag, 1994), 67–84; Elke Seifert, "Lot und seine Töchter: Eine Hermeneutik des Verdachts," in Jahnow et al., eds., *Feministische Hermeneutik und Erstes Testament,* 48–66; Elaine Wainwright (see 3.1.2); Renita Weems, "Gomer: Victim of Violence or Victim of Metaphor?" *Semeia* 47 (1989): 87–104.

3.2.5 Semiotics

Another Dutch exegete, Ellen van Wolde, became familiar with semiotic theory and method not least on account of her studies with Umberto Eco in Bologna. She has published a rereading of the paradise narrative of Genesis 2–3 from this perspective and now explores and writes on other texts of this "primordial history."

Ellen van Wolde, "Adam e Adamah: Gen. 2–4," in F. Vattioni, ed., *Sangue e anthropologia nella Liturgia* (Rome: Pia unione Preziosissimo Sangue, Centro studi Sanguis Christi, 1984), 219–77; idem, *A Semiotic Analysis of Genesis 2–3* (Assen: Van Gorcum, 1989); idem, *Words Become Worlds: Sematic Studies of Genesis 1–11,* Biblical Interpretation Series 6 (Leiden: E. J. Brill, 1994).

3.3   Approaches of Depth Psychology

The embrace of depth-psychological methods on the part of feminist exegesis has to be seen in the context of the current trend within theology to bid farewell to the historical methods. These methods are said to be no longer capable of bridging the "nasty ditch" between the texts of the Bible and the present in view of a biblically founded spirituality. There is a hermeneutic which is a primary guide throughout depth-psychological exegesis. It finds that the experiences of destructive as well as healing forces in the (individual and collective) inner core of the human soul that have deposited themselves in the Bible are comparable to those that are to be unearthed from the modern psyche. The Catholic woman theologian Maria Kassel came to feminist theology as a result of her depth-psychological interpretation of Scripture; the focus of her work is, consequently, to determine what ways the Bible offers to self-discovery. Her feminism manifests itself in the form of necessary and woman-centered corrections in the approach and methodology of depth-psychological analysis of biblical texts. In terms of hermeneutics, Kassel's work resembles that of the model sketched above in section 2.1.4, the main representatives being Christa Mulack and Gerda Weiler, both of whom work with Jung's theories. So far as we know, it is only the work of Mieke Bal that seeks to incorporate Freud's psychoanalytical theory into feminist interpretation of Scripture (see 3.2.2).

Mieke Bal (see 3.2.2); Maria Kassel, *Biblische Urbilder,* expanded edition (Freiburg, Basel, and Vienna: Herder, 1992)—see particularly the afterword, "Kritik am Jungschen Anima-Konzept," 281–88; idem, "Feministische Bibelauslegung" and "Tiefenpsychologische Bibelauslegung," in Wolfgang Langer, ed., *Handbuch der Bibelarbeit* (Munich: Kösel, 1987), 151–56 and 156–62.

3.4 Feminist Reception of History of Religion and Social History

In contrast to approaches that are orientated strictly by literary sciences and texts, terms like *history of religion* and *social history* bring into view methodologies that aim to explore historically the concrete world of biblical life and times. Since the approaches indicated in both those terms presuppose and critically extend historical criticism, one cannot simply speak of "methods" but must be attentive to the entire methodological continuum and the hermeneutical interest it expresses.

3.4.1 Social-Historical Approaches

At its first level, social-historical interpretation of Scripture means historically reconstructing life in the biblical world as comprehensively and concretely as possible. The material basis of its study includes for that purpose the whole range of extrabiblical as well as extratextual sources. It also expands the repertory of its theories by the use particularly of social-historical, sociological, and social-anthropological considerations. Traditional historical-critical practice is therefore submitted to a threefold critique. First, the approach implies the abandonment of writing history centered around great names or the winners in favor of a historiography of everyday life, of the "little people." Second, it submits to scrutiny exegesis that turns a blind eye toward power, thereby affirming power and, concomitantly, the existential appropriation of Scripture rooted in the advocacy of a purely individualistic piety. Instead, the social-historical approach recalls the political dimensions of faith that cannot forgo the analysis of power in church and society. Third, and related to the two preceding points, the approach implies critical reflection on the social location of one's own interpretation. These three aspects offer the prospect of taking up the social-historical interpretation of Scripture as a liberation-theological exegesis and of recommending it from a feminist point of view.

By proposing a "hermeneutic of remembrance," Elisabeth Schüssler Fiorenza has assigned social-historical methodology a place at the center of feminist reconstruction of women's heritage. Luise Schottroff went in the reverse direction when she incorporated feminist liberation theology into her social-historical approach, sharpening it thereby. Her critique of traditional historical-critical, as well as already existing social-historical, interpretations of the New Testament is directed throughout at patterns of theories, individual theorems, or stereotypes which, if taken over unexamined, tend once again to affirm existing power structures. She is especially attentive to the emergence, often in combination, of racism, Eurocentrism, and sexism/androcentrism. (See Part Three.)

A number of scholars working in the area of the First Testament have written social-historical studies which touch on topics specific to women. Among them are Jürgen Kegler, Hermann Schulz, Willy Schottroff, and Frank Crüsemann. Other relevant studies in this area are two explorations of so-called cultic prostitution. One of these incorporates comparative material from Hindu India (Marie-Theres Wacker) while the other examines material from Mesopotamia (Renate Jost). Finally, there is Carol Meyers' work on the everyday life of women (Eve as "everywoman") in early Israel. Renate Jost was the first in the German-speaking world to publish a monograph on the social-historical feminist interpretation of a First Testament theme. Basing her work on the declarations in the Book of Jeremiah concerning the worship of the Queen of Heaven (Jer. 7:16-20; 44:15ff.), she endeavors to provide, on the one hand, a more exact profile of this female deity and, on the other, a clearer grasp of the situation of Israel's women at the time of the Exile. By seeking the latter she extends the investigations of Susan Ackerman. Hannelis Schulte concentrates her research in history and social history on active, independently engaged women of the era before and immediately after the founding of the ancient state of Israel; she has developed stimulating hypotheses on the meaning of the *beenah* marriage. Christl Maier examines the figure of the "foreign woman" and seeks to understand it social-historically against the background of postexilic social conflicts.

From Berlin, and now New York, New Testament scholar Brigitte Kahl juxtaposes the feminist form of social history as practiced in Germany by Luise Schottroff and a number of her doctoral students, the French tradition of "materialist reading" (Fernando Belo, Michel Clévénot, Georges Casalis, Kuno Füssel), and the "Amsterdam School" and its reading of Scripture (Frans Breukelmann, Karel A. Deurloo, Rochus Zuurmond, Ton Veerkamp). Unlike the German tradition, "materialist reading" of Scripture takes up the structuralist challenge of the literary sciences and seeks to relate Scripture critically to its actual historical context. The reading of Scripture associated with the "Amsterdam School" is a specific form of the canonical approach to the Bible in that it always seeks to understand an individual text of Scripture in the context of the entire Bible. (As such it is not directly a social-historical method.) Other than in Luther's emphasis on "justification by faith alone," the principle governing all biblical writings is strongly determined by the First Testament and its option for liberation and justice. That option gives the principle a concrete ground. It is not set apart from a Jewish reading of Scripture since it was formulated precisely in light of that tradition. According to Brigitte Kahl both these forms of "nonidealistic" reading of Scripture offer feminist exegesis connections that have yet to be worked out. Using the tools of the "Amsterdam School," Klara Butting has recently published a fascinating feminist interpretation of the Books of Ruth, Esther, Ecclesiastes, and Song of Songs.

Susan Ackerman, *Under Every Green Tree: Popular Religion in Sixth-Century Judah*, HSM 46 (Atlanta: Scholars Press, 1992); Klara Butting, *Die Buchstaben werden sich noch wundern: Innerbiblische Kritik als Wegweisung feministischer Hermeneutik* (Berlin: Alektor Verlag, 1993); Frank Crüsemann, "'... er aber soll dein Herr sein!' (Gen. 3,16): Die Frau in der patriarchalischen Welt des Alten Testaments," pt. 1 of Crüsemann and Thyen (see 1.2.1); Renate Jost, *Himmelskönigin* (see 1.2.3); idem, "Von 'Huren und Heiligen': Ein sozialgeschichtlicher Beitrag," in Hedwig Jahnow et al., eds., *Feministische Herme-*

neutik und Erstes Testament (Stuttgart: W. Kohlhammer Verlag, 1994), 126–37; Brigitte Kahl, "Toward a Materialist-Feminist Reading," in Elisabeth Schüssler Fiorenza, ed., *Searching the Scriptures,* vol. 1: *A Feminist Introduction* (New York: Crossroad, 1993), 225–40; Christl Maier (see 1.2.3); Carol Meyers, *Discovering Eve: Ancient Israelite Women in Context* (New York: Oxford University Press, 1988); Luise Schottroff, *Lydia's Impatient Sisters* (see 1.2.3); Jürgen Kegler, "Debora—Erwägungen zur politischen Funktion der Frau in einer patriarchalischen Gesellschaft," in Willy Schottroff and Wolfgang Stegemann, eds., *Traditionen der Befreiung 2: Frauen in der Bibel* (Munich: Kaiser Verlag; Gelnhausen: Burckhardthaus-Laetare, 1980), 37–59; Willy Schottroff, "Der Zugriff des Königs auf die Töchter: Zur Fronarbeit von Frauen im Alten Testament," *EvTh* 49 (1989): 268–85; Hannelis Schulte (see 1.2.3); Hermann Schulz, "Zur Stellung der Frau in Stammesgesellschaften," in Schottroff and Stegemann, eds., *Traditionen der Befreiung 2,* 11–36; Mary Ann Tolbert, "Social, Sociological, and Anthropological Models," in Schüssler Fiorenza, ed., *Searching the Scriptures,* 1:255–71; Marie-Theres Wacker, "Kosmisches Sakrament oder Verpfändung des Körpers? Zur sogenannten 'Kultprostitution' im biblischen Israel und im hinduistischen Indien," in Renate Jost et al., eds., *Auf Israel hören: Sozialgeschichtliche Bibelauslegung* (Lucerne and Fribourg: Edition Exodus, 1992), 47–84.

3.4.2 Approaches of the History of Religion

As a method, *history of religion* refers to the work of examining the religious context of a culture which is itself studied historically. In terms of our focus, it is especially the cultures of the period of biblical Israel and of early Christianity during the Pax Romana. Biblical texts convey only a particular outlook on the religious reality of that time; they interpret it in terms of specific theological presuppositions. Including extrabiblical sources in one's studies shows that the practice of religion was more multifaceted than the Bible indicates. This often allows one to adjust images of reality distorted by polemical depiction in the biblical texts. The currently applied approaches of history of religion may be distinguished by what constitutes the core of their material, such as extrabiblical texts, archaeology, items bearing images, or by how they make use of biblical texts as "sources" of a history of the religion of Israel. Silvia Schroer integrates aspects of this method into her feminist exegetical work as do Renate Jost and Marie-Theres Wacker.

Reference to extrabiblical sources is indispensable precisely for the history of women—which in the biblical texts appears in such a fragmented manner—so that a part of the religion practiced by women may come into view. Sources of that kind are extrabiblical texts from Israel and Palestine and surrounding cultures; they allow for conclusions to be drawn by analogy. Then there are artifacts gathered from archaeological sites and material remains in the wide sense, if and when they are of cultic-religious relevance. Finally, there are the media of images as interpreted by iconography. The material used for comparisons should on principle come, wherever possible, from the immediately closest context, that is from Israel and Palestine and Syria. The greater the temporal or geographic distance between the biblical text and the documents used, the weaker their demonstrative force, unless, for example, it can be demonstrated that a motif has progressed through the ages or across great distances to the biblical text.

The work of the history of religion is not to approach biblical texts with different methods but, rather, to draw on and examine material in addition to those texts and to do so with the methods of textual analysis, archaeology, or iconography, as the case requires. Every one of these fields poses its own problems for the reconstruction of women's history. For example, extrabiblical texts may present an explicitly androcentric outlook on reality, as the Egyptian texts of banishment do. Whereas archaeology has arrived at conclusions to the contrary, these texts suggest that in the Middle Bronze Age there were only male deities in Palestine. Yet texts may also reveal a good deal about the religious world of women. The archaeology of the ancient Near East and especially of Palestine has always been subject to changes in research interests. Interest was greatest in palaces, temples, and big political events that had connections with the findings of excavations. Gradually, the questions of social history have become significant with the growing interest in reconstructing everyday life, large-scale settlement, and conduct. Unfortunately, questions specifically related to women have as yet made little inroad into this field of study. It is often not possible, given the form of reports about excavations, to distinguish female from male skeletons, with the result that important information is lost (see chap. 5). The domain of images, which in Israel/Palestine consists chiefly of small works and miniatures, has the advantage over biblical texts in that it represents the world of religion more directly and, thus, with less ideological filtering. If a motif or constellation of images is found in quite diverse media from a specific period, one may conclude that it had a significant meaning in the symbol system. Because in Middle Bronze Age Palestine the Goddess was portrayed consistently with branches, one may draw particular conclusions about what her image or type of appearance was. But this does not mean that in those images the world of women and that of men are documented in the same manner. We still know very little about the people who produced particular groups of media. Who carved the expensive ivory disks for the bedrooms of the upper class? Who cut the many thousand scarabs worn by men and women in Israel and Palestine? Did women and men have the same subjects engraved on their sealing amulets? Who produced the innumerable pillar figures, made sometimes by hand and sometimes in serial production by the use of modules?

There is clearly a connection between various media and certain social classes. Ivory and metal were costly and, hence, reserved for the rich. Large works of art, such as statues and reliefs, could be produced only when so ordered by the powerful. Amulets, seal rings, or terra-cottas, on the other hand, could be made from cheap materials and were, accordingly, within everyone's means. When the images of goddesses begin no longer to be made of metal but of cheap material, one may conclude that profound changes have taken place in the religious symbol system. Therefore, the development of the symbolism of images over extended periods of time offers broad orientation, allowing for a better ordering of phenomena such as the cult of the Queen of Heaven in Jeremiah 7 and 44. Since biblical texts present the cult of the Goddess only in a polemical style, pictorial documents are of particular significance for this thematic area. Even early Jewish or New Testament texts may be significantly illumined by a knowledge of the traditions of images (e.g., the *hokhmah* as tree goddess in Sirach 24, the dove as a messenger of love—originally the messengers of the goddess of love—in the baptism of Jesus in the Jordan). Other tools are listed in 5.4.2 and 5.5.

Renate Jost, *Himmelskönigin* (see 1.2.3); Othmar Keel, *Studien zu den Stempelsiegeln aus Palästina/Israel*, vol. 4, *OBO* 135 (Fribourg: Universitätsverlag; Göttingen: Vandenhoeck und Ruprecht, 1994); Silvia Schroer, "Elfenbein," "Göttin," "Ikonographie, Biblische," and "Lebensbaum," in Manfred Gorg and Bernhard Lang, eds., *Neues Bibel-Lexikon* (Einsiedeln and Düsseldorf: Patmos Verlag, 1991–); idem, "Der Geist, die Weisheit und die Taube: Feministisch-kritische Exegese eines neutestamentlichen Symbols auf dem Hintergrund seiner altorientalischen und hellenistisch-frühjüdischen Traditionsgeschichte," *FZPhTh* 33 (1986): 197–225; idem, "Die Zweiggöttin in Palästina/Israel: Von der Mittelbronze IIB-Zeit bis zu Jesus Sirach," in Max Küchler and Christoph Uehlinger, eds., *Jerusalem: Texte—Bilder—Steine,* Festschrift für Hildi und Othmar Keel-Leu, NTOA 6 (Fribourg: Universitätsverlag; Göttingen: Vandenhoeck und Ruprecht, 1987), 201–25; Silvia Schroer and Othmar Keel, *Religionsgeschichte Israels in Bildern,* forthcoming in the series ATD Ergänzungsreihe (Göttingen: Vandenhoeck und Ruprecht); Marie-Teres Wacker, in Wacker and Zenger, eds., *Der eine Gott und die Göttin* (see 1.2.3); idem, *Figurationen des Weiblichen* (see 1.2.3).

See also the anthology of Ross Kraemer (2.4.3) on the history of religion in New Testament times.

Part Two

TOWARD A FEMINIST RECONSTRUCTION OF THE HISTORY OF ISRAEL

Silvia Schroer

Chapter Four

Feminist Hermeneutics and the First Testament

For Jewish and Christian women, the writings of the Hebrew Bible are the heritage, or a part thereof, to which they refer. But each of these two groups of women relates to these writings differently. To this day, Jewish feminist exegesis belongs to a living and ongoing tradition of interpreting these books, whereas Christian theology has approached them much more selectively and from a greater distance. The history of Jewish exegesis includes both historical criticism, to the beginnings of which Baruch Spinoza contributed, and rabbinic interpretation of Scripture which, in general, shows little interest in historical questions. The scholarship of Christian Scripture has long placed great importance on questions such as what took place historically, what a text originally intended to say, and when it was written. It has become clear in the last few years how important the conversation is between Jewish and Christian women theologians, particularly in relation to the biblical books they have in common. Judith Plaskow's book *Standing Again at Sinai* develops a Jewish-feminist theology that is closely related to the tradition, which raises questions of history. Christian women exegetes, on their part, have learned from Jewish women to be more attentive to what historical consequences texts have had and to discern the liberating message of texts by reading them, not with a hermeneutic of skepticism, but with a prior positive expectation (e.g., Phyllis Trible).

The structure of what is to follow in this basic course is itself intentionally oriented in terms of historical explorations. The reason for this choice is that there are still no such schematic overviews, particularly for the First Testament; a gap exists here. Another reason is that we cannot do without historical reconstructions. Loss of history means loss of power: in the movements of blacks for liberation, it is such insight that motivated them ever anew to search for their own roots ("back to the roots").

Results from the reconstruction of the history of women adherents of the religion of YHWH as an integral part of the history of Israel may initially appear disenchanting. Such reconstruction confirms the suspicion that Israelite society, as well as the religion of YHWH, were highly patriarchal. How is this understanding to be reconciled hermeneutically with messages that liberate women? As presented repeatedly in feminist exegesis, such messages are found in certain texts and in entire biblical books. They are discernible in the tenor of narratives critical of patriarchy, dating from ancient and recent times. Why do many of the First Testament's traditions speak of an unmistakable identification of women with this YHWH-God, from whom they hoped to receive liberation and salvation for themselves and their concerns? Whence this critique within the Bible of patriarchal conditions, such as in certain texts about women in the Books of Samuel and so forth?

There is a tension between the hermeneutic of skepticism and that of positive expectation, both of which have proven themselves extraordinarily fruitful for feminist work with texts. In my judgment, this tension may be resolved only by what is once again a historical question: were there influential groups (which ones and when?) that were able to get the perspectives of women's identification with this YHWH-faith incorporated into the written tradition? Were there revisions of existing writings, possibly undertaken very late, for example, by one Salome Alexandra (first century B.C.E.), who reintroduced the *Ketubbah,* the marriage contract stipulating financial arrangements in the event of divorce? Did such revisions, while going against the stream of androcentric traditions, still firmly anchor in history the religious subjecthood of women? The second hypothesis may be supported from materials in the Books of Ruth, Esther, and Judith (see especially the explorations of Klara Butting; however, she does not pursue the question of exactly which groups created such texts or images of women and when). But what is striking is that two chapters of later origin have been prefixed to the Books of Samuel. They tell of a believing adherent of the YHWH religion who unites herself with her God against the threatening fate of childlessness. In the Song of Hannah a revolutionary program emerges from her lips. In reference to Israel's history, it speaks of YHWH as the God who stands every existing order on its head. Such women-centered perspectives are quite often found at the margins of biblical books, for example, in Proverbs 1–9 and the novella of the Book of Job. Further research into these background materials will assist significantly in determining how we, as women of today, may deal with the heritage of the First Testament. If there were women (and men) before the change to the common era who approached this heritage with the same critical questions and opposed it at crucial points, then this tradition of resistance would be an important reason for acknowledging the First Testament as part of our own tradition and to keep it alive. Clarification of all these fascinating questions will also tell us whether the "hermeneutics of remembrance," which plays such an important role in Elisabeth Schüssler Fiorenza's work, may be applied to Israel's history of women.

Klara Butting, *Die Buchstaben werden sich noch wundern: Innerbiblische Kritik als Wegweisung feministischer Hermeneutik* (Berlin: Alektor Verlag, 1993); Hedwig Jahnow et al., *Feministische Hermeneutik und Erstes Testament: Analysen und Interpretationen* (Stuttgart: W. Kohlhammer Verlag, 1994), 9–25; Judith Plaskow, *Standing Again at Sinai: Judaism from a Feminist Perspective* (San Francisco: Harper and Row, 1990); Silvia Schroer and Othmar Keel, "Von den schmerzlichen Beziehungen zwischen Christentum, Judentum und kanaanäischer Religion," *Neue Wege* 88 (1994): 71–78.
See also Part One for additional literature.

4.1 Specific Problems

By now, there exist comprehensive hermeneutical proposals for feminist readings of the New Testament (see chap. 2). For several reasons, however, development of a feminist hermeneutic for the First Testament is incomparably more difficult. For one, we are dealing with quite different writings whose period of composition encompasses nearly a millennium, on the assumption that it was during the early monarchy that the first collections of texts came into being and that the Wisdom of Solomon was composed only shortly before the change to the common era. There are almost no books in the First Testament that can be unambiguously traced back to a single and nameable author (such as Jesus Sirach); there are some that may have been composed by an individual, whether an anonymous or pseudonymous male or female author (Ruth, Qoheleth, Esther, Judith, Wisdom of Solomon). Most of the writings—the Pentateuch, the historical and prophetic books, as well as the wisdom writings—are literature of tradition and were composed by collectives. This means that the process of composition may have gone on for a longer period, sometimes for centuries, during which collecting, expanding, and revising took place (e.g., the collection of laws by the superior court in Jerusalem). Until recently the representatives of traditional critical-historical exegesis believed that this process of tradition could be constructed on the basis of literary-critical findings (such as breaks and incongruencies in the text). Many of the reconstructions developed by that procedure, however, have collapsed like a house of cards. Texts may, indeed, gain in harmony and uniformity over an extended period of growth so that one may not necessarily find criteria for identifying a text's layers and dates. More recent approaches concentrate therefore on the final form of the text (Erhard Blum, Frank Crüsemann) and seek from this position to determine older and younger narrative circles.

To regain the history of women on such unsure ground is clearly difficult. Feminist exegesis of the First Testament has reacted to this problem by developing very different methods and approaches. So far it has been deemed best to determine fixed points only within systems of coordination that are merely sketched out. This means drawing on limited, well-studied areas of research (e.g., Hosea), carrying out studies focused on themes and how concepts developed historically (e.g., Karen Engelken; see 5.3), and then eventually connecting individual results so that a larger, more comprehensive picture may emerge.

Since it is also our intention to stimulate work in feminist research, particular deficits of research already undertaken need to be cited. While individual women as well as texts and themes about women have been studied on an ongoing basis, whole areas are almost completely missing in feminist exegesis, such as the engagement of individual bodies of writings like the Books of Kings, Chronicles, and the literary prophets. That there is still no research in the books of the Law, that is, the Torah in the narrower sense, is particularly aggravating, because this deficit is part of the androcentric Christian tradition. Theologically the lack is highly problematic. The Torah and the question about the law that is valid for Christians must be a prior concern for Christian women. (See Crüsemann, 4.4.)

4.2 Keys to Concealed Information

Our point of departure must be the fact that the texts of the First Testament originated in a patriarchal world, that the majority of them transmit androcentric ways of seeing, and, for that reason, have to be read with a hermeneutic of skepticism. There is selective depiction of the world of women, exclusion, polemics, distortion, idealizing, and ideology. The texts may well contain important information about women's everyday life, religion, and history, if we learn to unmask them as such. Several keys help to unlock this problem.

1. Today's experience of women can alert us to backgrounds of a text that the text does not itself name. The narrative of Lot's daughters is on the surface a story of two women who surreptitiously obtain progeny by sleeping with their father, while deep down it is a tale of incest (Elke Seifert).

2. Different texts may present contrary ways of seeing the same circumstance so that we learn something from the contradictions. For example, priestly circles have in actual fact strongly controlled female sexuality by the purity-impurity models; prophetic groups favored the polemical defamation of eroticism and sexuality while the Song of Songs shows itself wholly unimpressed by it all. This collection of secular love songs testifies to a quite unburdened love life and proud self-awareness on the part of women. The "foreign woman," who on her own initiative looks for a/her lover, can in this text speak in her own name; she can be idealized in the Book of Ruth (Ruth with Boaz on the threshing floor) and be presented in the wisdom literature as a frightful specter against which young men must be warned.

3. Biblical texts may be corrected, supplemented, relativized, or even refuted in their assertions, not only by other biblical writings but also by extrabiblical texts and archaeological findings. This insight, which at this point is quite general in its meaning, is nevertheless of particular significance for feminist research (see 3.4.2). For example, the conquest of the land happened in a far friendlier way than described in the Book of Joshua; the prohibition of images must be seen in connection with the many references in the First Testament to the art of painting and with the paintings discovered by excavations (see 6.6.2). What Asherah meant in Israel cannot be reconstructed on the basis of biblical texts alone; benedictions found in inscriptions of the ninth/eighth century B.C.E. throw somewhat more light on the relation of Asherah and YHWH. Of

decisive importance in answering the historical questions related to this matter is iconography, which in comparison to biblical texts provides much more material (Keel and Uehlinger 1992; see 4.4).

In reconstructing the history of Israelite women or of women who embraced the religion of YHWH, great care and skepticism are required in evaluating the texts of the Bible as *historical* documents. That is because these texts came from those who had mastered writing and could, therefore, document their views. Text and reality may correspond in greater or lesser measure. The worlds of women and of men in Israel may well have coexisted separately and in contact with one another. Wherever they lacked access to dimensions of women's lives such as childbirth, feasts like the feast of the New Moon, or certain rituals, male writers lacked information, so that knowledge of those dimensions was passed on in fragmentary fashion or not at all. In each case, one needs to examine whether certain text genres possibly document authentic women's voices or were even written by women. It is generally to be assumed that traditions of women were far more a part of oral tradition. As examples, we may cite the narrative circles of the stories about Israel's primordial parents, songs of victory and derision connected with events of war, love songs, songs of birth, speeches and stories around the giving of names, the latter of which may have come from midwives (see 3.1.4). In the process of writing down traditions, the traditions of women received a strongly androcentric revision. Second Kings 8:6 speaks of the great woman of Shunem as the narrator who at the royal court tells of Elisha and his deeds. But as long as the opposite has not been proven, one must keep in view that women were the writers, for example, of parts of the Books of Samuel (Schroer 1992, 115), of Psalms, and of women's books like Ruth, Esther, and Judith, or of a writing such as the Wisdom of Solomon. In this connection, Athalya Brenner and Fokkelien van Dijk-Hemmes (1993) look systematically for "female voices" in biblical texts. They believe that *sex* and *gender* are not necessarily identical when certain texts are assigned to women or men. For example, in Proverbs 1–9 a teacher-father speaks to his pupil-son according to the genre of this text, but it is quite possible to read all these teachings as a mother's instructions to her son.

In what follows, it is presupposed that Israelite society was patriarchal. By patriarchy I mean a complex system of domination in a differentiated sense in which certain men, as well as women of certain classes or groups, exercise domination over other men, women, and children (see 2.2.1 and 2.2.2). But one must warn against comparing ancient Israelite patriarchy with that of today's industrialized, technological, and individual-oriented societies. In an agrarian culture where they are part of the process of production, women are often in positions of equal power to men even when they are excluded, for example, from politics and public activities. The free space of an Israelite woman (and related to it, her self-awareness as a woman) may at certain times have been considerably bigger than what bourgeois society could ever have conceded to women in the last one hundred years. In Arabic countries, where in many ways the worlds of women and men are widely set apart, how women themselves assess their influence and freedom does not necessarily coincide with how Western women see it. That is why care must be exercised when ancient Israel is under consideration. The rules on purity that seem discriminatory to us may well have been experienced as positive by women at that time. What we perceive as restrictive may not have been a restriction to an Israelite woman in those days. A clear criterion for assessing such cases is often provided when the sources themselves indicate that there were conflicts between women and men or between distinct groups about particular questions (contra Carol Meyers's all-too-positive description of the statues of Israelite women in the ancient world).

Athalya Brenner and Fokkelien van Dijk-Hemmes, *On Gendering Texts: Female and Male Voices in the Bible* (Leiden: E. J. Brill, 1993); J. Cheryl Exum, *Fragmented Women: Feminist (Sub)versions of Biblical Narratives*, JSOT Suppl. Ser. 163 (Sheffield: Sheffield Academic Press, 1993); Carol Meyers, *Discovering Eve: Ancient Israelite Women in Context* (New York: Oxford University Press, 1988); Silvia Schroer, *Die Samuelbucher*, NSK-AT 7 (Stuttgart: Verlag Katholisches Bibelwerk, 1992); Elke Seifert, "Lot und seine Töchter: Eine Hermeneutik des Verdachts," in Hedwig Jahnow et al. (see first bibliographical list in this chapter), 48–66.

4.3 Questions, Procedures, and Goals

As was indicated already in Part One, there are no specifically feminist methods of exegesis. But every method may be combined with a feminist option. Elisabeth Schüssler Fiorenza has put in place the requisite tools of historical criticism for a feminist reading of the Second Testament. She has developed a series of particular working steps which may be usefully transposed into the exegesis of the First Testament. As the following examples indicate, in actual practice such steps have already been applied there. In First Testament writings as well, one must reckon with androcentric translation, selection of texts, canonization, and projection: in other words, a broad common basis exists for feminist exegesis of the First and Second Testaments while the differences may well be greater in hermeneutical and other issues.

4.3.1 Androcentric Translations

The texts of the First Testament have been translated from the Hebrew and Greek almost exclusively by men. This very fact challenges women exegetes to uncover the androcentrism in the translations and so to recover information which was lost or systematically suppressed. In this area, impressive individual studies already exist. One of the major problems is the peculiarity of Hebrew and Greek (and of German) in using male forms of words, not only in gender-specific but often also in an inclusive (generic) manner. This means that women may also have been envisaged but left invisible. This has enormous consequences, for example, for how we understand the texts of the law; they are linguistically addressed to a "You" that is male, but in terms of their contents are valid for both men and women. The androcentric prejudgments of translators and commentators become drastically apparent—especially when positions occupied by women are involved—when a text assigns strong or even quasi-divine abilities to a woman or when images of God contain unexpectedly female elements.

According to Gen. 4:1, after giving birth to Cain, Eve breaks out in a shout of joy: "I have brought forth a man like YHWH" (Schüngel-Straumann 1989, 146ff.). Standard translations reduce this reminiscence of the mother (goddess) of all living by rendering this text, for example, as follows: "I have gotten a man with the help of the Lord" (RSV).

The already very androcentric text of 1 Kings 1:1-4 is made even more so by its translations. The text portrays Abishag the Shunammite as a pretty hot-water bottle for the aged King David. While translating the word *soken*, when applied to a man (as in Isa. 22:15), as "steward" or "prefect," translators have declassified the title *sokenet* in 1:4, which certifies Abishag to be a woman holding an office, by the use of verbal circumlocutions like "nursing, ministering" (Häusl).

Helen Schüngel-Straumann has demonstrated that in Hosea 11, YHWH is not the father of Ephraim, as the standard German translations make us believe (with the singular exception of the Buber-Rosenzweig translation). Instead, she is a mother who takes the baby in her arms and nurses him, and who later, because of her mother-love, cannot raise her hand against the child. The pointed declaration of Hosea 11:9, "for I am God and not man" (RSV), has been deprived of its critique of patriarchy in many translations, "for I am God and not human," even though the Hebrew text unquestionably speaks of man (*'ish*) and not of human being (*'adâm*). The distorted rendition of the original text has massively advanced the impoverishment of the traditions of our images of God; a similar case is given in Num. 23:19. It is of crucial significance for the interpretation of Genesis 2 that *'adâm* means human being and not man. For contrary to the effects of the text in history, the man is not the first to be created; rather, it was an "earth creature," an *'adâm*, of no specific gender who obtained his identity as a man only through the creation of a woman (see the synopsis of Schüngel-Straumann 1989).

Stefanie Schäfer-Bossert has researched the giving of names recorded in Gen. 35:18. Rachel names her second son *ben-'oni;* she dies while giving birth to him. His name is translated as "son of my misfortune, my sorrow, child of my pain." Subsequently, his father names the child *ben-jamîn,* "son of the right hand, child of fortune." However, in Gen. 49:3, the word *'oni,* also used in connection with naming and characterization, is translated very differently. Jacob says there that Reuben is the firstling of *'oni:* "[Y]ou are my first-born, my might, and the first fruits of my strength" (RSV). Stefanie Schäfer-Bossert undertakes a meticulous study of the words and shows that in Gen. 35:18 the name of the child should also be translated as "son of my life's strength, of my potency." The translators did not want to consider this possibility at all because they preferred to attribute sorrow to a woman, rather than strength and procreative potency. They proceeded to secure the meaning of "sorrow, misfortune" by means of complicated deviations.

One could add many more examples. The translations of and commentaries on the Song of Songs bristle with androcentrisms and clichés hostile to women. (An example to the contrary is Othmar Keel's commentary, which is suitable as a basis for the work of feminist exegesis.) The image of the personified Wisdom of Proverbs 8 is distorted when the textually difficult verse 30 is so bent out of shape that Wisdom becomes the "pet" or "plaything" of YHWH. This is despite the fact that from ancient Oriental traditions onward she is a young woman and not also necessarily a "daughter" (see Schroer 1991 for a synopsis and literature). The translations of the Wisdom of Solomon have almost totally excised the erotic undertones in the Greek words that describe the relationship of Solomon to Sophia or even of God and Sophia. (Dieter Georgi's translation is an example to the contrary.)

Collecting individual observations is, of course, only a beginning. These critical revisions of Scripture translations aim toward a new (German) translation of the First Testament, guided by feminist criteria, which would also offer firm ground for reading the Bible to nonexpert women (see the New Revised Standard Version).

Dieter Georgi, *Weisheit Salomos (Jüdische Schriften aus hellenistisch-römischer Zeit)*, vol. 3, no. 4 (Gütersloh: Gütersloher Verlagshaus Gerd Mohn, 1980); Maria Häusl, *Abischag und Batscheba: Frauen am Königshof und die Thronfolge Davids im Zeugnis der Texte 1 Kön 1 und 2*, Münchener Universitätsschriften (St. Ottilien: Eos Verlag, 1993); Othmar Keel, *Das Hohelied*, ZBK-AT 18 (Zurich: TVZ, 1986); Stefanie Schäfer-Bossert, "Den Männern die Macht und der Frau die Trauer? Ein kritischer Blick auf die Deutung von *'vn* oder: Wie nennt Rahel ihren Sohn?" in Hedwig Jahnow et al. (see first bibliographical list in this chapter), 106–25; Silvia Schroer, "Die göttliche Weisheit und der nachexilische Monotheismus," in Marie-Theres Wacker and Erich Zenger, eds., *Der eine Gott und die Göttin: Die alttestamentliche Rede von Gott im Horizont feministischer Theologie*, QD 135 (Freiburg: Herder Verlag, 1991), 151–82; Helen Schüngel-Straumann, *Die Frau am Anfang: Eva und die Folgen* (Freiburg: Herder Verlag, 1989); idem, "Gott als Mutter in Hosea 11," *ThQ* 166 (1986): 119–34.

4.3.2 Androcentric Composition of Texts

In the domain of the Second Testament, the synoptic comparison of the Gospels or the comparison of the Gospels and Acts with the epistolary literature yields interesting information on whether a text was an androcentric composition from the outset. For the exegesis of the First Testament such "wide-angle" comparisons are equally important, but it is much more difficult to ascertain the traces. Most of the examples will be presented in terms of diachronic and synchronic sections. Three examples will be presented.

The figure of Miriam is firmly associated in the Bible with the Exodus from Egypt and the trek through the desert. Exodus 15:20 depicts her positively as a woman prophet who, timbrel in hand, sounds the song of

Israel's victory after the crossing of the Red Sea. This image has established itself in Jewish tradition. Micah 6 names her next to Moses and Aaron as a leader of the people sent by God. Even the monastic Therapeutae of whom Philo writes recalled Miriam in their liturgy, as a leader of the Exodus of the same stature as Moses; innumerable Jewish women everywhere and in every century bore her name (Schroer, *Ein Gott allein?* and "The Book of Sophia"). The narrative in Numbers 12, on the other hand, uses every means to defame her as a rebel. Her punishment is disproportionately greater than that of Aaron, who is accused of the identical transgression: refusing to submit to the authority of her brother Moses. Miriam is struck with leprosy and sent from the camp; only her brother's intercession causes her divine punishment to be reduced. One must ask what interests the writers of this text had in putting this woman down in such a manner. What is clearly at issue are matters of authority and power, as well as of claims on direct revelations from God and the order of rank of the leading figures of Israel's faith history. Frank Crüsemann may have provided a clue (1992; see 4.4) when he proposes that Moses was a kind of corporate personality in the Pentateuch, one who is representative of the authority of the superior court of Jerusalem. Of what or of which group is Miriam a representative in that case? Does she represent Israelite women, who themselves also claimed functions of leadership, authority, charisma, and divine revelation and refused to submit to that court's instructions?

The Books of Samuel and Kings and their reception in the Books of Chronicles make for a useful synoptic comparison. There is no difficulty at all in demonstrating the androcentric selection and redaction at work there. Often the traditions in which women had played an important role are simply left out and minor additions reinforce negative images of women (e.g., the bad influence of King-mother Athaliah, 2 Chron. 22:3). Chronicles finally cleanses even the Deuteronomistic tradition of everything that even remotely reflects veneration of the Goddess (Frevel 1991).

Another example of a demonstrably androcentric editing of a text is the Book of Jesus ben Sirach from the second century B.C.E. A notably large section of the work deals with women, good and bad wives, daughters who are in need of their fathers' control, and so forth (Schroer 1996). Under this topic, the author clearly pursues a pastoral concern. According to Jesus ben Sirach, the ideal woman has to honor the husband (26:26), obey and support him (36:26), see to it that he reaches old age in peace, while she has to keep quiet (16:1-2). On the other hand, he demonizes all women who do not submit to the authority of their *pater familias*. His counsel to the man—"do not surrender yourself to a woman and let her trample down your strength" (9:2, NEB)—is a program to reinforce patriarchal order. That order must have been challenged somewhere in the author's environment, probably by women who did not accept strict submission to male domination, but perhaps also by men who had no wish to take on the role of rulers. The statements of Jesus ben Sirach are not to be taken, therefore, as a description of reality but as an androcentric projection of it. Next to his wish list, this teacher has left us a catalog of deeply misogynist assertions, among them the one that has had such horrendous consequences. "Woman is the origin of sin and it is through her that we all die" (25:24) (Küchler 1986; see 4.4). Neither did he shy away from using theological means in his war against the autonomy of women. Jesus ben Sirach develops a theological model in which Wisdom, itself depicted as a person and who in ancient writings often represents the God of Israel in the image of a woman, is strictly subordinated to the male God as a hypostasis.

Christian Frevel, "Die Elimination der Göttin aus dem Weltbild des Chronisten," *ZAW* 103 (1991): 263–71; Silvia Schroer, "The Book of Sophia," in Elisabeth Schüssler Fiorenza, ed., *Searching the Scriptures,* vol. 2: *A Feminist Commentary* (New York: Crossroad, 1994), 17–38; idem, "Die göttliche Weisheit und der nachexilische Monotheismus" (see 4.3.1); idem, "Die personifizierte Sophia im Buch der Weisheit," in Walter Dietrich and Martin A. Klopfenstein, eds., *Ein Gott allein? JHWH-Verehrung und biblischer Monotheismus im Kontext der israelitischen und altorientalischen Religionsgeschichte,* OBO 139 (Fribourg: Universitätsverlag; Göttingen: Vandenhoeck und Ruprecht, 1994), 543–58; idem, *Die Weisheit hat ihr Haus gebaut: Studien zur Gestalt der Sophia in den biblischen Schriften* (Mainz: Matthias-Grünewald-Verlag, 1996).

4.3.3 Patriarchal Formation of the Canon and Tradition of Texts

The process of canonizing the Hebrew writings began in the fourth century B.C.E. and came to a close at the change to the common era or even later. As of yet there are no feminist studies about the so-called Apocrypha and pseudepigrapha of the First Testament as a body. Surely reconstructing women's history cannot ignore these writings; an important issue would be whether nonacceptance into the canon was motivated in individual cases by reasons of misogyny. A large part of these early Jewish works is clearly hostile to women (an excellent groundwork for studies on this question is provided by Küchler 1986; see 4.4), whereas the writings incorporated latest into the canon are more integrated in relation to several questions. As far as we know there are also no feminist studies in the area of textual criticism and history. (But see 2.2.1 and Häusl on 1 Kings 1–2 and Wacker 1994 on the traces of the Goddess in the text of Hosea and its history.) Is there evidence of texts that, like the renowned Codex D of the Book of Acts, introduce themselves into existing texts in order to make information about women unrecognizable?

The Septuagint translation of the Hebrew text (ca. 300 b.c.e.; see Küchler 1992) offers drastic demonstrations of androcentric tradition of texts; it requires a separate feminist examination. For example, the Hebrew and Greek texts diverge noticeably in the long discourse between Jeremiah and the women and men who worship the Queen of Heaven (Jeremiah 44; Jost 1995, 221–26). The Septuagint could not bear the elevated valuation and praise of woman at the end of Proverbs 31 and has significantly changed the text in 31:28 and following (Schroer 1991, 161). It is not the woman who fears YHWH but the sensible woman who is to be praised; she is to extol the fear of YHWH and it is not she, but her man that is to be honored in the city gate. Sibylle Mähner has examined the textual history of Josh. 10:12c-13c and 1 Kings 8:12b-13 (changes made in the Septuagint, cuts in the Masoretic text) and has done so on the supposition of the sun (god or goddess?) as the precursor of YHWH in Jerusalem

Maria Häusl (See 4.3.1); Renate Jost, *Frauen, Männer und die Himmelskönigin: Exegetische Studien* (Gütersloh: Gütersloher Verlagshaus Gerd Mohn, 1995), 221–26; Max Küchler, "Gott und seine Weisheit in der Septuaginta (Ijob 28; Spr 8)," in Hans-Josef Klauck, ed., *Monotheismus und Christologie: Zur Gottesfrage im hellenistischen Judentum und im Urchristentum*, QD 138 (Freiburg: Herder Verlag, 1992), 117–42; Sibylle Mähner, "Die Sonne als Vorgängerin JHWHs in Jerusalem: Studien zu Jos 10, 12c–13c und 1 Kön 8, 12b–13b" (diss., Fribourg); Silvia Schroer, "Die göttliche Weisheit und der nachexilische Monotheismus" (see 4.3.1); Marie-Theres Wacker, *Figurationen des Weiblichen im Hoseabuch* (Freiburg, Basel, and Vienna: Herder Verlag, 1996).

4.3.4 Patriarchal History of Effects and Theological Attenuation of Misogynist Effects

The history of what is effected by a biblical text often does not coincide with the text's original intention. Christian feminist exegesis, whether it likes it or not, is part of the decidedly Eurocentric interpretive tradition of the West (see Schottroff and Schroer 1993). It is generally accepted that this heritage has to be critically reworked. And then there are problem areas specific to women. The best-known example is the J narrative of creation in Genesis 2–3. It is difficult to bring into focus the reception over many centuries of this text with its heavy emphasis on the man being created first and the seductive power and sin of the woman (Göss-mann and Schüngel-Straumann). Influenced by Hellenism, early Jewish writings already systematically eroticized and demonized biblical women and women's stories. Often, teachings of the Second Testament hostile to women built on the history of the effects of earlier texts (Küchler 1986; see 4.4). That history has an important place in feminist exegesis. That a text brought continuous misfortune on women may become the reason for dispossessing its authority as "God's word." In less drastic cases, that history may also be used as a beacon that helps exegesis to avoid walking into major traps. Finally, it is often very profitable to compare the Jewish and Christian histories of a text's consequences. The exegesis of Proverbs 31 found particularly in Reformation churches is one which depicts the industrious and pious wife who cares ever so much for husband, children, and home. The exegesis has been drawn on so strongly for this image that it is nearly impossible for Christian women to discern the original picture of the autonomous and strong Israelite women found in the text (Schroer 1991, 159ff.; see also the different view of Jahnow 1914). Jewish exegesis has done far less violence to the text (Navè Levinson 1989, 29).

The example cited next is used because it is one on which feminists appear to have reached consensus. It is not centered in a single biblical text but encompasses an entire motif tradition. It is in Hosea 1–3 that the relation of YHWH to Israel is depicted for the first time in the imagery of patriarchal marriage. In this image-event, the woman whom the prophet takes as his wife is known to be a street worker. The aim of the image is to portray Israel's demeanor toward its God in terms of sex-trade dynamics. Even though well treated by the master of the marriage, the people run after alien deities. Feminist exegesis has brought out the peculiarities of this prophetic metaphor (Balz-Cochois 1982; Wacker 1987;

Stienstra 1993). A male god is no longer brought together here with a female partner of equal status, a goddess, but with a land or people, which from the outset establishes a hierarchical relationship. In addition, the relationship is imaged as marriage in order to depict this patriarchal hierarchy. The female component of this unequal relationship, however, is not only shown to be subordinate but is also defamed as sexually unruly, unfaithful, and stupid. An ominous development took shape in Hosea. For one, this metaphor identifies the male with transcendence and the female with immanence (and, of course, subordinates the immanent to the transcendent). Then, being woman becomes the image for a licentious craving for sex without regard for human relationships. This motif achieved extensive success within the Bible itself: Jer. 2:23-25, chapter 3, and 13:20ff. take it up, and Ezekiel 16 and 23 develop it extensively. The elaboration given to this motif, sometimes in a variety of circumlocutions, has now come to be named without much ado as pornography (Brenner, van Dijk-Hemmes, Maier). In Christian traditions, these texts have had an unquestionably profound influence on the image of woman and especially on that of female sexuality. Therefore, it is urgent to make people aware that these texts cannot be proclaimed as the life-giving word of God. It is not only the demonization of female sexuality but also the fateful assignation of gender roles to transcendence and immanence that give rise to this. Much later, in Christian tradition, Hosea's image of marriage was applied to Christ and the church. The metaphor served to oblige women to be obedient to their men partners in marriage; this is made abundantly clear in Ephesians 5—a text that belongs to the patriarchal household code tradition. By this metaphor, resisting the patriarchal order is made a sacrilege; the man is drawn onto the side of transcendence (Christ) and the woman is excluded from it.

Helgard Balz-Cochois, *Gomer: Der Höhenkult Israels im Selbstverständnis der Volksfrömmigkeit. Untersuchungen zu Hosea 4,1-5,7* (Frankfurt: Peter Lang Verlag, 1982); Athalya Brenner and Fokkelien van Dijk-Hemmes (see 4.2); Elisabeth Gössmann and Helen Schüngel-Straumann, "Eva," in *WbfTh*, 90–97; Hedwig Jahnow, "Die Frau im Alten Testament," *Die Frau* 21 (1914): 352–58 and 417–26 (reprint in Hedwig Jahnow et al., *Feministische Hermeneutik und Erstes Testament*, 30–47; see first bibliography in this chapter); Christl Maier, "Jerusalem als Ehebrecherin in Ezechiel 16: Zur Verwendung und Funktion einer biblischen Metapher," in Hedwig Jahnow et al., *Feministische Hermeneutik und Erstes Testament*, 85–105; Pnina Navè Levinson, *Was wurde aus Saras Töchtern? Frauen im Judentum* (Gütersloh: Gütersloher Verlagshaus, 1989); Luise Schottroff and Silvia Schroer, "Bibelauslegung im europäischen Kontext," in *Feministische Theologie im europäischen Kontext*, Jahrbuch der Europäischen Gesellschaft für die theologische Forschung von Frauen 1.93 (Mainz and Kampen, 1993), 56–67; Silvia Schroer, "Die göttliche Weisheit und der nachexilische Monotheismus" (see 4.3.1); idem, *Die Weisheit hat ihr Haus gebaut* (see 4.3.2); Nelly Stienstra, *YHWH Is the Husband of His People: Analysis of a Biblical Metaphor with Special Reference to Translation* (Kampen, 1993); Fokkelien van Dijk-Hemmes, "The Metaphorization of Women in Prophetic Speech: An Analysis of Ezechiel 23," *VT* 43 (1993): 162–70; Marie-Theres Wacker, "Biblische Theologie und Männerphantasie: Das Beispiel Hosea 1–3," in Hubert Frankemölle, ed., *Die Bibel: Das bekannte Buch—das fremde Buch* (Paderborn: F. Schöningh, 1994), 155–72; idem, "Frau—Sexus—Macht: Eine feministisch-theologische Relecture des Hoseabuchs," in Marie-Theres Wacker, ed., *Der Gott der Männer und die Frauen* (Düsseldorf: Patmos, 1987), 101–25.

4.4   Important Resources

In addition to the literature listed in individual sections above, a number of indispensable sources or books for feminist exegetical study of the First Testament ought to be mentioned.

Crüsemann, Frank. *The Torah: Theology and Social History of Old Testament Law*. Minneapolis: Fortress Press, 1996.

———. *Leviticus: A Commentary*. Louisville: Westminster/John Knox Press, 1996.

Gerstenberger, Erhard S. *Yahweh—The Patriarch: Ancient Images of God and Feminist Theology*. Minneapolis: Fortress Press, 1996.

Goodenough, Erwin R. *Jewish Symbols in the Greco-Roman Period*. 13 vols. New York: Pantheon Books, 1953–68.

Hengel, Martin. *Judaism and Hellenism: Studies in Their Encounter in Palestine*. Philadelphia: Fortress Press, 1981.

Ilan, Tal. *Jewish Women in Greco-Roman Palestine*. Texte und Studien zum Antiken Judentum, vol. 44. Tübingen: Mohr und Siebeck, 1995.

Keel, Othmar, and Christoph Uehlinger. *Göttinnen, Götter und Gottessymbole: Neue Erkenntnisse zur Religionsgeschichte Kanaans und Israels aufgrund bislang unerschlossener ikonographischer Quellen.* QD, vol. 134. Freiburg, Basel, and Vienna: Herder Verlag, 1992.

Keel, Othmar, Max Küchler, and Christoph Uehlinger. *Orte und Landschaften der Bibel: Ein Handbuch und Studien-Reiseführer zum Heiligen Land.* Zurich: Benziger; Göttingen: Vandenhoeck und Ruprecht, 1982, 1984. Two volumes have been published to date.

Knauf, Ernst Axel. *Die Umwelt des Alten Testaments. NSK-AT,* vol. 29. Stuttgart: Verlag Katholisches Bibelwerk, 1994.

Küchler, Max. *Frühjüdische Weisheitstraditionen: Zum Fortgang weisheitlichen Denkens im Bereich des frühjüdischen Jahweglaubens.* OBO, vol. 26. Fribourg: Universitätsverlag; Göttingen: Vandenhoeck und Ruprecht, 1979.

————. *Schweigen, Schmuck und Schleier: Drei neutestamentliche Vorschriften zur Verdrängung der Frauen auf dem Hintergrund einer frauenfeindlichen Exegese des Alten Testaments im antiken Judentum.* NTOA, vol. 1. Fribourg: Universitätsverlag; Göttingen: Vandenhoeck und Ruprecht, 1986.

Kuhnen, Hans-Peter. *Palästina in griechisch-römischer Zeit (Vorderasien II and 2).* Munich: C. H. Beck, 1990.

Rostovtzeff, Michael. *The Social and Economic History of the Hellenistic World.* 3 vols. Oxford: Clarendon Press, 1953.

Weippert, Helga. *Palästina in vorhellenistischer Zeit (Handbuch der Archäologie, Vorderasien II and 1).* Munich: C. H. Beck, 1988.

Winter, Urs. *Frau und Göttin: Exegetische und ikonographische Studien zum weiblichen Gottesbild im Alten Israel und dessen Umwelt.* OBO, vol. 53. Fribourg: Universitätsverlag; Göttingen: Vandenhoeck und Ruprecht, 1983.

Note: See also volumes in the series Jüdische Schriften aus hellenistischrömischer Zeit, Gütersloh: Gütersloher Verlaghaus Gerd Mohn.

Chapter Five

Diachronic Sections

Reconstructing the history of Israelite women or of the women adherents of the YHWH religion has high priority in feminist exegetical study of the First Testament. This history needs to be released from silence and invisibility, its subjects remembered and identity for women achieved through the process of seeking our roots. In what follows there is deliberately no distinction made between Israelite women, that is, women who from the formation of the tribal union and of the territorial states lived in Israel and Judah or in exile, and the women adherents of the YHWH religion. It is not likely that the women who worshiped other deities completely distanced themselves, for that very reason, from the official YHWH cult. There is also an ideological-theological problem in the two designations. For as soon as Israelite women, for example, those who worshiped the Queen of Heaven, are no longer regarded as adherents of the YHWH religion, we are taking on notions of orthodoxy, heresy, or syncretism. These notions correspond to a great extent to the prophetic and Deuteronomistic construction of history, but not necessarily to the self-understanding of these women or the perspective of other contemporary groupings.

In feminist construction of the history of the religion of Israel, I consider it equally problematic to make use of models that strongly rely on the juxtaposition of state cult and popular piety (often associated with the differentiation of the center from the province), or temple cult and official theology over and against private religiousness (e.g., Balz-Cochois or Ackerman). Such classification may be appropriate in individual instances, but it is not suitable as a model. This is because, according to the sources, there never was a clear demarcation between the entities so named. Therefore, a model based on this juxtaposition would be anachronistic. (Similarly, since it has been used in today's sense only since 1789 C.E., the concept of *nation* ought not to be used in a history of Israel.) While the cult of the Goddess gained strength during the reign of Manasseh in private homes, the state cult also came under the sway of such developments. For a feminist exegetical approach, the particular danger of classifying conceptions is that women are quickly ranged on the side of popular piety, private religiousness, and domestic cults, whereas YHWH religion of the state becomes a purely male domain. But we know that even at the highest levels of politics, women attempted to exercise influence on the religion of the land. Conversely, men—occasionally even the rulers of the land—participated in all the cults that are defined as belonging to popular or private piety. Future feminist research in the history of Israel may, on the contrary, be oriented by a conceptuality such as the identification of women with the YHWH religion and the elements in this religion that liberated or strengthened women, and the alienation of women from the YHWH religion as a result of needs left unmet or the expulsion of women from the cult of YHWH.

That it is not yet possible to produce a continuous diachronic historiography is quite obvious. Therefore, the following represents no more than an attempt to draw some of the lines that have already become visible. The sources employed are not only biblical texts but also pictorial material from Palestine/Israel that help to trace large developments. What suggests itself is a division into periods, including the period before the founding of the state, the monarchy, and the exilic and postexilic periods, because the classic question about "woman" or "woman's place" in Israel is much too broad. The question fails to do justice to the massive changes in living conditions that occurred in the various periods of time. It is problematic to examine the biblical material on the basis of the traditional groupings: Pentateuch (Deuteronomistic history), major and minor prophets, and writings (as in Alice L. Laffey). Such examination is problematic for historical reconstruction since it fails in making lateral connections that are sufficiently visible. From the point of view of canonical history, however, it is interesting to examine the three traditional parts since they were edited by different groups.

The reconstruction of the history of the women who were adherents of the YHWH religion should not base itself on the development models of redemptive or unredemptive history, for the history that is to be reconstructed does not begin with a golden age of matriarchy. Nor were there liberating impulses for women at the beginning of Israel's history with YHWH that subsequently were pushed aside by patriarchalization. Nor is it true, conversely, that Israelite women through the centuries attained greater freedom and power as women because of the religion of YHWH. In other words, there is no ascent or descent, but rather a fluctuation of liberation and suppression, power and powerlessness, side by side.

The following subjects are very important for the reconstruction of women's history, but to a large extent they have not yet been addressed. It is urgent that they be dealt with in textual studies and archaeology.

1. The archaeology of Palestine has been advanced not only by men but also by great women archaeologists, though the discipline has paid little attention to the distinction between male and female skeletons in graves, urns, and so forth, even though it is easy to make that distinction. This practice should be an obligatory aspect of precise documentation. Hence much evidence about the age of women and the cause of their death is lacking. Also lacking is evidence about specific features of burials of women and what was placed in their graves. Were there differences in status that became manifest in the customs of funerals? and so forth. In this context I call attention to Robert Wenning's forthcoming, groundbreaking publication on graves and funeral rituals in Judah in the Iron Age.

2. It would be useful to have an idea of the size of the population of Palestine, of individual settlements, and statistics for life expectancy, infant and child mortality, and so forth. According to Israel Finkelstein (1988), 55,000 Israelites may have lived in Palestine in the first Iron Age. The average life expectancy was under forty years (Walter Wolff 1974, 119ff.; see 6.7); for women it was closer to thirty years. Stillbirths and deaths in early childhood are mentioned in many a biblical text. Although next to hunger and sword the First Testament again and again names epidemics as the third biggest threat to the population, the presence of devastating epidemics, such as pestilence, cannot be substantiated archaeologically. Unlike mass graves of soldiers, nowhere have mass graves of people who died of pestilence been found. The question is whether epidemics decimated the population (as Carol Meyers assumes), so that Israelite women were constantly constrained to bear children.

3. We know too little about the degree of literacy of the Israelite population in general and the two sexes in particular. The only thing that can be said without ambiguity on the basis of the biblical texts is that members of the upper class, probably men and women alike, could read (Hul-

dah in 2 Kings 22:14ff.) and write (Jezebel in 1 Kings 21:8). Archaeological findings of ordinary, everyday dishes with writing on them would suggest that a wider segment of the population had some knowledge of reading. Were "simple folk" able to read and write? Since we have no indications of any kind of school system, instruction must have taken place at home. Did young girls and women have access to this sphere of knowledge or was the whole world of letters the domain of men?

Israel Finkelstein, *The Archaeology of the Israelite Settlement* (Jerusalem: Israel Exploration Society, 1988); Alice L. Laffey, *An Introduction to the Old Testament: A Feminist Perspective* (Philadelphia: Fortress Press, 1988); Carol Meyers, *Discovering Eve: Ancient Israelite Women in Context* (New York: Oxford University Press, 1988); Robert Wenning, "Grab," in *Neues Bibel-Lexikon* (Einsiedeln and Düsseldorf: Patmos Verlag, 1991), 1:942–46.

5.1 Prehistory to the End of the Late Bronze Age

The land of Palestine was inhabited for thousands of years before Israel constituted itself there as a tribal confederacy and later as a state. It is worthwhile to look at the cultural history of these epochs, for it assists in classifying and understanding developments from 1250–1150 B.C.E. There are no especially noteworthy textual documents from Palestine predating the middle of the second millennium B.C.E., so for questions specifically related to women we are also dependent on archaeology and iconography. In contrast to research in matriarchy, I refer here to material from Palestine and not to the Near East in general. The numerous catalogs and collections of the Biblical Institute in Fribourg, Switzerland, are a particularly good source of information. Othmar Keel and this author are currently preparing a comprehensive history of the religion of Palestine from the Mesolithic Age to the Persian Period based on iconographic material. I present some results of that work in process and do so in the form of theses.

During the Mesolithic and Neolithic Ages (ca. 12000–4500 B.C.E.), Palestine was part of huge cultural regions which extended from Anatolia and Mesopotamia, across Syria and Palestine, all the way to the Sinai Peninsula and Egypt. The cult of the dead is predominant during the pre-ceramic Neolithic Age. The dead are buried beneath people's dwelling places, their skulls artfully decorated and frequently displayed in the homes in order to make the dead present again. Masks may be used as a substitute; it has been noted that in a few instances those masks were clearly designed to be a man's head, with holes for the hairs of a beard and the arched bone above the socket of the eye that is typical of the male skull. The cult of the dead, quite likely a cult of the ancestors, was presumably determined patrilineally. During the Chalcolithic Age (4500–3200 B.C.E.), too, male ivory figurines and basalt heads seem to have had great significance in the cult of ancestors. In Palestine during the ceramic Neolithic Age, extensive production of miniature figures of women begins, figures known also from Catal Huyuk and other sites in Anatolia as well as Mesopotamia and Syria. During that epoch, being human is portrayed chiefly as being female, with a heavy accentuation on reproductivity and sumptuousity of living. There is no male equivalent to this plentifulness of female figures of clay and loam. However varied, these figures comprise the most constant element in the iconography of Palestine during the next several millennia, an iconography that is only partially influenced by changes in culture or politics.

While the he-goat and his horns play a significant role in the religious symbol system of the Chalcolithic Age, the cow occupies that position in the Early Bronze Age (third millennium B.C.E.). The breeding of large livestock, namely cattle and donkeys, creates in Egypt and the Near East the economic foundations for the development of advanced cultures. (The cultivation of large parcels of land, plowed with cattle power, allows for increased storage of goods and results in the establishment of communities of a thousand or more inhabitants, while donkeys favor trade and transport.) During the third millennium B.C.E., Palestine is the "Third World" of the Near East although, being at the edges of those cultures, it has a share in the huge changes. The town or city now comes to be seen as the place where life is lived. Cities are planned and fortified at costs that are in no relation to any imaginable threat from wild animals or aggressors. City life is characterized by division of labor, centralization, and hierarchical order. The head of the city governs in the palace and is looked on as the chief shepherd and protector of the flocks, a successful warrior, chief justice, and high priest. Worship moves from the home or the occasional open-air sanctuary into various temples, often double-temples, within the city. Which deities were worshiped in Palestine cannot be determined. Inanna, the goddess of flocks, of reproductivity, and of culture in general, bestows authority on the heads of cities in Uruk. In Egypt and Mesopotamia, temple and palace become the centers of the economy and of a class society with employees, slaves, and large administrative staffs. Writing, another of the great inventions of the third millennium B.C.E., creates the precondition for large-scale administrations. Together these developments create the basis for culturally astonishing achievements in all spheres; at the same time, women's free spaces most likely become noticeably smaller, since most of public life was taken over by men.

In Egypt the social order is already unambiguously founded on patriarchal family structures; ownership of the land, exalted offices, and the oldest wisdom writings have passed into the control of men and the god of the state is male. In that same millennium, Palestine also experiences changes of direction that have significance for Israelite time (such as the breeding of large livestock, or the characteristic image of the head of the city, and so on). This is also the millennium in which war is invented. A wave of destruction of hitherto unknown dimensions destroys the city cultures after the rulers of Accad waged their imperialistic wars against neighboring states. War, subjugation, fighting, and domination are a central motif in the iconic art of the Early Bronze Age. These advanced cultures must have built up a huge potential for conflict, which in the end led them and the cities around them into demise.

It is only in the eighteenth century B.C.E. that living conditions in Palestine improve enough for a new culture of city-states connected with Syria to take shape. At the beginning of the Middle Kingdom, Egypt's influence is weak and the Palestinian heads of cities grow strong. In the course of two centuries in the Middle Bronze Age (first half of the second millennium B.C.E.), Canaanite culture comes into existence and develops an autonomy that the region was never again able to replicate. Its influence extended as far as the Egyptian Nile delta, where in about 1650 B.C.E. the Hyksos ("the rulers of the foreign lands," i.e., the Canaanites) take power. The standard of living is quite high in the cities of Canaan. Everyone has furniture and there is no separation between rich and poor city areas (Weippert 1988, 227 and 242; see 4.4). Even smaller communities have their own temples. Evidence of iconography indicates that political power in the cities is in the hands of men, for only enthroned male rulers—no female rulers—are portrayed there. These heads of cities appear to have been deified after their death. Funeral customs suggest that within families and clans a patriarchal chief was accorded special privileges (Jericho, chamber-grave H18; Weippert 1988, 242ff.). There are no textual sources yet from the Middle Bronze Age in Palestine that yield relevant information. Among the deities depicted in the iconography of the time, it is the erotic goddess of twigs or trees, associated with vegetation and growth, who predominates. Her partner, the weather god, has a subordinate role, at least in personal piety. Even though they are displaced in the sixteenth century B.C.E., when Egypt's domination is established, Canaanite culture and religion continue to influence many areas of Palestinian life.

At the beginning of the sixteenth century B.C.E., Syria/Palestine up to the Euphrates comes under Egyptian rule. Canaan is not able to break free from Egyptian dominance at any time during the Late Bronze Age (1550–1250 B.C.E.). Hard pressed, part of the Canaanite population abandons its rural and urban ways of life and adopts a nonsedentary one, leaving behind very few archaeological traces. Next to these groups of déclassé or deracinated people (*'apirû*) of Canaanite society, there is a rural population to which Egyptian sources refer as *shasu*. They lived in the extensively cultivated regions between the city-states that were ruled by Egypt; the biblical narratives of the first progenitors give fragmentary evidence of their way of life. Both of these peoples had contact with the sedentary Canaanite population.

From the Late Bronze Age, the iconographic materials that yield usable evidence focus on the urban centers in the Palestinian plains, leaving the religious conceptions of the majority of the population undocumented. Only male deities hold sway in centers under Egyptian rule, especially deities associated with fighting and war. Goddesses and the whole motif of vegetation recede into the background in the iconography of those centers and in the valuable iconic media of the period. However, in private religiosity, they continue to play their role, as the great number of terra-cotta figures of the Goddess would suggest. Occasionally, a goddess is militarized by being mounted on a cavalry horse. Whenever images depict political life, they clearly show that upper-class women have become subordinated; they are portrayed as servants of the heads of cities who govern by the grace of Egypt. Royal might, fighting, and war are the motifs that predominate in this epoch, with a clear correlation between politics and conceptions of God. The bullies are taking over on earth as in heaven.

In relation to the history of Israel, it is important to note that no later than the Early Bronze Age, if not earlier, patriarchal forms of society are clearly in evidence in Palestine. In the Late Bronze Age, the world of symbols for God, as well, is already shaped by patriarchy; the Goddess has been supplanted. There can be no talk, therefore, about the destruction on the part of Israel of matriarchal orders.

The times of which the biblical legends of the patriarchs speak correspond in part to the Late Bronze Age. Condensed and repeatedly worked over, the narratives reminisce about nonsedentary life and the transition to sedentariness, as well as contemporary subjects from the time when the texts themselves came into being. Reminiscences of the Late Bronze Age probably contain the following narrative traits: famines caused by drought which again forced nonsedentary people to migrate (Abram and Sarai in Egypt, Joseph's brothers, the Israelites in Egypt); the great significance of pregnancy and progeny and the low life expectancy of women resulting therefrom (the ancestral mothers Sarah, Rebekah, and Rachel all die before their husbands); the importance of small livestock herds and the latent or open skepticism vis-à-vis Egyptians and city people.

Othmar Keel and Christoph Uehlinger, 1992 (see 4.4); Ernst Axel Knauf, 1994 (see 4.4); Silvia Schroer, *Die Samuelbücher*, NSK-AT 7 (Stuttgart: Verlag Katholisches Bibelwerk, 1992).

Othmar Keel and Silvia Schroer are working on a two-volume work on the history of religion in Palestine from the Mesolithic Age to the Persian age; no title has yet been fixed. The work is to be published in the series ATD Supplements (Göttingen: Vandenhoeck und Ruprecht).

5.2 The Period before the State Was Formed (1250–1000 B.C.E.)

Toward the end of the Late Bronze Age, Egypt increasingly loses control of the Palestinian region. Deurbanization is accelerating, and almost all extant city-states under Egyptian governance collapse. Similar dislocations of power from the cities to tribes occur at that time in the region of what today is southeast Turkey (Knauf 1994, 111–16). This could well be the reason why Israel later so emphatically insisted on the kinship with the Arameans who had settled in that region.

One result of this destabilization is the invasion by maritime people, who advance by land and sea toward Egypt and in doing so lay waste to coastal towns. They take possession of southwest Levantine. At nearly the same time, in southeast Levantine, a process may be described whereby groups of previously nonsedentary peoples once again become sedentary. To these groups belong a part of what later are called the Israelites; in the era of Egyptian domination, they move about as sheepherders at the edges of and between the settled regions. Now they begin to establish small, unfortified settlements, at first in the hill country of Samaria and then also in Judea; in addition to breeding livestock they also engage in agriculture, horticulture, and viniculture. They build their houses on stilts, which could well have been a further development of the provisionally constructed harvest huts on the edges of their cultivated fields. In shaping their settlements, characterized by huts with animal pens and the absence of walls around the settlement, and in their material culture, these newly settled men and women look more to the achievements of sedentary people than to their nomadic traditions. The absence of public buildings, rulers' mansions, and storage facilities is quite typical of these early settlements. Surplus grain is stored in underground silos. More often than not, the cultic places of this period are open-air sanctuaries built outside the settlements or within them. In addition, there is archaeological evidence of house cults. Already around 1250 B.C.E. (Iron Age IA, 1250–1100 B.C.E.), the "conquest," of which the Bible speaks above all in the Book of Joshua, begins sporadically in certain regions. However, the decisive events do not occur until the eleventh century B.C.E. Israel Finkelstein estimates the number of Israelites at that time to be about 55,000. Only at the beginning of the monarchy is there territorial expansion in the boundary regions of Ephraim and in the Judean hill country.

Between 1100 and 1000 B.C.E. (Iron Age IB)—in biblical terms, the time of the "Judges"—the number of Israelite settlements increases. The tribes, now sedentary, have to fight again and again for control over larger territories. They fight with the Philistines who attack from the coastal plains; often the attackers succeed in pushing the Israelites back for sustained periods. More than anything else, the need to defend themselves against the maritime peoples forces the newly settled men and women to organize themselves politically, no longer in loose tribal confederations only, but as a monarchy (as the neighboring peoples east of the Jordan, Aram, Ammon, Moab, and Edom had done before them). Only in 995 B.C.E., after the Philistines had been pushed back for good into the southern coastal plain, does a "united monarchy" under David come into existence. It is governed from Jerusalem and completely integrates into itself all extant Canaanite cities in the hill country and the plains (Iron Age IIA, 1000–900 B.C.E.).

Concerning the history of religion, the trends observed in the Late Bronze Age continue in Iron Age I. Female deities are depicted in symbols or through substitutions (such as a mother animal suckling her off-spring, a tree, a scorpion); when represented in the form of a woman, it is only as terra-cotta figurines. Lordship, domination of the enemy, and superior aggressivity are symbolized in triumphant male gods, rulers, and warriors, or in wild animals on the attack. Aggressivity is experienced as a value. In the iconographic symbol system of Israel at this time, two form-giving factors may be discerned. They exist side by side. One is aggressivity, seeking superiority and domination; it is reflected especially in the biblical narratives of the Exodus, of the Book of Judges, and the battles with the Philistines, told in the Books of Samuel. The other factor, also playing an important role, is fruitfulness of both humans and animals; the groups that had settled the hill country depended on it for their survival. This motif is addressed particularly in the biblical narratives of the foreparents (the Jacob-Laban cycles).

In reconstructing the history of women of the time before Israel became constituted as a state, parts of Genesis, Judges, and 1 Samuel are of greatest use among the books of the Bible (given all the reservations about the historicity of the narrated times). What do the texts reveal concerning the everyday life, work, and religion of women in clan, tribe, and state, in nomadic, rural, and urban ways of life? Generally speaking, the diversity of women's stories from that early time is quite astounding. A broad spectrum of all facets of women's life is recounted, while such information is much rarer for the period of the monarchy, which is due also to the official, annals-like recording of history for which high politics was of chief interest.

The narratives of the ancestors (Fischer 1994, 1995) are marked by men and women alike who, moving about as nomads, try to make a living for themselves and their flocks. An important theme that runs right through the narratives is that of pregnancy and progeny. Childlessness is a blow of fate that is almost unbearable; polygamy was probably widely practiced due to the high mortality rates of women and infants. Polygamy prevailed even though it was fraught with legal obstacles, since the right of primogeniture of the first born male was of high prominence in the life of clan and tribe (Gen. 25:19-34). A steady source for tales of jealousy was provided by the lives of wives or women of different status living in the same household. Having no children, or not having given birth to a sufficient number of sons, existentially threatened the self-awareness of women (Sarah and Hagar, Leah and Rachel; see also Judges 13 and 1 Samuel 1–2). Yet particularly in this area, all the ancestral mothers are portrayed as full of initiative, and little inclined to be resigned to their fate. Midwives play a very important role in the world of women (Gen. 35:17; 38:27; 1 Sam. 4:20). At that early time, it was the undisputed right of mothers to name children (Winter 1983, 22–25; see 4.4). It is possible that originally women, too, circumcised newborn boys (Exod. 4:24-26).

Nonsedentary peoples' way of life presupposes extensive freedom of movement on the part of women who keep watch over flocks in fields or at wells. That freedom of movement allows contact between marriageable men and women. It is the head of the family (Gen. 29:1-30) or the entire family (Genesis 24) who gives daughters to be married.

There was great fear of predatory encroachment of the urbanites on men and women of these unprotected groups (Gen. 12:10-20; 34; and elsewhere), since contact between them is unavoidable but also sought. This makes for collision of norms, as the urbanites disregard the right of hospitality, for example, a right that is sacred for nomad or newly sedentary people. In case of conflict, a woman's life is valued less than that of a male guest (Genesis 19; cf. Judges 19). On the other hand, sexual assault on a woman from one's clan is avenged by vendetta (Genesis 34; Judges 19). At that time, mediation or resolution of conflicts resides basically in the power of the clan elders; in particular cases a charismatic personality, known beyond the region, was consulted (e.g., Deborah).

The holy places to which these nomadic people return again and again are, above all, sacred trees (Gen. 12:6ff.; 18:1; 21-33; 35:4; cf. Judg. 4:5; 9:6), sacred rocks (Gen. 28:10-22), river fords (Gen. 32:22-32), and mountains (Genesis 22). A clan or large family keeps the household god (the *teraphim*) holy; as the patron of protection, the *teraphim* is given into the care of the clan's patriarch. The figurines of the *teraphim* probably represent quasi-divine ancestors. As indicated in Genesis 31 (or 1 Sam. 19:13-16, the story of Michal's use of the household god in helping David escape), women were used to dealing with these images in a liberal manner.

The Book of Joshua contains hardly any authentic recollections of the time when the Hebrews took on sedentary life. And yet, the colorful figure of Rahab, given the type she is intended to portray, is no purely fictitious creation. In the urban communities there were women who lived alone and who were apparently quite autonomous; in the manner of ancient Oriental tradition, they combined hostelry and prostitution in their houses (see Judg. 16:1). These women had much contact with strangers and were, for that reason, perspicacious and politically well informed. At that time women of every part of the population (see Dinah in Gen. 34:1 and later Abigail) were particularly open to contact with the various other groups, as is reflected in the androcentric perspective of the Bible—for example, in the persistent concern with the dangers of mixed marriages (Judg. 14:1).

The figures of the women in the Book of Judges are very colorful. Here, too, the texts themselves are not as old as the time of which they tell. According to Ulrike Bechmann, even the Song of Deborah in Judges 5, which is considered to be quite old, should be dated only in the time of the northern kingdom's demise. As a charismatic and nationally known personality Deborah has significance for Israelite women and men who have now become sedentary. She is a counselor and a mediator in conflicts but is for that reason also called on to be a leader in war. As female warriors, Deborah and Jael correspond to the image of the "militarized" goddesses of the Late Bronze Age (Qudshuh, Anath, Astoreth); however, like these goddesses they are an exception, since the business of war was to a very great extent the affair of men. Nonetheless, using rocks in defending the city, women take part successfully (Judg. 9:53 and 2 Sam. 20:14-22). In the politically tense time of the Philistine wars and in the fight for living space, violence is part of everyday existence. It also brutally affects women, as the hair-raising story of the sexual assault on and murder of the concubine of the Levite in Judges 19 demonstrates. In the days before Israel became a state, it was no rarity for tribes to buy and sell women among themselves. If a deal turned out to be less than satisfactory, men did not shrink back from wholesale raids on women (Judges 21).

At first, the holy places mentioned are sanctuaries of YHWH, whose importance was not confined to their local region, such as Shiloh (see also Judges 17). They are attended to by a male priesthood. However, the gods of the Philistines were also known to the Israelites, such as the war goddess Astarte (1 Sam. 31:10) to whom the Philistines make an offering of Saul's armor, or Dagon (1 Samuel 5). Among the charismatic chiefs of the Book of Judges is one Shamgar ben-Anath, Shamgar the son of Anath (Judg. 3:31), whose clan still traces its military prowess back to the goddess Anath. During the feasts that may well be rooted in Canaanite tradition (the feast in the vineyards of Shiloh, Judg. 21:19-23; cf. 11:37-40), young women dance and celebrate among themselves. Most likely of greater importance than the sanctuaries of YHWH was the worship in families with the *teraphim*. In connection with the religious practices of women, the narrative of the spirit woman of Endor in 1 Samuel 28 is highly informative. However, the text itself is strongly permeated by later interests and ideologies. But it is historically probable that at the time of Saul women practiced necromancy and divination unscathed. On account of this ability, which they put at the service of the community, they become widely known and were utilized in private as well as political affairs. In the days before the united monarchy came into being, there existed no prohibition of divination and necromancy, like that which became part of the ordinances to centralize both state and cult. The "wise women" were highly regarded as counselors on the highest political and military levels of the time. Second Samuel 14 recounts the diplomatic role that a woman from Tekoa, who was well known outside her own community, plays in achieving clemency for Absalom at the royal court. In 2 Sam. 20:14-22, it is a wise woman from a small northern town who succeeds by her diplomacy in bringing an end to a war that was in progress. The portrait of these women gives testimony to their strong self-confidence, political wisdom, and oratory, which permits them to exercise remarkable influence on the men's world. (Sophia Bietenhard is preparing a study on David's general Joab, a figure of much interest in this connection.)

One of the strong women of early Israelite village culture is Abigail, who comes from a well-to-do family from southern Judea (1 Samuel 25). Together with her marriage partner, she manages a large farm. In enterprises of this kind at the edge of the desert, agricultural and horticultural business is combined with animal husbandry. Frequently and for extended periods, this practice makes it necessary for men and women to go about their work separately and to rely on their own resources. The narrative involving Abigail provides an excellent sociogram of society at that time (Staubli 1991, 238–44). Local potentates like Abigail's partner hire (nonsedentary) shepherds on a daily-wage basis to guard their flocks. Nabal provided work for a sizable number of people in the region—relatives, impoverished folk from Judah, transients, and male and female slaves. From the desert regions foreign nomads carry out raids on the areas where the sedentary people live. To protect themselves, the villagers hire people who, not succeeding in becoming part of the village culture, receive a kind of soldier's pay for their services. Contrary to her surly partner, Abigail recognizes the relationships of mutual dependence among the several groups of the population. Without informing her partner, she resolutely pays the tribute demanded by David and his men because she realizes that refusal would have deadly consequences for the whole village. In this narrative, much attention is given as well to the wise woman's oratorical skills.

While all the women referred to may be seen as belonging to the newly emerging and prosperous village culture, indications at the edges of the narratives suggest bitter hardships suffered by many women and children at that time. Men who failed to provide for themselves through agriculture or animal husbandry and who had fallen into debt or other tribulation (1 Sam. 22:2) formed marauding bands. They supported themselves by plunder or as vigilantes. David surrounded himself with such people who retreated to caves or rocky terrain; with their help he strengthened his hold on Judea. When these guerrilla troops went on their expeditions, women, children, and the aged were in the way. Therefore, they were lodged in the towns (1 Sam. 22:3; 30:5) where they were only inadequately protected against the raids of pillaging nomads from the Negev, and from deportation.

Ulrike Bechmann, *Das Deboralied zwischen Geschichte und Fiktion: Eine exegetische Untersuchung zu Richter 5,* Dissertationen Theol. Reihe 33 (St. Ottilien: Eos Verlag, 1989); Sophia Bietenhard, "Des Königs General: Eine exegetische Untersuchung der Joabgestalt in 2 Sam 2—1 Kön 2" (working title of a dissertation being prepared at the Protestant faculty at the University of Bern); Israel Finkelstein, 1988 (see first bibliographical list in this chapter); Irmtraud Fischer, *Die Erzeltern Israels: Feministisch-theologische Studien zu Genesis 12–26,* BZAW 222 (Berlin: Mouton; New York: de Gruyter, 1994); idem, *Gottesstreiterinnen: Biblische Erzählungen über die Anfänge Israels* (Stuttgart: Katholisches Bibelwerk, 1995); Othmar Keel and Christoph Uehlinger, 1992 (see 4.4); Ernst Axel Knauf, 1994 (see 4.4); Silvia Schroer, "Abigajil: Eine kluge Frau für den Frieden," in Karin Walter, ed., *Zwischen Ohnmacht und Befreiung: Biblische Frauengestalten* (Freiburg: Herder, 1988), 92–99; idem, *Die Samuelbücher* (see 5.1); idem, "Und als der nächste Krieg begann . . . Die weise Frau von Abel-Bet-Maacha," in Angelika Meissner, ed., *Und sie tanzten aus der Reihe: Frauen im Alten Testament,* STB 10 (Stuttgart: Verlag Katholisches Bibelwerk, 1992); Thomas Staubli, *Das Image der Nomaden im Alten Israel und in der Ikonographie seiner sesshaften Nachbarn,* OBO 107 (Fribourg: Universitätsverlag; Göttingen: Vandenhoeck und Ruprecht, 1991), 238–44.

5.3 The Time of the Monarchy (1000–587 B.C.E.)

During the transition to the Iron Age IIA, that is, the tenth century B.C.E., a new pattern of settlement emerges. In the hill country many settlers abandon tiny communities; people now live in sizable villages, some of which grow into fortified towns. New towns come into existence. This change in settlement patterns occurs at nearly the same time as the birth and solidification of the Israelite-Judean monarchy. An increasing interaction between the hill country and the plains favors the development into a territorial state; a steady bartering trade of surplus agrarian products, among other things, leads to the emergence of regional and, finally, interregional powers as well.

The life of women in Palestine is significantly affected by the founding of the twin monarchy under David. Saul still belongs to the tradition of the charismatic chiefs and, even though he maintains a small court, the rural population is relatively little touched by it. What brings Saul down are the Philistines, his chief enemies. It is not until David that their threat is finally brought to an end, and it takes years of preparatory work to lay the foundations for a stable, territorial kingdom. Contrary to Saul, David stakes everything on the integration of every segment of Palestine's population, including the Canaanite urbanites. In order to achieve this goal, he makes concessions that make political and cultic sense. For his residence he chooses the ancient city of the Jebusites, Jerusalem, which lay on the boundary between the northern and southern kingdom. He establishes a royal household with administrative offices (partially modeled on Egypt), founds a standing army as well as a sizable harem. The court is supported by high taxes and services imposed on the population; young men are conscripted for military service and the conduct of war. Others have to work on the royal estates or in the royal weapons manufacture. Young women are brought to the court to provide for physical needs (preparing food, caring for the body, and so forth). The finest land is given to the court administrators. Taxes are considerable: one-tenth of the income from the harvest and the herds of sheep. Free Israelite citizens must donate part of their work time (their own as well as that of their work animals) to the court (1 Sam. 8:10-18). In order to monitor this system efficiently, the census is introduced (2 Samuel 24). Eventually Solomon turns the existing temple to the sungod into the central sanctuary of YHWH in the twin monarchy.

The changes that took place at the beginning of the first millennium
B.C.E. are not only very decisive but also remain the basis of all the internal and external political changes to which the country is subjected in
the next four centuries. The separation of the northern and southern
kingdoms after Solomon's death basically changes nothing in the centralization of politics and worship. The biblical sources available to us
for reconstructing that period's history of women are numerous and
quite diverse. The official recording of history (2 Samuel and 1 and 2
Kings) concentrates on the major political events and the happenings at
court and temple. All the texts are more or less permeated by Deutero-
omistic theology, which after the fall of the northern kingdom introduces its outlook into the presentation of events. If the Books of Kings
are reliable on this subject, women in public life tend to diminish in
importance in the course of the monarchic period and as the country
increasingly comes under the threat of its neighbors' imperialistic poli-
cies. The literary prophets (Amos, Hosea, Isaiah 1–39, Micah, Jeremiah,
Nahum, Zephaniah, Habakkuk, Ezekiel's retrospection) provide an important corrective and complement to the court historians' work. The
criticism of society and worship life made by those prophets brings into
focus very different aspects of Israelite reality. Certain parts of Genesis
and the Psalms also originate in this period, as does the main body of
Proverbs (chaps. 10–30) and the songs of the Song of Songs. Important
sources related to the area of justice and law are the so-called book of
the covenant (Exodus 20, 22–23, 33), which dates from the end of the
eighth or the beginning of the seventh century B.C.E., and the preexilic,
Deuteronomistic book of the law (Deuteronomy 12–26). (Dating according to Crüsemann 1996; see 4.4.)

Careful examination of the narratives of the ancestral forebears in
Genesis 12–36 yields interesting information about the developments
during the monarchy (in relation to the time when these narratives are
told rather than to the time about which they tell) as Irmtraud Fischer
(1994) has demonstrated. It is, above all, a comparison of the three narratives of husbands abandoning their marriage partners for fear of their
lives (Gen. 12:10-20; 20; and 26) and the narratives of Hagar and Ish-
mael being cut off (Gen. 16:21) that shows that the most ancient narrative cycle—dating from the early monarchy, according to Fischer—is
not really about the great promises made to the primal ancestor but
about YHWH's intervening in favor of women. YHWH saves Sarah,
promises Hagar freedom and a future for her son, and takes to heart
Sarah's interest by promising her a son. The oldest of the abandonment

narratives in Genesis 12 depicts Abraham as a scared and egocentric man who puts his partner in grave danger (see Lanoir). His demeanor is in no way excused; rather, God stands decisively with Sarah. Only in the later texts are the male actors increasingly exonerated and the patriarchs placed at the center. This allows one to demonstrate through literary history the trend toward patriarchalization within the texts.

Karen Engelken, *Frauen im Alten Israel: Eine begriffsgeschichtliche und sozialrechtliche Studie zur Stellung der Frau im Alten Testament,* BWANT 7, no. 10 (Stuttgart: Verlag W. Kohlhammer, 1990); Irmtraud Fischer, 1994 (see 5.2); Corina Lanoir, "Era Abraham un hombre violento con su esposa?" *Servicio Evangélico de Prensa* (Managua) 37, no. 7 (1992).

5.3.1 Woman at Court and in the Affluent Strata of Society

The Second Book of Samuel already moves women who belong to the elite of the land into the center. Their lifestyle differed significantly from that of simple Israelite women in the villages, although it did not protect them in any way from the violent assault of men. David, no less, carries off Bathsheba, a married woman, gets her pregnant, has her partner done away with, and marries her. David's daughter Tamar (2 Samuel 13) is sexually assaulted at court by her half brother Amnon and spends the rest of her life with her brother Absalom, as a woman banished. One of Saul's concubines, Rizpah (2 Sam. 21:8-14), loses two sons in a political murder; she puts up her own kind of struggle to have her sons properly buried. In case of war, women at court, be they mothers of kings, princesses, women of the harem or palace, share the same fate as men: they are deported (2 Kings 24:8-16; Jer. 38:22f.; 41:10; 43:6).

The splendor of the royal court is reflected, among other things, in the wealth and beauty of the king's wife (or wives), the princesses, and the other young women there (portrayed positively in Psalm 45). These women live in separate quarters of the palace (2 Samuel 13; 1 Kings 9:24). Their influence on politics is not insignificant.

Maria Häusl has demonstrated clearly that Abishag, the Shunammite woman, who occupied a position of trust in the household of old David (1 Kings 1:1-4), was responsible for the entire female staff or the chief overseer of the harem, for she bears the title of *okenet* (a term known from Akkadian sources and from documents relating to the Assyrian court). The male form *oken* or "steward" in Isa. 22:15 corresponds to this term. In the confusion around who will succeed to the throne, it becomes quite important which of David's sons may marry this woman (2:13-23), indicating that being a *okenet* meant being a politically powerful person at court.

Throughout the whole period of the monarchy, the influence which the king's mother (*gebîrah*) wielded in the southern kingdom was considerable. It may be that Ezekiel 19 is about *gebîrah* Nehushta, the mother of Jehoiachin. At times, the king and the king mother even shared the throne together (1 Kings 2:19; Jer. 13:18).

Bathsheba successfully intervened in the succession to the crown on behalf of her son Solomon (1 Kings 1–2). In similarly critical situations, particularly in the irregularities of succession to power, women again and again became active. When they became king-mother, they took on the role of special advisor to their sons; their influence could well be compared to that of the counselors at court (cf. Prov. 31:1-9). But no longer are wise women called to court to give counsel. According to 1 Kings 15:13, the king-mother also functions in the cult of the state (see Ackerman 1993), but can only do so with the consent of her son and never in opposition to him. Renate Jost has demonstrated a connection between the Deuteronomist's evaluation of the Judean kings and the more or less solid loyalty to YHWH manifested by the various king-mothers (as indicated by their names). This suggests that those women also held a powerful position in the affairs of religion. It is possible that the rare title of *gebîrah* is related chiefly to religious functions.

It seems that the sisters of kings and the wet nurses of princes also exercised considerable influence on political developments (2 Kings 11:1-3). In the ancient Orient, the daughters of kings often assumed the role of priestesses, whereas in Israel the priestly office was obviously restricted to men, while women were assigned certain tasks at the various sanctuaries (2 Kings 23:7, see below 6.5).

In the northern kingdom, Jezebel, daughter of the king of Sidon, plays an important role as regent next to Ahab. We are dealing here with a woman who is accustomed to taking political matters in hand, making decisions, and achieving her goals. While the Deuteronomist's caricature of Jezebel shows only that women who exercised power were more and more demonized in Israel, Elijah's criticism of the royal household is well founded. King Omni's men shamelessly enriched themselves at the expense of the population (see the story of Naboth, 1 Kings 21), for example, by abrogating the existing prohibition to sell inherited land. It is quite apparent that women of the upper class were part of this exploitation; some, like Jezebel, actively corrupted the law and justice. One of King Omni's granddaughters, Athaliah, was a woman with a character like Jezebel; as Ahaziah's mother, she took on the position of ruler of Judah upon her son's murder; she governed for six years, until her reign was overturned and she herself was murdered (2 Kings 11).

To date there has been no examination in connection with particularly powerful or wealthy women in Israel, whether the names of towns and so forth are to be traced back to women, that is, whether they were founded by them or given to them as dowry or inheritance at marriage (see Josh. 15:13-20, the pools of Achsah). This is certainly so in the case of Uzzen-sheerah (the "ear of Sheerah," 1 Chron. 7:24) and may also be so for Abel-beth-Maacah (the lord of the house of Maacah).

The narrative of the great woman, the wife of Shunem, in 2 Kings 4 reflects the living conditions of a well-to-do village woman. Her freedom of action and independence (hospitality, rebuilding the house, travel by donkey, her demeanor with the servants, purposefulness in conversing with Elisha) are reminiscent of Abigail in 1 Samuel 25.

It is Amos and Isaiah in particular who are critical of women of the upper class (Amos 4:1, the "cows of Bashan" of Samaria; Isa. 3:16-25, the haughty women of Jerusalem; cf. 26:9). They live in luxury, just like the men, in expensive houses while, at the same time, they took the last piece of clothing from impoverished people who could no longer pay their debts, or sold them into slavery and then made sure that the law would not help them. Women of the upper class, especially when they were at the royal court, had legal competence, that is, they could conduct business in their own name, make contracts, and so forth. This is what a small number of seals with women's names would suggest (Avigad 1987, 195–208). The women to whom these seals belong (about one dozen, or 5 percent of the signature seals known) are always designated as the daughter of a man X or the wife of Y. One of the seals belonged to a princess Ma'adanah. In Jerusalem the imprint of a seal belonging to one Hannah was found on a pitcher handle from the seventh century B.C.E.; therefore, it is certain that there were Israelite women active in trade and commerce (Avigad, "A Note").

Nahman Avigad, "The Contribution of Hebrew Seals to an Understanding of Israelite Religion and Society," in Patrick D. Miller et al., eds., *Ancient Israelite Religion: Essays in Honor of F. M. Cross* (Philadelphia: Fortress Press, 1987), 195–208; idem, "A Note on an Impression from a Woman's Seal," *IEJ* 37 (1987): 18ff.; Maria Häusl, *Abischag und Batscheba: Frauen am Königshof und die Thronfolge Davids im Zeugnis der Texte 1 Kön 1 und 2*, Münchener Universitätsschriften (St. Ottilien: Eos-Verlag, 1993); Renate Jost, 1995 (see 4.3.3).

On *gebîrah*: Susan Ackerman, "The Queen Mother and the Cult in Israel," *JBL* 112 (1993): 385–401; Renate Jost, 1995, 141–46, chap. 3.2.5 with additional literature; Silvia Schroer, "Weise Frauen und Ratgeberinnen in Israel: Vorbilder der personifizierten Chokmah," in Verena Wodtke, ed., *Auf den Spuren der Weisheit: Sophia—Wegweiserin für ein weibliches Gottesbild* (Freiburg: Herder, 1991), 15–18 (with additional references); Eng. trans.: "Wise and Counselling Women in Ancient Israel: Literary and Historical Ideals of the Personified Hokma," in Athalya Brenner, ed., *The Feminist Companion to the Bible*, 9 (Sheffield: Sheffield Academic Press, 1995), 67–84.

5.3.2 Women of the Less Affluent Population during the Monarchy

Administration of Justice. Conflict resolution was something that in the days before the monarchy belonged to clans and families. In the period of the united monarchy, the king himself took on special cases of justice until King Jehoshaphat established the high court in Jerusalem in the ninth century B.C.E. (2 Chron. 17:7-9); it had to prepare the foundations for the administration of justice of the elders in the gate. It is possible that "wise women," called on as neutral references, played the role of arbiters before the court was established.

In the transition period, it appears that women, in particular those who were not given adequate legal protection by their relatives, were the ones who appealed to the king to settle issues, like the wise woman from Tekoa and her fictive case (2 Samuel 14). Widowed, she begs the king's protection for her son, who is in danger of his life for the murder of his brother. The otherwise sensible procedure of avenging bloodshed, however, would threaten the woman's livelihood, so she calls on the king's help against her own relatives. The case of the two women in the sex trade who appear before Solomon is more famous (1 Kings 3:16-28). They seek a ruling on who is the mother of the surviving infant after the other infant was smothered by his mother during sleep. The women were single mothers who, on account of their work, apparently could or would not claim legal protection from their relatives. Even 2 Kings

8:1-6 presupposes that a woman, who spent time out of the country and had been widowed, could regain her house and land only through the king's judgment.

During the monarchy, the elders in the gate administer justice in the name of the king. The oldest written codes of law of the First Testament are concerned throughout with free, property-owning men and heads of clans; these codes are, in other words, class laws, and only a free man is fully a subject of law. It is true, the *mishpatim* (or legal "instructions" of Exodus 21f.) lay down a certain number of minimal rules for the protection of the poor and slaves, but in general the law protects the interests of the free and the owners. The growing money economy enables creditors to demand compensation in silver from debtors. The laws and decrees mentioned in Isa. 10:1f. may refer to the *mishpatim*, written laws fashioned in the eighth century B.C.E. by members of the rich upper class of Judah and which deprive the poor, especially widows and orphans, of all legal recourse (Crüsemann 1996; see 4.4). Even though inscriptions on everyday utensils like ceramic wares suggest that a sizable portion of the population could read (Weippert 1988, 583; see 4.4), those persons on the margins of society would have had difficulty upholding their rights against written laws without assistance. The Book of the Covenant recites the *mishpatim* but corrects and supplements them with the *lex talionis* and the protective laws for strangers, the poor, widows, orphans, and animals. Only the Deuteronomist's laws significantly improve the legal situation of women by including the domain of family law (marriage, sexuality, matrimony, inheritance laws). It is quite safe to assume that the "You" in the laws is addressed to free men and women (generic language). Whether women were given the same fundamental legal competence as men, for example in commerce, contracts, witnessing at court, and so forth, cannot be deduced from these laws (contrary to Crüsemann 1996, who somewhat hastily deduced general legal competence from a dozen signature seals). The laws of inheritance governing the sons of different wives of the same man are fixed with binding force (Deut. 21:15-17; but see the quarrels about the rights of the first-born in the narratives of the patriarchs). According to Deut. 21:18-21, both parents must bring charges at court in case of conflicts within the family. A widow is given the right to lay claim to levirate marriage before the elders in the gate (25:5-10). If a young woman is accused of having entered marriage with her virginity defiled, the defamation becomes subject of a public process. A woman caught in the act of adultery can no longer be killed by her husband without due process of law (and the testimony of two witnesses). If a young woman engaged to be married is sexually assaulted, she need only prove her innocence before the court of her town and the man is regarded as guilty. Premarital (forced?) intercourse with a young woman who is not engaged to be married obliges the man to marry her.

Impoverishment and Enslavement for Indebtedness. During the monarchy, it was again and again women who were particularly hard hit when natural disasters, especially droughts and wars, came over the land. When a town was besieged and starved into submission, the distress was later recalled in images of women slaughtering and eating their children (2 Kings 6:24-30). The most vulnerable group among women were widows and their children (an excellent source here is Willy Schottroff 1992, 54–89). Their hardships seem to have become very acute in the seventh and sixth centuries B.C.E., as the numerous appeals in their favor on the parts of the prophets of that time would indicate. Whereas the welfare of a married woman was quite well protected by her clan, widows have no social net to fall back on. Part of their image in society is that they will (and really should) not survive for long (Jer. 49:11). Since they cannot inherit the land of their husbands, they are without means and depend on the benevolence of their relatives. Most often what they have left is the house and a small plot of land (see 2 Kings 8:3) and perhaps a cow or donkey (see Job 24:3). Yet, the avaricious must have had their sport with twisting the law (Isa. 10:1f.) or secretly replacing the property markers of widows in particular, so that the wisdom literature puts their property bounds directly under the protection of YHWH (Prov. 15:25; 23:10f.; and elsewhere). According to 1 Kings 17, during the big drought Elijah is sent to the widow of Zarephath, who with her son is facing death by starvation. When a husband was in debt, the creditor would come for the children after his death (2 Kings 4:1f.). (Nancy Cardoso Pereira has studied the place of women and children in the Elisha narratives.) The death of children often sealed the terrible fate of those women (note the raising of the dead child in 1 Kings 17:17-24). To a widowed woman, the only way out of the catastrophe was when the next male relatives of the dead husband agreed to a levirate marriage. Legally, the children were then the deceased man's children. Israelite men clearly reneged on their duty on many occasions, meaning that a woman like Tamar (Genesis 38) has to resort to trickery to have her right to progeny met. It is quite possible that relatives often sold widows into slavery so that they would be burdensome to nobody. Before the period of the Exile, Deut. 25:5-10 reinforced the pressure on men to enter levirate marriage by granting widows the right to bring a complaint, even though no sanctions against the man in question were stipulated.

In the period of the monarchy, many Israelite women lost their freedom due to indebtedness. They became their creditors' slaves or were sold again, while the right of the slave owner to the slave woman's body was protected even in cases of gross abuse (Exod. 21:20f.). Exodus 21:2-6 compels male slaves who had become married during their time of service to remain slaves permanently. In an emergency situation, the head of the family would first sell daughters into slavery, from which there is no chance to return to freedom. Women have to render service not only with their labor but also their body; they are turned into a cheap family whore (Amos 2:7). Exodus 21:7-11 endeavors to establish an arrangement that envisages a secure sexual relationship with one man only.

The beginnings of a social legislation are discernible in the Deuteronomic law book (Deut. 14:22-29). The tithe, a taxlike levy, is abrogated in actual practice, but is channeled directly as a social impost every three years to the landless, that is, to the strangers, widows, and orphans. Regular debt cancellations are to assist in keeping slavery for indebtedness under control. Not only male, but also female slaves are to be released after a period of service of six years (Deut. 15:12-18). But Jer. 34:8-17 shows how the free men and women of Judah were very much against releasing slaves. Wage labor is introduced, and those in direct poverty are given the right to enter fields and vineyards to satisfy their hunger.

War. Sexual assault and brutal murder of pregnant women were very likely part of how armies in the ancient Near East normally fought their wars (2 Kings 8:12; 15:16; Hosea 14:1; Amos 1:13; Isa. 13:16; Jer. 8:10). Women are torn from their children (Micah 2:9; Jer. 18:21), are carried off by the enemy and made into slaves (Judg. 5:30; Jer. 6:9-15; 8:10-12). Infants are killed (2 Kings 8:12; Isa. 13:16; Hosea 10:14; 14:1; Nahum 3:10; Ps. 137:8f.). When Sennacherib laid seige to Lachish (701 B.C.E.) about 1,500 young men died and their bodies buried in a mass grave (Keel, Küchler, and Uehlinger, 2:895; see 4.4). Losses of such magnitude rest on the female population for years to come (see Isa. 4:1). In times of war the crying of (professional) wailing women is heard constantly (Jer. 9:17-22). The work of mourning is predominantly left to women (only in 2 Chron. 35:25 and Zech. 12:11-14 do we find men in this role), as was the case among the Philistines, whose art portrays wailing women and never any wailing men (Keel and Uehlinger 1992, 141; see 4.4).

In military campaigns, children are also taken as booty and have to work as slaves (2 Kings 5:2). According to Num. 31:18, 35, girls and young women who had not yet had sexual intercourse were preferable to boys. Foreign prisoners of war in Israel are given some protection only by the Deuteronomic laws; there it is laid down that a man must marry a woman prisoner when he desires to have sexual intercourse with her (Deut. 21:10-14).

There must have been large streams of refugees, particularly after the fall of the northern kingdom, who settled chiefly in Jerusalem. For that reason, the Book of the Covenant speaks extensively in its social legislation about the issue of strangers.

5.3.3   The Perception and Self-Perception of Women

Proverbs 10–30 and the collection of love songs in the Song of Songs, probably written between the eighth and sixth century B.C.E., represent a source for discerning how Israelite women were imaged or how they saw themselves. In line with its Egyptian models, the androcentric wisdom literature consistently highlights the elevated position of the mother who is to be accorded esteem and respect. Generally, the Israelite man considered a good wife to be a gift of God, less so in terms of her role as housewife than as counselor to her husband (Schroer 1991/1995). How tenaciously women took advantage of giving counsel is indicated in numerous sexist sentences that lament how unbearable, in a man's view of things, a quarrelsome woman is in the home (Prov. 21:9 and elsewhere).

In the Song of Songs, an equality of man and woman becomes apparent that is made possible perhaps only by the experience of untroubled love beyond all social institutions and claims. Rejoicing in the beauty of the partner, woman and man at times speak of themselves in terms of the same metaphors. To the man the woman is desirable; she is close, then at other times far away and as unapproachable as a goddess. Pride and aloofness are as much a part of her image as a deep longing for the man, unbridled wildness and seductiveness as much as hesitant waiting. The curse put on the woman in Gen. 3:16—her desire for the man is requited with domination—is lifted in Song 7:10 by an assertion put into the woman's mouth: "I am my beloved's, and his longing is all for me." Part of the relation of woman and man is the feeling of kinship. In comparison to Egyptian love poetry, the eroticism of the Song of Songs is not oriented by genital intercourse. Amorous glances, affectionate touches, kisses, the bare breasts of the woman, or the ivory-colored skin of the man are quite capable of creating every condition of bliss. Klara Butting (1993, 117–60) seeks to provide a political reading of the Song of Songs. However, her reading does not take the genre of this kind of literature into consideration.

The First Testament frequently refers to relationships between women, for example, between sisters (Leah and Rachel), women and their wet nurses or female servants, women friends (Ruth and Naomi), or women and their mothers (Song 6:9). Basically, the mother seems to have been a person in whom one confided. On several occasions, the home of a woman is referred to as the mother's house (Gen. 24:28, Ruth 1:8) contrary to the customary language of Scripture that speaks of the father's house; the establishment of domicile was firmly tied to one's mother (Meyers 1991). In Song 3:4 and 8:2, the lover pictures in her mind how she would bring her friend to her mother's house.

Klara Butting, 1993 (see the first bibliographical listing in chap. 4); Carol Meyers, "To Her Mother's House: Considering a Counterpart to the Israelite Bêt 'ab," in David Jobling, Peggy Day, and Gerald Sheppard, eds., *The Bible and the Politics of Exegesis: Festschrift for Norman Gottwald* (Cleveland: Pilgrim Press, 1991), 39–52; Nancy Cardoso Pereira, *Profecia e cotidiano* (São Bernardo do Campo, 1992); Willy Schottroff, "Die Armut der Witwen," in Marlene Crüsemann and Willy Schottroff, *Schuld und Schulden: Biblische Traditionen in gegenwärtigen Konflikten* (Munich: Chr. Kaiser Verlag, 1992), 54–89; Silvia Schroer, "Weise Frauen und Ratgeberinnen in Israel," 1991/1995 (see 5.3.1).

5.3.4 Religious Developments

During the period of the "united monarchy" (Iron Age IIA, 1000–900 B.C.E.), as a result of the calm in foreign politics, the significance of war and the military recedes in favor of the establishment of a central administration and the representation of royal power. Since the cult of the state had already been centralized in Jerusalem, there was no longer a temple architecture indigenous to the towns. The god of the temple in Jerusalem no longer fights wars; rather, he is enthroned in sovereignty as the highest royal god on the cherubim (without pictorial presentation). The significance of female deities continues to shrink. In place of the Goddess, there are more and more pictorial substitutes, such as caprids suckling and men and/or women offering veneration at small trees. Terra-cotta figurines depicting women beating drums in worship replace nude goddesses more and more. In the tenth century B.C.E., the only still relatively unambiguous traces of goddess worship are found in the towns, in the domain of local piety. All developments indicate that even the domains of prosperity and fertility, which in the history of Palestine had long belonged to the Goddess's area of competence, were seen to be within the powers of YHWH, the male god of the state.

In the two centuries during which Israel and Judah exist side by side as distinct monarchies (Iron Age IIB, 900–ca. 700 B.C.E.), religious development in the two kingdoms is not totally parallel. In terms of iconography, the northern kingdom is oriented very much by Phoenician miniature art; it introduces into the religious imagination the symbolism of the sun and the sky that originated in Egypt. The elite of the northern kingdom worships YHWH as the royal sun-god and the lord of the sky. Within the cult of YHWH, one finds figures of all sorts of beings, many of which are hybrids, who are venerated for their powers of protection and prosperity.

As early as the ninth century B.C.E., there arises a conflict in the northern kingdom between one of the YHWH prophets and the royal house of the Omri who, culturally and religiously, are strongly influenced by Phoenicia (Canaan). Jezebel and Ahab share de facto in governing the country; perhaps for reasons of state she supports a cult of Canaanite character (1 Kings 18:19). A self-confident ruler, she adopts the image of the goddess of the land. It belongs to a tradition that is already found in the pictorial art of the Middle Bronze Age (see Winter 1983, 577–88, on Jezebel and the motif of the woman at the window; see 4.4). It would appear that women customarily went alone to religious celebrations of the new moon and the sabbath (2 Kings 4:23).

The prophet Hosea's attacks on the cult brings about changes in direction that have special consequences for women. Hosea holds men primarily responsible for the mountain and tree cults associated with the Goddess and the sexual rites carried out there (Hosea 4:13f.). With mixed success he tries to integrate lost aspects of the Goddess into the image of YHWH. However, his attempt to describe the relation between YHWH and Israel in the imagery of a patriarchal marriage increasingly develops a misogynist dynamic.

In the southern kingdom as well, tensions emerge at the beginning of the ninth century B.C.E. that have to do with the religious practices of powerful women. King Asa deprived his grandmother Maacah of the rank of *gebîrah* because she had commissioned a cultic image of Asherah.

Literature on Hosea: Helgard Balz-Cochois, 1982 (see 4.3.4); Helen Schüngel-Straumann, 1986 (see 4.3.1); Brigitte Seifert, *Metaphorisches reden von Gott im Hoseabuch*, FRLANT 166 (Göttingen: Vandenhoeck und Ruprecht, 1996); Yvonne Sherwood, *The Prophet and the Prostitute: Hosea's Marriage in Literary-Theoretical Perspective*, *JSOT* Supplement 212 (Sheffield: Sheffield Academic Press, 1996); Ruth Thornkvist, "The Use and Abuse of Female Sexual Imagery in the Book of Hosea: A Feminist-Critical Approach to Hos 1–3" (diss., Uppsala University, 1994); Marie-Theres Wacker, 1987 (see 4.3.4); idem, "Biblische Theologie und Männerphantasie: Das Beispiel Hos 1–3," in Hubert Frankemölle, ed. (see 4.3.4), 155–72; idem, *Figurationen des Weiblichen im Hosea-Buch*, HBS 8 (Freiburg, Basel, and Vienna: Herder, 1996).

In the century between the fall of the northern kingdom and the Babylonian Exile (Iron Age IIC, ca. 700–600 B.C.E.) the religious symbol system of Judah, resulting from Assyrian and Aramaic influences, massively accommodates aspects of astral religiosity; the nocturnal constellations are now at the center of cultic acts. Many a biblical text recalls sacrifices offered in the hill country and on the roofs of Jerusalem under the open night sky (2 Kings 22:5 and elsewhere). Explicitly naming both men and women as potential delinquents, and on the pain of death, Deut. 17:2-7 (see also Deuteronomy 13) prohibits astral cults in the land. There are other indications that support the view that these cultic forms were part of popular religion. Archaeological findings show that the host of heaven is very much present in family worship in the form of horse and rider terra-cotta figurines. It is in this context that the cult of the Goddess experiences a unique revival in Judah. Three thousand pillar figurines, that is, female terra-cottas, many of them with strongly emphasized breasts, were found in the archaeological strata of that time, two thousand alone in Jerusalem. The influence of this renewed worship of Asherah in the family circle was also felt in the cult of the state. This is the only way to explain why King Manasseh had a cultic image of Asherah placed in the temple of Jerusalem (2 Kings 21:7; 23:6f.) for which women at the temple regularly wove vestments. Asherah is probably perceived as a type of Queen of Heaven. According to Jer. 7:16-18 and Jeremiah

44, not only women, but men and often the whole family, see their hope in the Goddess who is to secure peace, safety, and food. The god in Jerusalem is not regarded as capable of satisfying these existentially very important needs, a view totally contrary to that of Jeremiah, who regards the cult of the Goddess as one reason for the catastrophe of the Exile. Jeremiah 44:21 registers explicitly that the influential persons of the land, including those at the royal court, had also turned to the Queen of Heaven, suggesting that this was in no way a matter of mere private religion. The veneration of the host of heaven had become a state cult. The Book of Ezekiel claims that the cultic activities of both men and women increased rapidly shortly before the Exile, with the temple in Jerusalem being used heavily for all of these activities, with lay people carrying out priestly functions denied to them in the worship of YHWH. Most of the Levites adapted themselves quickly to the new requirements and made their services available (Ezek. 44:9-13). A cultic image was set up in the area of the gate, according to Ezekiel 8. It was most likely an image of Asherah or the Queen of Heaven (Schroer 1987; Jost 1995). Upper-class men offer incense to animal deities reminiscent of those from Egypt; other men offer worship to the sun-god Shamash, whose horses and chariots Josiah had recently ordered removed from the temple in a major clean-up action.

Ezekiel 8:14f. cites a cult especially for women. At the gateway facing north, women sat and wailed for Tammuz; this rite had ancient rootage in the Sumerian tradition of Dumuzi. Every year, when vegetation dies, the dead Dumuzi and Tammuz, Ishtar's partner, is mourned. The Babylonian influence is apparent, and it is also likely that there is a connection with the worship of the Queen of Heaven (Ishtar). The reason for this ritual wailing may be sought more in the disorders resulting from the wars than in the annual events of nature (Jost 1995; see 5.3.2, "War," on the wailing women). According to Ezek. 13:17-23, there is a noticeable increase before and during the Exile in the mantic practices offered chiefly by women. Mention is made for the first time of a whole group of women prophets who may have been connected to the cult of Ishtar. Recognizing them as prophets and as his competitors, Ezekiel attacks them for their ideas. He accuses them because they make use of magic to decide about who lives and who dies; how exactly this happens cannot be clearly determined from the text. But Ezekiel refuses to give recognition to independently operating dealers in magic (Jost 1994).

In the Deuteronomists' historiography (as in that of Zephaniah) the kings of Israel and Judah are judged primarily according to how they went about eradicating cultic installations (hilltops, cultic rocks or *masseboth*, places holy to Asherah), which were well attended in town and country by followers of YHWH as part of their ancient Canaanite tradition. Their sweeping condemnations also include the *teraphim* and all forms of soothsaying. The reform kings Hezekiah and Josiah, who sought to rid the religion of YHWH of this old heritage, found great favor in their eyes. The impulse for Josiah's reform came from a book of the Torah found in the temple, and from the oracle of Huldah, a woman prophet and follower of YHWH to whom an official government delegation had been sent (2 Kings 22). In the time of the monarchy, there was another woman prophet besides Huldah of whom mention is made in writing, namely Isaiah's partner in marriage (Isa. 8:3).

Renate Jost, *Frauen, Männer und die Himmelskönigin*, 1995 (see 5.3.1); idem, "Die Töchter deines Volkes prophezeien," in Dorothee Sölle, ed., *Für Gerechtigkeit streiten: Theologie im Alltag einer bedrohten Welt. Festschrift für Luise Schottroff* (Gütersloh: Gütersloher Verlagshaus Gerd Mohn, 1994), 59–64; Silvia Schroer, *In Israel gab es Bilder: Nachrichten von darstellender Kunst im Alten Testament*, OBO 74 (Fribourg: Universitätsverlag; Göttingen: Vandenhoeck und Ruprecht, 1987); idem, "Der israelitische Monotheismus als Synkretismus: Einblicke in die Religionsgeschichte Israels/Palästinas auf der Basis der neueren Forschung," in Anton Peter, ed., *Christlicher Glaube in multireligiöser Gesellschaft: Erfahrungen, Theologische Reflexionen, Missionarische Perspektiven* (Immensee, 1996), 268–87.

These various pieces of information provide a multileveled picture. The cult of YHWH was promoted as the state-cult. Personal names from the ninth/eighth century B.C.E. that incorporate a god's name also indicate that the population oriented its life strongly by this highest deity. But the cult of YHWH could not satisfy every religious need of the Israelites' everyday life. For ages, the Goddess governed the fruitfulness and thriving of plants, animals, and humans, as well as love. Even in the Deuteronomist's sentence "the offspring of your herds and the increase of your lambing flocks" (Deut. 7:13; 28:4, 18, 51), the names of goddesses are mentioned, namely Astarte and the north Syrian Shagar (note Gen. 30:37ff. and the twigs on which Jacob's animals feed). Many were not prepared to give up the feasts and rites of the hill country and among mighty trees that are to assure fruitfulness. Sacred rocks and trees, oracles, and soothsaying had proven their value; so why give them up? How strongly Canaanite religiosity was rooted in Israel may also be seen in the aspect of Israelite tradition reflected in the Song of Songs. The lovers swear by the gazelles of the love-goddess (2:7 and 3:5), and the woman is depicted in the image and according to the various types of the ancient Orient's goddesses; the Goddess's palm tree and apple tree, beneath which the lovers' play takes place, are referred to positively and without polemics. The God of Israel is simply not mentioned in these love songs. The guardians of the state religion had no control over family worship; this is why Deuteronomic law (Deuteronomy 13) called on people to denounce neighbors and even closest members of the family in case they offered worship to alien gods. It proscribed the penalty of death for such offenses. Resistance against a pure YHWH religion was also frequently offered at the highest political levels.

It would appear, therefore, that goddess worship and other Canaanite traditions inherited by the Israelites were more or less suppressed but never really eradicated. From time to time, they blossomed forth again. The knowledge and practice of such cults was presumably guarded by men and women, but chiefly by the latter. Their readiness to identify themselves (wholly) with the cult of YHWH, which was administered by men and obviously insufficient for women, could not have been very strong. Perhaps this may explain why Israelite women's names were formed much less frequently than men's with the name of the God YHWH (Winter 1983, 21f.; see 4.4). There was an unwritten law that gave women the right to continue adhering to the religion which they had come to embrace in their home country. Foreign women who came to Israel through marriage kept their religion (1 Kings 11:1-5 and elsewhere). Israelite women who went to a foreign country also did not have to renounce their religion (see 2 Kings 5:1-3). Later on, the Deuteronomists came to see in this arrangement one of the chief offenses of which the Israelite people were guilty. The commandment to worship YHWH alone (found in Exod. 34:12-16 and originating from the circle of Hosea, according to Crüsemann) seeks to undercut the participation of Israelite women and men in the religious festivals of Canaanite origin and to prevent groups who are not rigorous adherents of the YHWH religion from marrying Israelite youth. These daughters of Canaan (Deut. 7:1-4 and elsewhere) were not necessarily particular groups in the population, but simply Israelite women who were not prepared to give up the religious traditions rooted in the country. Most likely, the centralization of the cult of YHWH in specific official sanctuaries and, finally, in Jerusalem alone, contributed to many Israelites continuing to frequent traditional sacred spaces.

5.4 The Exilic-Postexilic Period to the End of Persian Rule (600/587–333 B.C.E.)

Nebuchadnezzar's troops captured Jerusalem in two stages between 600 and 587 B.C.E. Twice, thousands of Jerusalem's and Judah's upper classes (among them Ezekiel) are deported to Babylon in the vicinity of Nippur; Jehoiachin and the royal family of Judah live at the Babylonian court. Many people of Judah escape to Egypt, where part of the men hire themselves out as soldiers. A Jewish garrison is settled on the Elephantine island. Jeremiah and Baruch are also taken to Egypt, against their will. Judah becomes part of the Persian province of Samerina, losing territory—the Negev and the southern Shefelah, ceded to the Edomites and Arab tribes—while in the coastal region several city-states keep a partial autonomy. From the time of the Exile onwards, we need to keep in view several groups of peoples as well as diverse carriers of the religious tradition, all of which lived in highly different political, social, and cultural contexts. All of this diversity had an impact on the religious imagination. That within three generations developments diverged noticeably can be seen in the social and religious tensions that emerged when the Babylonian exiles (at most forty thousand people) were allowed to return home in approximately 520 B.C.E., after the Persians had conquered the ancient Near East. In all these controversies, a central role is played by women, the image of women, and the question of goddess worship. Generally speaking, the collapse of the monarchy and the destruction of the temple in Jerusalem shook profoundly the well-fortified orders of patriarchy, giving new chances to women, since the traditional role models or faith structures were no longer automatically valid. Suddenly, Israel's religious identity was once again solidly tied to family or clan, as it had been before Israel became a state.

In order to reconstruct these processes, we are dependent primarily on texts, since the information offered by pictorial art is quite meager.

The religious traditions of the motherland were gathered and reworked by the Golah in Babylon; in the process a priestly and a Deuteronomic school emerged. The so-called Priestly writing (including the holiness laws of Leviticus 17–26) and the so-called Deuteronomistic history are to be traced back to these schools, respectively. At work in the exile in Babylon was the so-called Deutero-Isaiah, most likely a group of disciples of Isaiah. The Book of Ezekiel, which is close to the Priestly source, provides some information about the situation of the exiles, as does the Book of Jeremiah. (On the so-called Book of Consolation in Jeremiah 30–31 and its strongly feminine metaphors, see Bozak 1991.) The Book of Lamentations may have originated in Judah itself. The first voices from postexilic Judah are the so-called Trito-Isaiah (Isaiah 56–66), Haggai, and Zechariah. About a century later, the books of the Chroniclers' history (Ezra, Nehemiah, and 1 and 2 Chronicles) inform us about the period until the end of Persian rule (333 b.c.e.); the voices heard there are primarily those of restoration-minded circles. Malachi and Obadiah are additional prophetic works. Distinct traditions are those of the wisdom schools (Proverbs 1–9, Job, and parts of the Psalms). The world of women after the Exile is made visible in an extraordinary manner in Ruth and partly in Esther. By the end of the fourth century b.c.e. the Pentateuch would have been completed, the final form of which is permeated with exilic and postexilic texts.

Barbara A. Bozak, 1991 (see 3.2.3).

5.4.1 The Exile (Egypt, Judah, Babylonia)

Aramaic texts from the fifth century b.c.e. inform us about the life of women and men of Judah in Upper Egypt. To a very large extent, these texts deal with legal matters from private life, such as marriage, divorce, and property. These documents indicate that the Judaic colony did not seek isolation but lived together with other foreigners and Egyptians and intermingled with them through marriage. In addition, one notices that the legal status of female persons of the Elephantine was unusually elevated. They could file for divorce, own property, and were authorized to buy and sell. It was even possible that a female slave of Egyptian origin held office in the Temple of Yaho in the Elephantine (Eskenazi 1992 and the literature cited there). Sixty percent of women's names are religious names, a high proportion in comparison to the usual quota of names found in exilic and postexilic texts.

It becomes clear as early as in Jeremiah's conflict with exiled women and men of Judah in Egypt (Jeremiah 44) that they were not at all prepared to give up the worship of the Goddess in favor of the cult of YHWH. The Jewish military colony in the Elephantine built a temple to

Yaho but venerated YHWH and Anath as a divine couple. Such openness to intercultural relations and polytheistic forms of religion characterized subsequent developments of Judaism on Egyptian soil. As late as the first century B.C.E., the Wisdom of Solomon endeavors to speak of the God of Israel and his *paredros* Sophia (his female consort on the throne).

Life changed fundamentally in what remained of Judah after the fall of Jerusalem. Most likely, those who remained behind were chiefly simple rural women and men (2 Kings 24). The country's elite had been deported; the temple lay in ruins. There is no palace and no functioning superior court. The administration was wholly in the hands of the occupying forces who confiscated the houses and hereditary lands left behind by those deported (Lam. 5:2), giving them to impoverished Jews (2 Kings 24:14; 25:12; Jer. 39:10, and elsewhere). In other words, an utterly different pattern of possession emerges. Misery was rampant, characterized by starvation, large numbers of widows and orphans, and widespread sexual assault; in addition, one must come to terms with the horrible catastrophe that had come on the state and religion (Lamentations). From the tensions that arose later between those members of the Golah who returned from the Exile and the people who had been left behind in Judah, one may conclude that during the sixth century B.C.E. the population of Judah, temporarily rid of the priestly and Deuteronomic elite, continued to give themselves over to popular religious imagination and practice. In the regions adjacent to Phoenicia, northern Arabia, and Edom, the Goddess, now often depicted as a goddess-mother with child, played an important role.

Those deported to Babylon are people of the upper class, officials from the court, priests, rulers of towns, able-bodied males of political age, and skilled workers. They are left free to exercise their vocations. To a certain extent, they are self-governing, with the elders looking after the administration. The exiles soon prepare for a long stay: they build houses and plant gardens (Jeremiah 25). Marriages and business connections make for closer relations to the Babylonian population. While the Priestly circles have no objectives to such contacts (see Neh. 13:28f.), other groups rigorosly insist on endogamy. In order to protect identity, the traditions of the homeland are cultivated in a special manner in the midst of the strangeness the Exile has imposed. New legal codes come into being at that time, as does a new historiography. During the Exile, theological developments take place that were to shape the Israelite-Jewish religion for a long time. There is now an explicit formulation of and reflection upon the prohibition of images and monotheism. The

Deuteronomists apply their model of dealing with guilt to the whole history of Israel. Again and again the cult of the Goddess is held to be the chief cause of the great historical catastrophe. Jerusalem's fornication is the prophet Ezekiel's key metaphor for salvation squandered (chaps. 16 and 23).

The Priestly schools (as well as Ezekiel) construct a wholly new view of the world that builds on the understandings of pure and impure, sacred and profane; the Priestly group needs to replace the utterly impossible cultic traffic of Jerusalem if there is to be perfect life "before God." The system of pure and impure (see 5.5 as well as Gerstenberger, *Leviticus* [reference in 4.4], Feld 1996, and Batmartha 1996), which is based fundamentally in culturally conditioned (and, consequently, culturally different) tabooing of any kind of intermingling, has nothing to do with moral perception. An impurity, such as caused by spilling semen, is not anything prohibited or a matter of subjective guilt; it usually disappears by itself when night falls or by washing oneself. But the domain of the sacred, and most of all the temple, is absolutely pure and, for that reason, set apart from the profane world. Thus the exclusion of everything impure from cultic spaces takes on special significance. At this point the Priestly view of the world becomes utterly hostile to women, since their monthly impurity, and giving birth (Leviticus 12; 15:19-33), renders them unable to attend worship for weeks and months. The new temple Ezekiel conceives of, and with which he offers consolation to his compatriots, is under the care of the high priestly king and the Zadokite priests; as a result of the rules concerning purity, they may not even marry a widow or divorced woman but only a virgin or a priest's widow (Ezek. 44:22; cf. Leviticus 21 and 22:13). In the Priestly system of God's presence, in which the distinction between Israelites and strangers is all but abrogated, women have no place. Later this becomes quite apparent in the designation of a special antecourt for women in the temple in Jerusalem. This comes into effect even though the creation account of that same Priestly writing firmly upholds the equality of both sexes and their both being in the image and likeness of God (Gen. 1:27; but cf. Num. 5:20 and its formula of subordination). The holiness laws (Leviticus 17–26), in contrast to the Deuteronomic laws, clearly reinforce the orders of patriarchy. The priests watch over women's fidelity in marriage and carry through a humiliating ordeal (Numbers 5) on mere suspicion of infidelity. These laws in part reverse the Deuteronomic social legislation, for example in relation to cancellation of debts and releasing of slaves (Leviticus 25). As a result of the new situation, the law no longer affects free landowners alone but all Israelites. A supplement dealing with buying release from vows, found in Leviticus 27, graphically states the values assigned to the life of a man and a woman in terms of shekels. These values presumably correspond to the productive capacity of the men and women involved.

AGE	MALE	FEMALE
over 60	15	10
20–60	50	30
5–20	20	10
up to 5	5	3

The theology of the Deutero-Isaiah movement in the Exile set out from a very different starting point. This populist movement is borne by an integrative universalism that points beyond Israel and dares to portray the Persian king Cyrus the Great as the messiah of YHWH (Isaiah 45). In the hope of an imminent end of the Exile, Second Isaiah preaches in comforting words a new beginning in the history of Israel with YHWH. One notices that frequently in this work daughters are explicitly referred to next to sons, and women next to men (Isa. 43:6; 49:22). The work reminds people not only of Abraham, their father, but also of Sarah "who gave you birth" (51:2). Incorporated into the image of YHWH are images drawn from the world of women's experience (such as God as a woman in labor pain, 42:14) and comforting motherly aspects (49:15; cf. already Hosea 11).

Ina Johanne Batmartha (Petermann), "Machen Geburt und Monatsblutung die Frau 'unrein'? Zur Revisionsbedürftigkeit eines missverstandenen Diktums," in Luise Schottroff and Marie-Theres Wacker, eds., *Von der Wurzel getragen: Christlich-feministische Exegese in Auseinandersetzung mit Antijudaismus* (Leiden: E. J. Brill, 1996), 43–60; Tamara C. Eskenazi, "Out from the Shadows: Biblical Women in the Postexilic Era," *JSOT* 54 (1992): 25–43; Geburgis Feld, "'... wie es eben Frauen ergeht' (Gen. 31,35): Kulturgeschichtliche Überlegungen zum gegenwärtigen Umgang mit der Menstruation der Frau in Gesellschaft und Theologie," in Schottroff and Wacker, eds., *Von der Wurzel getragen,* 29–42; Keel and Uehlinger, 1992 (see 4.4); Silvia Schroer, "Die göttliche Weisheit und der nachexilische Monotheismus," in Marie-Theres Wacker and Erich Zenger, eds., 1991 (see 4.3.1).

5.4.2 Developments in Judah after the Exile

In relation to the situation of women, the period immediately after the Exile seems to have been much like the period before the state came into existence. For a short time, the end of the monarchy and the temple opened up new liberties; social roles needed to be defended anew. The return of the exiles from Babylon, made possible by an edict of King Cyrus II, created problems that would not have been dissimilar to those created by the reunification of West and East Germany. Ownership of property has to be regulated anew; those who return, armed with ancestral charts (see Nehemiah 7), lay claim to their houses and lands, now long inhabited by other families. New houses need to be built. A drought in approximately 520 B.C.E. drastically intensifies the situation. Then there are social differences between those who had been left in the country and the Golah-Israelites, who return with their pockets by no means empty. It might be that the dramatic depiction of the homelessness and pauperization of the country poor, found in Job 24:2-14 and 30:2-8, describes this situation after the Exile. The country is under Persian rule, with the two provinces Yehud and Samerina administered by governors. In matters of religion and cult, as well as in politics, the ones returning claim orthodoxy and power for themselves.

Trito-Isaiah links up anew with the prophets' traditional social criticism. In the land, he says, there are people who go without food, shelter and clothing (Isaiah 58; see Job 24:2-14 and 30:2-8). YHWH stands on the side of these broken and humble ones (57:15). From all Israelites YHWH demands solidarity with their impoverished compatriots. The message Trito Isaiah has for the poor is full of comfort. These missionar ies of YHWH, who were close to the people, also incorporate women and men into their religious language; they speak of God as mother (66:13) or as reliable father (63:16; 64:8). Social justice (57:1; 58) is more important to them than a new temple (66:1). The miserable and those who mourn are to be the priests of YHWH (61:6). The cult of YHWH is to be open to strangers and all peoples (56:7). It is an open question whether the descriptions of social problems found in Proverbs 1–9 (e.g., in 3:27-29) and in the Book of Job (chap. 24) are to be dated precisely in the first period of this new beginning or later.

In the first generation of those who had returned there are groups around Zerubbabel and the high priest Joshua with strongly restorative aims. For them, orthodoxy and especially the rebuilding of the temple are the highest priority (Haggai, Zechariah). Right from the start, the rural population that had not been carried off into exile and the people from the former northern regions (in the province of Samerina) were excluded from building that temple (Hag. 2:10-14; Ezra 4:3). In a programmatic vision (5:5-11), Zechariah equates foreign cult with the cult of the Goddess by personifying all wickedness of the land in the form of a woman (the Goddess) and having her shipped off to Babylon in a sealed barrel. This "one-way ticket to Babylon" would have been an unambiguous message especially to women (Schroer 1991, 176; Uehlinger 1994, 93–103).

Nehemiah, the governor of Judah (445–425 B.C.E.), and Ezra, "priest and scribe of the law of the God of Heaven" (398 B.C.E.), continued the restorative tradition. In the name of the Persian monarch, Nehemiah pushes the construction of the Jerusalemite wall, work in which women are also very active participants (Neh. 3:12, the daughters of Shallum). But obviously, women are also part of the resistance against this project; among them is the prophetess Nadiah, an opponent of Nehemiah (Neh. 6:14). Social conditions are still marked by harsh injustice. In Nehemiah 5 we read of the complaints laid before the governor, particularly by the women of the impoverished rural population. They are forced to pawn off their children, fields, vineyards, and houses in order to obtain food or to pay their taxes. Affluent residents of Judah reap profits from the women's distress and heap up riches. (This is perhaps the concern of Proverbs 1–9 and its critique of feudalism.) Nehemiah legislates a general cancellation of debts and the restitution of property. (Cf. the postexilic regulations of Leviticus 25.)

We are explicitly told that Ezra reads the Torah in the presence of every man and woman gathered at the Water Gate in Jerusalem. On account of the Persian edict of tolerance, it is made the law code of Judah. A number of criteria are to determine who may belong to the new community. The prohibition of mixed marriages and the separation of foreign populations within the land and in neighboring countries play a significant part. It is likely that these men and women of Judah were reckoned among the nations within the land who did not practice their religion according to orthodox perceptions, along with Jews, including returners from the Exile, who had married women from neighboring regions (see Neh. 13:23, discussing women from Ashdod, Ammon, and Moab, and Ezra 9:1f. and its stylized listings) or indigenous Jewish women who had not come from the Golah clans. When the patriarchal narratives of Genesis tell of the men (Isaac, Jacob) fetching themselves women from their own kin in Mesopotamia, a highly current issue of postexilic times is addressed. By means of such endogamous marriage, many returners maintained contact with members of their class that had remained in Babylon. Indeed, such practice was most congenial to the conception of an orthodox religious community.

Ezra urges the expulsion of the so-called foreign women and children. He and Nehemiah establish a strictly monotheistic veneration of the high God of Heaven. This God of Heaven has long lost any competition from male deities. The cult of the Goddess, still alive in Judah and neighboring regions, alone offers challenge; Astarte, Atargatis, and Aphrodite had come to be worshiped as the highest of city-gods. Composed in the fourth century B.C.E., the Books of Chronicles rigorously erase from Israel and Judah's past every trace of the Goddess that is still to be found in the Deuteronomists' history (see Frevel 1991, 263–71). Even reminiscences of strong women are nearly completely eliminated, while certain women are thoroughly incriminated (e.g., 2 Chron. 22:2 accuses Athaliah, the king's mother, of counseling godlessness). On the other hand, at the time of Chronicles, women could have the image of city builders, as a note incorporated into the tribal history of Ephraim indicates (1 Chron. 7:24). According to the text, Sheerah built Lower and Upper Beth-horon and Uzzen-sheerah.

The forceful opposition to mixed marriages and goddess worship and the latent hostility against women in several writings of the fifth/fourth century B.C.E. may serve as a mirror in which certain social and religious developments of this time became visible. To a significant degree, women take part in the rebuilding of the country and in carrying forward the religious tradition; women exercise influence that enables them to make demands on men in places of responsibility. The sixth-century B.C.E. seal of a Shulamite woman, referred to as an official of Governor Elnatan, shows that women too played their part in the Persian administration (Avigad 1987). It may be that this Shulamite woman is the daughter of Zerubbabel, Shelomith (1 Chron. 3:19), and that it is her descendants that are mentioned in Ezra 8:10 (Eskenazi 1992, 39f.). Among the clans which returned from the Exile was a family who, interestingly, is referred to as "Sophereth," that is, "woman scribe" (Ezra 2:55, Neh. 7:57).

The wisdom literature and the Books of Ruth and Esther add to this picture in a variety of ways. These writings all look at the questions of foreign women, a purely male image of God, and patriarchal order differently than the groups concerned with restoration. Literary fiction would have us believe that Proverbs 1–9 and 31 are a father's teachings to his son, but feminist exegetical studies have shown that the text may well presuppose a mother who gives her son instruction (Torah) (Brenner and van Dijk-Hemmes). The term "wisdom of women" connects the postexilic framework of this writing with the older corpus of sayings (Proverbs 10–30). According to Prov. 14:1, the wisdom of women builds the house whereas foolishness tears it down with its own hands. The strong woman in 31:10-31 owns a house and conducts her own business. Women who build houses, who teach and give counsel, along with images of goddesses from the ancient Near East, become incorporated into the complex image of *hokhmah,* of wisdom personified. The image meets us here for the first time in literary form. Most likely she is not a goddess as such (with her own cult). Rather, she embodies the endeavor to firmly establish feminine discourse of God that is positively related to women's reality within an already firmly structured monotheistic symbol system that still admitted pluralistic approaches (see Camp 1985 and Schroer 1991: "Die Göttliche Weisheit"). For example, the image of the prophetess and the woman advising kings and mighty men is taken up positively (Prov. 8:14; 31:1-9) in contrast to Nehemiah, Ezra, and Chronicles. Not the whole of the country's wickedness but, rather, its whole righteousness, creative power, and vitality are personified in a woman. Another long-felt need in research has in the meantime been met by an outstanding exegetical, social-historical study by Christl Maier (1995). In her monograph, she examines with minute care the concept of "foreign woman" in Proverbs 1–9. In this context she makes reference to the opposed image of the personified *hokhmah.* Maier demonstrates that during the late Persian period in the province of Judah, young men of the upper classes were to be integrated into the time-honored patriarchal family structures by means of warnings against the "foreign woman." Contact with women outside the circle of one's kin is regarded as endangering respected and successful life; an extramarital sexual relationship with one of them is out of the question. According to Maier, the figure of wisdom personified is used as a positive image of identification to tie women into patriarchal structures just as the figure of the "foreign woman" is used for the same purpose as a negative image. What this interpretation fails to explain is why in Proverbs 1–9 wisdom never appears as a mother figure. That would have been the desired role for women par excellence. In some aspects, the image of *hokhmah* probably goes beyond traditional roles. Therefore, it is to be regarded as a constructive reaction to changing conditions and images of women (see Maier 1996; Baumann, "Zukunft" and "Wer mich findet").

A similar situation applies to the novelette of Ruth, which puts relations among women at its center (Fischer 1991 and 1995). It recounts a typical situation of women after the Exile. Dislocated by a drought, a family from Bethlehem emigrates to neighboring Moab. While there, the husband dies and later the two sons, who leave behind their Moabite widows. Naomi sets out to return to Judah because she hopes to find support there from her relatives. While one of the daughters-in-law goes back to her mother's home, the Moabite Ruth stays with Naomi. The two women succeed in establishing a new existence for themselves by claiming the ancient right of levirate marriage. They escape the total poverty of widows and preserve the family name. The narrative is about a "foreign woman" who is depicted, however, as an ideal follower of YHWH and whose praise is sounded in the gates (3:11; see Prov. 31:31). She stands next to Rachel and Leah as a builder of the house of Israel (4:11), thus resembling in many ways the wise woman or Wisdom. As one in that time's chorus of voices, the novelette is to be seen as an attempt to counter, with concrete examples, positions hostile to women and strangers. In addition, Klara Butting (1993, 21–48) has shown how this story consciously replaces the "history of fathers and procreation" with "history of women." It is a perspective which documents the hope of Israelite women for an end to patriarchal power in society and religion.

On every page of the Book of Job, one may study the deficits of the male-dominated religion of YHWH after the Exile. The supreme God of Heaven does not solve the problems that follow upon political and religious ruin. The pattern of "you fare according to what you do" no longer works: many affluent patriarchs like Job have to face an undeserved failure and take God and traditional wisdom to task. God and *hokhmah*, depicted to resemble the Egyptian Maal (Job 28), are inaccessible and distant; just order is found nowhere. One notes that explicit reference is made to Job's daughters by name (!) at the end of the book, where Job experiences rehabilitation; the three women are given an inheritance with their brothers (42:13-15; see Ebach 1994, 35–40). A connection has to be made between this reference and the Priestly laws governing inheritance in Numbers 27 and 36. Mahlah, Noah, Hoglah, Milcah, and Tirzah, the daughters of Zelophehad—all of them mentioned by name—make a presentation before Moses, that is, the highest court of the community, that they be recognized as inheritors, seeing that their father had no sons. Their plea is granted. Later writings on the law, however, add a restriction stipulating that women eligible to inherit property, such as those five, may only marry men from their own tribe so that the inherited land may not be lost to the tribe.

The writings cited provide perspective on the religious developments of the fifth/fourth centuries. In matters of social and religious conflict, the women and men who had returned from exile for all intents and purposes gain control. The worship of goddesses is abolished through drastic measures and, quite likely, primarily at the expense of women. In spite of the strong position enjoyed by women in the period of reconstruction, a highly patriarchal order of society establishes itself in a short time. Worship is again centralized in the temple. The symbol system is monotheistic. The less exclusive position in relation to monotheism adopted by Proverbs 1–9 is an attempt to safeguard the legacy of the Goddess (and with it the traditions of women) within the boundaries set out by orthodoxy. A certain kind of pluralism was quite possible, as the language alone of Second and Third Isaiah would suggest. There are similar approaches in the Psalms which, without any polemics and claims to exclusivity, fuse the God of Zion and of creation with old traditions of Baal, for example, by transposing a Canaanite rain hymn from its context to that of the worship of YHWH (Psalm 65; Schroer 1991: "Psalm 65—Zeugnis eines integrativen JHWH-Glaubens?").

Again and again, the difficult position of women in a religion dominated by men becomes visible. Numbers 12 may be seen as a highly concentrated version of this subject (see 4.3.2). In this text, Miriam is thoroughly tarnished, even though for centuries her image as a prophetic or charismatic leader of the Exodus was held up high. Together with Aaron, her brother, she rebels against Moses by claiming that they and not only Moses alone had received direct revelations from God. At issue here, clearly, are subsequent questions of authority. If Moses embodies the Jerusalemite court of justice (Crüsemann, 1996; see 4.4), one needs to ask which collective entity might stand behind the figure of Miriam questioning the authority of Moses. Might it not have been women who were resisting that court's laws (see Numbers 27 and 36) or who were no longer prepared to acquiesce in the claim of men that they alone were leaders in religion?

The Book of Esther, set in the Persian period, which is difficult to date with precision (fifth–second century B.C.E.), offers a similarly abhorrent example from the political-social realm. Queen Vashti's refusal to be shown off by the king at a festive gathering of men results in her being deposed in an edict. Both of these are means of solidifying the patriarchal dominance of men. However, the main story is an impressive testimony of women-centered history of faith: a woman—cast in the type of Joseph—becomes a savior, indeed a messianic queen (Butting 1993, 49–86) through her resistance against anti-Semitism.

Nahman Avigad, 1987 (see 5.3.1); Gerlinde Baumann, "*Wer mich findet, hat Leben gefunden*": *Traditionsgeschichtliche und theologische Studien zur Weisheitsgestalt in Proverbien 1–9*, FAT (Tübingen: Mohr und Siebeck, 1996); idem, "'Zukunft feministischer Spiritualität' oder 'Werbefigur des Patriarchats'? Die Bedeutung der Weisheitsgestalt in Prov 1–9 für die feministisch-theologische Diskussion," in Luise Schottroff and Marie-Theres Wacker, eds., *Von der Wurzel getragen*, 1996 (see 5.4.1), 135–52; Anastasia Bernet, "Frauengeschichte(n): Eine Untersuchung über das literarische Schicksal ausgewählter Frauengestalten aus der hebräischen Bibel in der frühjüdischen und frühchristlichen Literatur" (diss., Fribourg, 1990); Athalya Brenner and Fokkelien van Dijk-Hemmes, *On Gendering Texts*, 1993 (see 4.2); Maria Brosius, *Women in Ancient Persia (559–331 BC)* (Oxford: Oxford University Press, 1996); Klara Butting, 1993 (see 5.3.3); Claudia V. Camp, *Wisdom and the Feminine in the Book of Proverbs*, Bible and Literature Series 11 (Sheffield: Sheffield Academic Press, 1985); Jürgen Ebach, "Hiobs Töchter: Zur Lektüre von Hiob 42, 13-15," in Dorothee Sölle, ed., *Für Gerechtigkeit streiten*, 1994 (see 5.3.4); Tamara C. Eskenazi, 1992 (see 5.4.1); Irmtraud Fischer, *Gottesstreiterinnen*, 1995 (see 5.2); idem, "Eine Schwiegertochter—mehr wert als sieben Söhne! (Rut 4,15): Frauenbeziehungen im Buch Rut. Ein Lehrbeispiel des Affidamento," in Herlinde Pissarek-Hudelist and Luise Schottroff, eds., *Mit allen Sinnen glauben: Feministische Theologie unterwegs: Festschrift für Elisabeth Moltmann-Wendel* (Gütersloh: Gütersloher Verlagshaus Gerd Mohn, 1991), 30–44; Christian Frevel, "Die Elimination der Göttin aus dem Weltbild des Chronisten," ZAW 103 (1991): 263–71; Keel and Uehlinger, 1992 (see 4.4); Christl Maier, *Die "fremde Frau" in Proverbien 1–9: Eine exegetische und sozialgeschichtliche Studie*, OBO 144 (Fribourg: Universitätsverlag; Göttingen: Vandenhoeck und Ruprecht, 1995); idem, "Im Vorzimmer der Unterwelt: Die Warnung vor der 'fremden Frau' in Prov 7 in ihrem historischen Kontext," in Luise Schottroff and Marie-Theres Wacker, eds., *Von der Wurzel getragen*, 1996, 179–98; Channa Safrai, *Women and Temple: The Status and Role of Women in the Second Temple of Jerusalem*, Studia Judaica 12 (Berlin: de Gruyter, 1995); Silvia Schroer, "Die göttliche Weisheit," 1991 (see 4.3.1); idem, "Psalm 65—Zeugnis eines integrativen

JHWH-Glaubens?" *UF* 22 (1991): 285–301; idem, *Die Weisheit hat ihr Haus gebaut,* 1996 (see 4.3.2); Dorothee Sölle, ed., *Für Gerechtigkeit streiten,* 1994 (see 5.3.4); Christoph Uehlinger, "Die Frau im Efa (Sach 5,5-11): Eine Programmvision von der Abschiebung der Göttin," *Bibel und Kirche* 49 (1994): 93–103.

5.5　Vistas

The Hellenistic period and the transition to the Pax Romana in the Near East are marked by an extensive, rich productivity as far as Jewish literature is concerned. Only a few milestones of the further development can be referred to now. A number of writings have not yet been, or, like the Book of Qoheleth, have just begun to be studied from feminist perspectives. On account of its pointed assertions (7:27) it may be accused not only of cynicism but also of hostility toward women. (Butting 1993, 87–116, offers a different interpretation.)

The Book of Jesus ben Sirach (see 4.3.2 and Schroer 1995) witnesses to the perduring virulence of the question of women and the Goddess in the second century B.C.E. It is Jesus Sirach's aim to solidify men's patriarchal dominance in every respect. He displays approval only for mothers and good wives; other than that his remarks about women are undisguisedly misogynous. At the level of theology this hostility toward women shows itself not only in the statement about women being the origin of sin (25:24). It can also be discerned in his adroit attempt strictly to subordinate the figure of Wisdom personified to the male God in the temple and to identify her with the Torah, the Law. As portrayed in Proverbs 1–9, the *hokhmah* probably offered women a language of religion and possibilities of self-identification that were beyond endurance for this teacher of the Law.

In the later Book of Wisdom, Sophia is cast in quite a different role. Most likely the book was composed in Alexandria during the three decades before the change to the common era; it may be connected with the Therapeutae, referred to by Philo of Alexandria (*De vita contemplativa*). They were a monastic group of Jewish male and female dropouts who in their common religious life participated on an equal footing, attended to special traditions of women in their liturgies, and devoted themselves to the study of wisdom. In the middle part of The Wisdom of Solomon (chaps. 6–11) the personified Sophia plays an important role. She embodies the whole of Hellenistic and Jewish wisdom tradition and is the advice-giving consort of Solomon, the legendary teacher of wisdom, and the *paredros*, the one who assists the God of Israel. But above all, Sophia is a Jewish response to the cult of Isis that was so attractive to, and demonstrably emancipatory for, Jewish women. A divine figure from Jewish tradition, equivalent to Isis, is set over and against her. It is Sophia who, in place of the male god, leads the Exodus from Egypt; it is this image of woman to which the Therapeutae reverted. The image is also at the foundation of the Book of Judith.

A huge and largely unplowed field for feminist research is the so-called early Jewish literature (the Apocrypha and Pseudepigrapha). There is a monograph by Angelika Strotmann (1991) on that period's image of the Father-God and one by Angela Standhartinger (1995) on the image of women in the Book of Joseph and Asenath. Max Küchler (see 4.4) has provided excellent foundations for such research. They give a good overview of these sometimes very difficult writings. His book *Frühjüdische Weisheitstraditionen* is a large compendium that contains indispensable materials in relation also to a Jesuanic or Christian wisdom theology. It contains Alexandrian wisdom traditions, the wisdom of the apocalyptics, wisdom in Qumran, wisdom of the early Jewish exegetes, historians, novelists, and poets, traditions of Achicar, the Testament of the Twelve Patriarchs, and others. In the section "Schweigen, Schmuck und Schleier" (silence, adornments, and veil), he sets out from Second Testament texts (1 Cor. 11 and the command to wear veils) and systematically traces the literary fate of those biblical figures of women in early Jewish writings (such as the Enoch traditions, the Book of Jubilees, and the Testament of the Twelve Patriarchs) who recount conflicts between man and woman. It becomes apparent that the foundational texts from the Bible are consistently raised to the level of eroticism through an emphasis on the seductive beauty of women and that the erotic is demonized throughout. The arguments in the writings of the Second Testament hostile to women follow those traditions.

Léonie J. Archer, *Her Price Is beyond Rubies: The Jewish Woman in Graeco-Roman Palestine*, JSOT Supplement Series 60 (Sheffield: Sheffield Academic Press, 1990); Ulrike Bail, "Susanna verlässt Hollywood: Eine feministische Auslegung von Daniel 13," in Ulrike Bail and Renate Jost, eds., *Gott an den Rändern: Sozialgeschichtliche Perspektiven auf die Bibel*, Festschrift for Willy Schottroff (Gütersloh: Gütersloher Verlagshaus Gerd Mohn, 1996), 91–98; Klara Butting, 1993 (see 5.3.3); Tal Ilan, 1995 (see 4.4); Amy-Jill Levine, ed., *Women*

Like This: New Perspectives on Women in the Greco-Roman World (Atlanta: Scholars Press, 1991); Silvia Schroer, "Die göttliche Weisheit," 1991 (see 4.3.1); idem, "Die personifizierte Sophia," 1994 (see 4.3.2); idem, *Die Weisheit hat ihr Haus gebaut*, 1996 (see 4.3.2); Angela Standhartinger, *Das Frauenbild im Judentum der hellenistischen Zeit: Ein Beitrag anhand von Joseph und Aseneth*, Arbeiten zur Geschichte des antiken Judentums und des Urchristentums 26 (Leiden: E. J. Brill, 1995); Angelika Strotmann, *"Mein Vater bist du!" (Sir 51,10): Zur Bedeutung der Vaterschaft Gottes in kanonischen und nichtkanonischen frühjüdischen Schriften* (Frankfurt: Verlag J. Knecht, 1991); Luzia Sutter Rehmann, *Geh, frage die Gebärerin: Feministische befreiungstheologische Untersuchungen zum Gebärmotiv in der Apokalyptik* (Gütersloh: Chr. Kaiser/Gütersloher Verlagshaus, 1995).

Chapter Six

Synchronic Sections

6.1 Who Is Eve?

Feminist exegesis has worked intensively and for a long time on the position of woman in Genesis 2–3 (Gössmann and Schüngel-Straumann, 90–97; Schüngel-Straumann 1989). The reason for the close attention paid to these texts is due to their great significance in the early Jewish and, above all, the Christian history of interpretation, and their anthropology, which is hostile to women. Nowhere does the Hebrew Bible make any reference to the Yahwist's narrative of creation and failure, or to the connection between the woman and the fall. On the basis of an exact reading of the text, feminist exegesis has refuted a number of traditional misinterpretations, and it was not the first or only school of interpretation to do so. The woman is not someone who was created second since it is only as a result of the creation of *'ishah* that the *'ish* ("man") receives his sexual identity. Before, there was only *'adām*, "earth creature," whose gender was not established. The woman is brought to the man as his counterpart (his *Gegenüber*), as someone who helps him as his equal, and who in her being is most closely related to him. On the basis of this relation, declares Gen. 2:24, every man will at some time or other neglect (not leave!) his parents in order to be attached to a woman. There are no indications in the text of ancient matrilineal orders according to which a man moved into the woman's family.

The so-called story of the fall, conscious that patriarchy is a distortion of the created order, seeks to explain how the distortion came about. It happened because, seduced by the serpent, the woman and the man did not respect a boundary set by YHWH. The texts of the curses set out etiologically why, ever since, the serpent—in Hebrew grammar a male

147

creature—moves about on his belly in the dirt, without feet; why women have to suffer numerous and difficult pregnancies; why men exercise domination over women; and why farming is so excessively laborious. It is important to note that in Genesis 2–3 the relation between the sexes and not the question of children is at the center. The woman is not explicitly fixed by the created order in her role as mother (see Ulrich 1994); only the reversal of the true order of creation constrains her to the hardships of pregnancy.

The precise date of the composition of Genesis 2–3 cannot be determined; different narrative motifs, woven one into another, point to an extended process of formation. The main part of the narrative was probably written down in the time of the monarchy. How several of the motifs are connected is still to be made clear. In pictorial art from the Late Bronze Age, the serpent is closely connected to the Goddess (Qadesh, who holds two serpents); yet, the symbolism of the serpent is so polyvalent in the ancient Near East that the background to the connection between woman and the serpent is not apparent. From earliest times in Palestine, the sacred tree was held to be a domain of the Goddess, whereas in this narrative it is said to be taboo. An old pictorial tradition tells of a dragon from chaos (serpent) threatening the tree of the world, that is, the order which guarantees life. In the Syro-Palestinian region, it is the weather-god who is to kill the serpent, while God and Goddess together protect the tree of the world. However, in the biblical narrative woman and man renounce the given order. The enticement of the tree— and here we face a whole bundle of motifs—lies in the desirability of its fruit, in its promise of immortality, knowledge of good and evil, likeness with God, and wisdom (cf. Sirach 24 where hokhmah is said to be rooted in different trees). Putting the tree under taboo must be connected with the Palestinian tradition of the Goddess and the sacred trees. Certain groups of adherents of the religion of YHWH increasingly maligned the sacred trees (eradication of the Asherah) because of their inseparable linkage with the Goddess cults. This may perhaps make plausible why the serpent in this narrative sought out the woman as its accomplice in order to break the taboo.

Carol Meyers has raised a question that could move us forward: who really is Eve? As havvah, the "mother of all life," she surely belongs to the tradition of an ancient mother-deity but is now replaced by the Israelite woman. The prominent place which Genesis 2–3 has in the Yahwist primordial history and in the Pentateuch suggests that Adam and Eve are corporate personalities, husband and wife in Israel as such. There are

several corporate personalities in the biblical tradition, Moses representing the supreme court of Jerusalem; Aaron representing the priesthood;
Miriam perhaps representing the Israelite woman, who after the second
exodus questions Israel's authorities; Shiphrah and Puah representing
the guild of midwives, and so on. Adam stands for the Israelite farmer
who with burdensome labor wrests food from the earth. Eve stands for
the Israelite woman whose life is marked and also threatened by pregnancies. By failing to bring into focus that in an agricultural village society Eve would have worked in the fields, the text thus renders women's
work invisible. The struggle for existence outside of paradise does not
affect man and woman in the same measure; it affects women twice as
much. In Israel, the relation of man and woman is marked on the one
hand by devoted attachment, and on the other by the man's dominance.
In this mythic narrative, the woman has the role of advice giver; she is
active and the man reacts to her impulses. She is interested in forbidden
things, things that transcend mere survival: immortality and wisdom.
She makes her decisions. The role of advisor to the man is actually the
most important task of married Israelite woman, more important than
her role as homemaker (Schroer 1991). It is a firm rule that the man
follow the advice of the woman and acquiesce in her instruction (Job is
the sole exception). This powerful position of women in the home, as
well as the king's mother's role of advisor to the king, must surely have
come under attack from Israelite men. Genesis 3 very clearly depicts Eve
in this traditional role but as a giver of bad advice, whose counsel was
not for the good but, rather, the downfall of all. The context would suggest that, in terms of the subject matter, women's influence on religious
affairs is at issue, their predilection for tree cults and serpents, their
search for autonomous wisdom, the capacity for knowledge and vitality
(immortality). This is how Eve competes with the God of Israel and
comes into conflict with the cult of YHWH.

Elisabeth Gössmann and Helen Schüngel-Straumann, "Eva," in *WbfTh*,
    90–97 (with literature list); Carol Meyers, 1988 (see first bibliograph-
    ical list in chap. 5); Silvia Schroer, see 5.3.1; Helen Schüngel-Strau-
    mann, *Die Frau am Anfang: Eva und die Folgen* (Freiburg: Herder,
    1989); Kerstin Ulrich, "Evas Bestimmung: Studien zur Beurteilung
    von Schwangerschaft und Mutterschaft im Ersten Testament," in
    Hedwig Jahnow et al., *Feministische Hermeneutik und Erstes Testa-
    ment. Analysen und Interpretationen* (Stuttgart: W. Kohlhammer Ver-
    lag, 1994), 149–63.

6.2 Woman's Work

The work of women, be they free or slaves, is frequently left unconsidered in the First Testament, so that one painstakingly needs to collect incidental observations. In an agrarian society, both sexes have to share in the necessary labor, such as tilling the fields, growing and preparing produce, caring for livestock, and so forth. Genesis 2-3 portrays the man and not the woman as the typical worker of the field. Judges 13 and the Book of Ruth, among others, clearly presuppose that especially at harvest time, women and men were busy in the fields. As Ruth 2:9 shows, out in the fields women seem to have been subject to sexual molesting by men. Their work appears to have included the processing of field produce and meal preparation, part of which was the time-consuming activity of grinding grain with a hand-operated mill (Exod. 11:5; cf. Deut. 24:6). A series of special tasks was assigned to women. At court, women cook, bake, and make ointments and perfumes (1 Sam. 8:11-13; see the informative article by Willy Schottroff 1989). They were trained as musicians and singers (Amos 8:3; see 2 Sam. 19:36). In postexilic writings there are references to women singers in Ezra 2:65 and Neh. 7:67.

The production of textiles was to a large extent women's work, certainly for domestic use but also outside it (Exod. 35:25ff.; 2 Kings 23:7; Tobit 2:11-14). Most skilled trades, such as those of smiths, fullers, potters, and bakers, were practiced in family workshops unless they had been incorporated into the king's factories (Isa. 7:3; Jer. 19:1; 37:21; Neh. 3:31f.). What is not clear is whether a trade such as seal engraving was reserved for men; Egyptian pictures show only men performing this task, but the generic use of Hebrew language suggests that women may also have engraved seals (Exod. 28:11; 39:30). The vocation of midwife or wet nurse was reserved for women. Wise women, prophetesses, women necromancers, soothsayers, and wailing women sometimes offered their services for pay and sometimes for free.

A later text, Prov. 31:10-31, describes a woman who rules over a household with servants and who earns an income through the manufacture and sale of textiles. The city of Tyre was well-known for its fabrics, so this image of a woman could reflect conditions in Phoenicia.

Carol Meyers, *Discovering Eve*, 1988 (see the first bibliographical list in chap. 5); Luise Schottroff, "Lohnarbeit," in *Neues Bibel-Lexikon*, 666f.; Willy Schottroff, "Der Zugriff des Königs auf die Töchter: Zur Fronarbeit von Frauen im alten Israel," *EvTh* 49 (1989): 268–85.

6.3   Female Sexuality

Judaism certainly did not develop an untroubled relation to female sexuality. But, at least, sexuality within marriage was not made problematic, whereas following Paul, Christian tradition regarded celibacy as a form of life more adequate for the reign of God. In this domain, the first course changes are already discernible in First Testament texts in which, quite obviously, female sexuality rather than male sexuality was the more important issue.

In the early times of Israel, under the influence of Egyptian and Aegean culture, there appear to have been homosexual relationships among men of the upper classes. This fits into the image of an epoch in which, for example, paintings of ceremonial events at court show only men with men. The narratives of Saul, Jonathan, and David recall that Israel's great king David and Jonathan were lovers. To this day the history of interpretation of those texts is much under taboo. However, precise exegesis indicates that homoeroticism is not merely to be assumed but can actually be demonstrated in the texts (Schroer and Staubli 1996).

Israelite men and women, who had entered sedentary existence and lived in villages, felt threatened by the sexual behavior of city dwellers and other nations. They feared sexual assault and harassment which, according to Leviticus 18 and 20, also occurred within the clans of Israel. Quite early, nudity and everything sexual seems to have been excluded from the cult of YHWH. Saul's daughter Michal despises David because he bares himself during a cultic dance. Later, priests are ordered to wear undergarments when serving at the altar so that their genitals are covered when they climb the altar steps, or else the steps are prohibited (Exod. 20:26b; 28:42; Ezek. 44:18). The creation narrative of Genesis 2–3 perceives the shame felt by humans as a result of the distortion of the order God had ordained.

The First Testament does not give us a coherent picture of sexuality. The Song of Songs reflects an uninhibited joy in eroticism and sexuality on the lovers' part; presumably, this writing was only accepted into the canon of Scripture thanks to its allegorical interpretation. Within the system of regulations governing purity, sexuality is a prime area of impurity which, however, affects men and women to an equal degree and is not as such a denigration of sexuality. The view that menstrual and other flows of blood make women impure has had a far-reaching impact on the discrimination against female sexuality and reproductivity. The greatest contribution to this defamation was made by the Israelite prophets. Hosea already describes the religious behavior of all of Israel as the fornication of a married woman. Once the refrain is invented, Ezekiel and Jeremiah take it up and provide it with pornographic overtones. Again and again, female sexuality and the body of woman are the image par excellence for infidelity, shamelessness, and the lowest form of behavior. It is Ezekiel too (36:17) who symbolically compares the Israelites' behavior before God to the impurity of menstruation. In so doing, the value-free circle of pure-impure thought is, as such, broken through once and for all with the categories of morality.

In questions of sexuality, Israel's patriarchal society was marked to some extent by the same moral double standards as today's societies. Women's sexuality was massively controlled. This became particularly evident in the harsh punishments for adultery. While a man could only break someone else's marriage and never his own, a woman was forbidden to have sexual relations outside her marriage. Even the slightest suspicion of adultery on the part of his marriage partner allowed the man to have her examined in an ordeal (Numbers 5) administered by a priest. Israelite men went to women in the sex trade (*zonah*), which was far less dangerous than a liaison with an unmarried or engaged woman or with a married woman. Women in the sex trade were paid money or produce. They may possibly have worn particular clothes. As unmarried women, they seem to have been in a strong position prior to the existence of the state. They earned their livelihood on their own (sometimes in combination with the hospitality trade), living alone or with other women in houses they owned, and they had children. But when they reached advanced age they often fell through the social net when their relatives did not look after them (see the song of the aged women in the sex trade in Isa. 23:15-18). It is worth investigating whether this shows the traces of so-called *beenah* marriages (visitation marriages in matrilineal families) as Hannelis Schulte surmises. Beginning with the monarchical period, a *zonah* is met with more and more contempt.

Whereas this form of "professional" sex trade was integrated into society by means of the moral double standard of patriarchy, the prophets attacked the forms of what they called "prostitution" that were practiced by a sizable portion of the population and quite likely had religious foundations. During cultic celebrations of Canaanite origin, there appears to have been rather free sexual contact between men and women. The prophets called this adultery because married people took part in these occasions. According to Lev. 19:29 (cf. Hosea 4:14), daughters were enjoined by their fathers to engage in this form of sex trade. It is still an open question whether these celebrations were rites of initiation or consummation of the so-called sacred marriage (Wacker 1992 and Jost 1994). In the judgment of Lev. 21:9, it is utterly abhorrent when the daughter of a priest "profanes" herself in practicing the sex trade (in a place consecrated to YHWH?). Sanctuaries also had their sacred prostitutes who served cultic functions; perhaps they acted as the representatives of the Goddess (Qadesh "the Holy One"—female) (1 Kings 14:24; 15:12; 22:47; and Hosea 4:14; 1 Sam. 2:22b is a later comment) and engaged in sex trade. In any case, their image was that of the *zonah* because they were similarly beyond the patriarchal family circle and enjoyed greater freedom, including in the area of sexuality (Jost 1994).

Mary Douglas, *Purity and Danger: An Analysis of Concepts of Pollution and Taboo* (London: Routledge and Kegan Paul, 1966); Monika Fander, "Reinheit und Unreinheit," in *WbfTh*, 349–51; Renate Jost, "Von 'Huren und Heiligen': Ein sozialgeschichtlicher Beitrag," in Hedwig Jahnow et al., 1994 (see 6.1), 126–37; Silvia Schroer and Thomas Staubli, "Saul, David und Jonatan—eine Dreiecksgeschichte?" *Bibel und Kirche* 51 (1996): 15–22; Hannelis Schulte, "Beobachtungen zum Begriff der Zonah im Alten Testament," *ZAW* 102, (1992): 225–62; Marie-Theres Wacker, "Kosmisches Sakrament oder Verpfändung des Körpers? 'Kultprostitution' im biblischen Israel und im hinduistischen Indien: Religionsgeschichtliche Überlegungen im Interesse feministischer Theologie," in Renate Jost, Rainer Kessler, and Christoph M. Raisig, eds., *Auf Israel hören: Sozialgeschichtliche Bibelauslegungen* (Lucerne: Edition Exodus, 1992), 47–84.

6.4 Women and Violence in the First Testament

For a number of years now, the First Testament especially has often been the focal point of criticism because it does not distance itself fundamentally and consistently from violence but, rather, readily documents and legitimizes its use and often has no problem with uniting faith in God with violence. The issue of violence has additional and women-specific dimensions for women reading the Bible. One reason is that women in every culture are affected by structural and direct violence or participate in it in a different way than men. Another is that Western Christian tradition declared the use of violence, as typified for example in the heroine, as against woman's nature. This incompatibility of womanness and violence or even womanness and acceptance of violence has sunk deeply into the self-image of women so that they not only find texts of violence and male, warlike images of God unbearable, but also react with abhorrence when women in the Bible resort or accede to violence.

We cannot deal now with the problems related to the assessment of biblical traditions of violence in general. But we recall that it is this subject which attracts ever and again anti-Jewish clichés that impute violence and inhumanity to the First Testament and thoroughly cleanse the Second Testament of every trace of them. For that sort of thing there is no warrant. Repudiating a tradition which expresses violence often has little to do with true pacifism and much to do with aversion to physical contact, or simple inexperience. Those who are in the comfortable position of not having to defend their existence against violence may readily adopt rigorist positions. How quickly such basic positions are shaken was shown by the reactions of many European women to the systematic sexual assaults during the war in Bosnia.

The remembrance of the violence in our biblical heritage, of the men and women who perpetrated it and who were its victims, may be wholesome if we do not back away from the fact that, like every human history, this heritage also interwove what makes for healing with what brings destruction. After the event, nothing coerces us women in particular to justify violence in this history. But much speaks in favor of finally putting aversions and taboos behind us. It is certainly worthwhile, as far as questions specific to women are concerned, to attend to the connection between women and violence in the First Testament in a more differentiated way, and to make connections where individual texts are usually studied in isolation. Above all, this reveals that the narrators not infrequently take the side of women and that it is precisely the violence of men that is again and again challenged in the name of God. The First Testament has preserved the memory of Israelite women, not of the pacifists but of the peacemakers among them, who *because* they believed in a deity who desired peace believed also that violence on earth must come to an end.

In the First Testament women are portrayed primarily as victims of male violence. Several years ago, Phyllis Trible devoted a widely noted feminist study to the "texts of terror." There are many examples of texts from all ages that speak of violence to women. Judges 21 speaks of women being sold and kidnapped, Deuteronomy 21 of women being taken as prisoners of war. More than anywhere else, however, violence to women takes place in the private sphere, in the circle of kin (Exod. 21:22 presupposes an accident). In a moment of extreme distress, the Levite in Judges 19 does not hesitate to hand over his concubine to the violent men of Gibeah in order himself to escape from the threatened sexual assault (see Lanoir and Rocha 1992, and Müllner 1996). Jephthah is prepared to keep his absurd oath and sacrifices his daughter (Judg. 11:30-40). But every year Israel celebrates a feast commemorating the tragic victim.

Israelite women consistently faced the threat of sexual assault. In addition to all her misery, a sexually assaulted woman must demonstrate her innocence and reckon with society's disdain or be given as a wife to the man who assaulted her. If we read the explicit legal instructions of Leviticus 19 as an indication of a contrary reality, incest seems not to have been a rare occurrence. Behind the narrative of Lot's daughters there is possibly the recollection of daughters being sexually abused by their fathers (Seifert).

With astonishing sensitivity to the situation of the woman, 2 Sam. 13:1-22 tells about her experience of sexual assault at the royal court. (On this text see Müllner, "Macht—Sexualität—Gewalt.") Amnon, one of David's sons, has fallen in love with Tamar, his half sister. He invents a ruse to be alone with her. Feigning illness, he asks that the king's daughter bake him some cakes and bring them to his bed. He unscrupulously exploits the situation and overpowers her, sexually assaulting his sister. No sooner has he seized what he wanted than his passion turns to disdain and hate. He throws the ravaged woman out on the street, socially ruined for life. But Tamar's voice of wisdom, her citing of the unwritten law, her moving appeals to Amnon's reason, and her pleas are powerless against this injustice and brutal violence.

The story of Tamar is anguishing testimony to the violence to which women are exposed in a patriarchal society. That is why a woman will read this text with other feelings and thoughts than a man. First, she will note that Tamar is indeed the object of a man's brutal violence and lust, the victim of men's vile compacts, of her own father's lack of care and legal protection and, finally, even though an innocent woman, the victim also of society's disdain. Second, a woman reading this text will note that the narrators of the story are on Tamar's side. They declare her to be free of any guilt, stress her wisdom and thoughtfulness, and feel sympathy for her. And this is how the story of a sexual assault at the royal court is at least snatched from the jaws of the final injustice, that of being silenced. In Israel, the victims of violence are remembered.

With loud cries and laments and by tearing up her clothes, Tamar makes known the injustice done to her. Another manner of breaking the silence that settles over such experiences of violence (see Burrichter) is perhaps depicted in Psalm 55. In her close, text-oriented exegesis, Ulrike Bail mounts many a sound argument that in this psalm a woman plaintively brings before God the terrible experience of being sexually assaulted by a man close to her.

Israelite women are involved directly in actions of war only in exceptional circumstances. But often they cannot comment on them. In a number of narratives, the First Testament documents the custom of Israelite women celebrating victorious military actions with festive and exuberant drumming, dancing, and singing, hailing the heroes' successes and showering the less successful with their ridicule. It is not at all difficult to find the reason for their cheering: these women were relieved. For surely, often enough, they had reason to fear for their own lives or their freedom, and for the lives of their men. After the Israelites had crossed the Red Sea, Miriam reaches for her tambourine and joins the women in song (Exod. 15:19-21). After the victory over Sisera, Deborah leads in singing a song of triumph (Judges 5; on the Song of Deborah, see Bechmann). Jephthah's daughter meets her father by dancing toward him after he and the Israelite army had defeated the Ammonites (Judg. 11:34). And Israelite women cheer David as he returns from battle with the Philistines: Saul has killed a thousand but David ten thousand (1 Sam. 18:7).

To these texts correspond many Iron Age terra-cotta figurines depicting women beating a tambourine. Participation in this manner in the activities of war was expected of Israelite women. Not in every case, however, is the jubilation over the death of the enemy completely unfettered; it is quite plausible that the women's sung commentaries in certain instances had ironic undertones (Brenner and van Dijk-Hemmes, 32–48). Marie-Theres Wacker presumes that originally the Song of Miriam still included a critical note as compared to the Song of Moses that precedes it. When Miriam sings "the horse and his rider he has hurled into the sea," she ascribes the victory over the Egyptians not to the Israelite forces but to God.

Women are affected in many ways by the results of political and war-related acts of violence. Already, Philistines and Israelites left chiefly to women the activities of mourning. Clay figurines show women, not men, in the actions of mourning. The vocation of wailing women (e.g., Jer. 9:17ff.) is not by coincidence a woman's job.

There is a memento to a remarkable Israelite woman in the midst of a report about the coldly calculating brutality of patriarchal politics (2 Samuel 21). In a very shady political deal, David handed two of Saul's sons and five of his grandsons over to the Gibeonites to expiate for the persecution they had suffered at Saul's hands. The seven are killed but not burned. Rizpah, the mother of two of the murdered men, does not speak out in mourning her dead but shows by extraordinary action that she does not acquiesce in this senseless killing. She remains loyal to her sons. For months she keeps her mournful vigil near the decomposing bodies, preventing animals feeding on carrion from getting to them. Touched by Rizpah's loyalty and determination, David has the remains of Saul and Jonathan, buried in Jabesh-Gilead, exhumed and reburied, together with those of the seven murdered men, in the hometown of Saul's father. Rizpah is a model of all those women who today seek to make sure that the disappearance of their children at the hands of violent governments is neither simply accepted nor forgotten, that the disappeared and the dead are remembered, and that there be no respite until the guilty are brought to justice.

A series of women's narratives about the earliest times of Israel shows that Israelite women frequently offered assistance in people's escapes (e.g., Michal in 1 Sam. 19:8-24). In Exod. 2:1-10 and 2 Kings 11:2 women save lives and engage themselves as "women for peace," countering with various means the violence caused by men. In this context, Shiphrah and Puah, the midwives who resisted the deadly orders of the state, should be mentioned (Exodus 1) or the far-sighted Abigail (1 Samuel 25), who prevented a large and senseless bloodbath that male pride and men's notions of honor had provoked. Her words provide interesting clues about her image of God. She tells David that it would be in accordance with the mind of God if he, as the future leader of Israel, were not to soil his hands with blood shed in an act of revenge. The narrative of the women of Abel-beth-maacah tells of a wise woman who is able to prevent war from breaking out in a politically tense situation (2 Sam. 20:14-22).

There are biblical women, albeit not too many, who use violence as a political tool. One thinks of Israel's and Judah's queens and king-mothers, who just like male rulers commit judicial murder (Jezebel) and cold-bloodedly have people done away with (Athaliah). I focus on these particular narratives in which acts of violence by women are approved of in the biblical presentation or are described as actions in accordance with the mind of God.

The narratives concerning Jael (Judges 4–5) and Judith are a case in point. Jael enticed the Canaanite commander Sisera to come into her tent, and she kills him with a tent peg. By her deed, Israel is liberated from the overwhelming power of the Canaanites; by means of it, God can bring freedom.

That such isolated actions occurred or were conceivable in extreme situations only becomes very apparent in the Book of Judith.

The Book of Judith was written in the second, perhaps even in the first century B.C.E. It does not recount historical events but, rather, retells in the form of a novel the ever recurring liberation of Israel from the hands of its oppressors. Judith, an affluent and devout widow, takes action when her hometown, Bethulia, comes under attack by Nebuchadnezzar's troops. Those responsible for the town do not know what to do next, and they wait desperately for God's intervention. Judith accuses them of lack of faith and wanting to force the hand of God with their hesitancy. Without revealing the details of her plans, she and her female servant enter the lions' den. With a woman's charms, she succeeds in enticing Holophernes, the commander of the enemy army, into the biggest trap of his life. As soon as Holophernes falls asleep, drunk on wine and with love, Judith beheads him with his own sword.

Women's reactions to the figure of Judith are often vehement. Many find utterly unbearable the idea that a woman kills a human being. But the Book of Judith itself does not at all paint the murderess of the tyrant as a femme fatale. In an extreme situation, Judith makes use of extreme means. Her prayer (chap. 9) and her song of thanksgiving (chap. 16) express a faith that fundamentally and in the name of God questions military power and violence (Schroer 1992). Judith's God is a God of peace who repudiates violence and the force of arms that are explicitly ranked with men. It is the God of Israel who often withdraws a great distance from men's virtues, and military power in particular. This God would rather enter into alliance with a David who confronts Goliath without armor or a Judith who goes without protection into grave danger.

It is the task of feminist theology and exegesis to deal with the open and concealed violence that a hierarchically structured, patriarchal society directs against women. Structural violence is more basic than the physical, visible violence or counterviolence elicited by it. But what is still lacking here are fundamental social-historical studies specific to women. In what way were Israelite women the victims of their society's structural patriarchal violence? What we can assert is that in Israel, widows in particular were those hit worst by social inequities and exploitation. One would also need to know which women of the upper classes contributed to structural violence against women, and so forth. But it is not only social history that gives rise to new questions; so does the history of theology and religion. Is the history of monotheism a history of triumph that made its way at the expense of the religious needs and convictions of women in Israel? Is it not also structural violence when women as religious subjects are demonized in connection with cults of the Goddess, when the relation between YHWH and Israel is symbolized in terms of the relation between husband and wife and, when after the Exile, Israelite men sought to destroy the practice of mixed marriages at the expense of foreign women, and so forth? It is to the credit of Jewish feminist theology (see especially Plaskow) that it has raised further and more radical questions on the whole problem of violence: is the theological idea of the election of peoples still tenable? Does not the consciousness of special election, of the exclusive possession of the truth, create the foundation of discrimination against other groups or nations? Does not the consciousness of unique election, of a special character and nature, spawn over and again new unholy hierarchies and violence-filled orders?

Ulrike Bail, "Vernimm, Gott, mein Gebet: Psalm 55 und Gewalt gegen Frauen," in Hedwig Jahnow et al. (see 3.2.4), 67–84; Ulrike Bechmann, *Das Deboralied zwischen Geschichte und Fiktion: Eine exegetische Untersuchung zu Richter 5*, Dissertationen Theol. Reihe 33 (St. Ottilien: Eos Verlag, 1989); Athalya Brenner and Fokkelien van Dijk-Hemmes, *On Gendering Texts* (see 4.2); Rita Burrichter, "Die Klage der Leidenden wird stumm gemacht: Eine biblisch-literarische Reflexion zum Thema Vergewaltigung und Zerstörung der Identität," in Christine Schaumberger, ed., *Weil wir nicht vergessen wollen: Zu einer feministischen Theologie im deutschen Kontext* (Münster: Morgana Frauenverlag, 1987), 11–46; Corina Lanoir and Violeta Rocha, "La mujer sacrificada: Reflexiones sobre mujeres y violencia a partir de Jueces 19," *Xilotl* 5, no. 10 (1992): 49–62; Ilse Müllner, "Macht—Sexualität—Gewalt: Die Geschichte von Tamar und Amnon (2 Sam. 13,1-22) im Kontext der 'Thronfolgeerzählung' Davids" (diss., Münster, 1996); idem, "Tödliche Differenzen: Sexuelle Gewalt als Gewalt gegen Andere in Ri 19," in Luise Schottroff and Marie-Theres Wacker, eds., *Von der Wurzel getragen* (see 5.4.1), 81–100; Judith Plaskow, *Standing Again at Sinai* (see first bibliographical list in chap. 4); Silvia

Schroer, "Frauen und die Gewaltfrage im Ersten Testament," *KatBl* 119 (1994): 676–86; idem, "Gepriesen vor allen Frauen: Biblische Heldinnen," *FAMA* 10, no.4 (1994): 5–7; idem, "'Zerschlage ihren Stolz durch die Hand einer Frau,'" *Bibel heute* 110 (1992): 126f., on the subject of Judith; Silvia Schroer and Othmar Keel, "Von den schmerzlichen Beziehungen zwischen Christentum, Judentum und kanaanäischer Religion" (see the first bibliographical list in chap. 4); Elke Seifert, "Lot und seine Töchter: Eine Hermeneutik des Verdachts," in Hedwig Jahnow et al. (see 6.1), 48–66; Phyllis Trible, *God and the Rhetoric of Sexuality* (Philadelphia: Fortress Press, 1978); Marie-Theres Wacker, "Mirjam: Kritischer Mut einer Prophetin," in Karin Walter, ed., *Zwischen Ohnmacht und Befreiung: Biblische Frauengestalten* (Freiburg: Herder, 1988), 44–52.

6.5 The Access of Israelite Women to the Cult of YHWH

Within the home and family, women were certainly assigned the duties of simple ritual acts. They have access to the images of the ancestors (*teraphim;* Gen. 31:30-35; 1 Sam. 19:13, 16). Exodus 4:24-26 would suggest that in the early days women had the right not only to name children but also to circumcise boys. As time passes, it becomes more and more the task of women to begin the dirges at a person's death (see already Jahnow 1923). Women and men took part equally in the cultic celebrations of Canaanite origin "on the hilltops." It is noteworthy that cultic activities of women are referred to most frequently in texts that speak of the times before Israel became a state, for example, the commissioning by his mother of an image of God for the chapel in Micah's house (Judg. 17:1-13; see Jost).

That there were no women priests in the cult of YHWH has long been the motive for traditional biblical studies to investigate the competence of Israelite women to conduct worship at all. Indeed, there exists no doubt that the priesthood of the central sanctuaries, as well as the Levites who offered their services in the provinces, were exclusively male. But because the Near East was quite accustomed to women priests, serving in the cults of female and male deities, this fact is certainly astounding. A few influential women are referred to as *nebi'ah,* "prophetess," two of whom had been accredited (2 Kings 22:14-20; Isa. 8:3). Yet no book has been passed on in the name of a woman writer-prophet. It was generally conceded that women received divine revelations, but the statement is always accompanied by arguments as to whether such revelations have real authority for faith (Miriam in Numbers 12) or are even credible. In Judges 13 the angel of YHWH has to appear twice, because Manoah does not want to believe his wife that an angel had appeared to her and given her a message.

What else do we know about the activity of women in the sanctuaries of YHWH? Both pictorial records and biblical texts indicate that probably as early as the beginning of the Iron Age, the responsibility for music in worship fell chiefly into the hands of men (the patron of cultic music is David!). Dancing and beating the tambourine belong nonetheless to the profile of women worshipers of YHWH (e.g., Miriam). According to Erhard S. Gerstenberger (1994, 349–63) about one-third of the Psalms originated in family worship; these psalms make no direct references to women's concerns, prayer language, or spirituality (with the exception of Psalm 55; see 6.4). This does not necessarily have to mean that women could not also find themselves in these prayers. The descriptions of distress, of the attacks of chaos and of salvation in direst straits could console a deeply indebted Israelite man as well as a widow, a sick person as well as a woman in labor. The Song of Hannah in 1 Samuel 2 makes no direct reference to her experience of salvation from childlessness; nevertheless, a theological interpretation is given to this experience, which is specific to women, in this programmatic hymn of praise to YHWH who overturns the orders of the status quo.

First Samuel 1–2 is a text which, even though it tells of the times before the monarchy, probably belongs to the final redactional phase of the historical writings. It presupposes innocently that at least once a year whole families would journey to the sanctuaries of YHWH to offer their sacrifice and share meals together. This is where the ruling should become apparent that had been in effect since Deuteronomy: women took part in the pilgrim festivities and Easter meals or were certainly not excluded from them (Braulik 1991, esp. 129–36). Nor were women obliged to participate in the same manner as men (Exod. 23:17; 34:23f.; Deut. 16:16). The sabbath commandment would have applied in the same way to the free Israelite woman and to the man. How such a ruling was handled in practice, when home, farm, and livestock could not be left unattended for several days or when children were still very young and could not be brought along (1 Sam. 1:22), is another matter. In any case, Hannah enters the temple in Shiloh, offers prayer, speaks with the priests in charge, and makes a vow. How much women were deprived in this aspect of their autonomy as religious subjects is shown in Numbers 30. The explicit instructions found there assume that the *pater familias* (the father of a daughter or the husband of a woman) has the basic right to veto a woman's vow. If he claims that right, the vow becomes null and void. These instructions represent what is an ambiguous, albeit also partial, patriarchal disenfranchisement of women in the domain of religion (but cf. Prov. 7:14; 31:2).

There are traces, dating from the period of the monarchy, of activities of women in the sanctuaries; but they are always related to deities other than YHWH. We hear of women weaving textiles for the Asherah in the Temple of Jerusalem (2 Kings 23:7) and of others, in the time before the Exile, wailing for Tammuz outside the temple (Ezek. 8:14). Exodus 38:8 contains a recollection of the mirrors that women used to bring to sanctuaries as part of their worship of the Goddess (Winter 1983, 58–65; see 4.4). In what activities the so-called holy women were involved is difficult to determine (see 6.3).

When the priests in exile created a new order of worship on the basis of the purity-impurity system, it must have created radical changes for women. Especially in their child-bearing years, women are from now on severely limited in their conduct of worship. Every menstruation and every birth made them impure for days or months, thus excluding them from visiting a sanctuary. In the areas of divination, oracles, and soothsaying not associated with the temple or other specific sanctuaries, the religious practice of women appears to have been increasingly suppressed. This may also have to do with notions of purity. In the eyes of those who think in terms of pure and impure, someone who takes up contacts with the realm of the dead or other spheres of reality becomes an ambiguous person. Such a person has power and also is dangerous. The prohibition of soothsaying and magic was not for women only (see Lev. 20:6, 27) but it did affect them in particular (Ezek. 22:18).

Therefore, for a woman adherent of the cult of YHWH, the possibilities for active participation in the worship of her God were quite limited. Small wonder then that women who adhered to other cults are depicted as taking much greater initiative. A shaded grove invited festivities where sexual encounters took place under the auspices of religion and smoked produce and baked goods were prepared for the Queen of Heaven. That there are so few feminine names that include the theophonic element

YH(WH) may possibly have to do with the relatively low degree of identification by women with the heavily male-centered cult of the state.

Ina Johanne Batmartha (Petermann) (see 5.4.1); Phyllis Bird, "The Place of Women in the Israelite Cultus," in Patrick D. Miller et al. (see 5.4.2), 397–419; Georg Braulik, "Die Ablehnung der Göttin Aschera in Israel: War sie erst deuteronomistisch, diente sie der Unterdrückung der Frauen," in Marie-Theres Wacker and Erich Zenger, eds., *Der eine Gott und die Göttin* (see 4.3.1), 106–36; Mary Douglas (see 6.3); Monika Fander, "Reinheit und Unreinheit" (see 6.3); Geburgis Feld (see 5.4.1); Erhard S. Gerstenberger, "Weibliche Spiritualität in Psalmen und Hauskult," in Walter Dietrich and Martin Klopfenstein, eds. (see 4.3.2), 349–63; Hedwig Jahnow, *Das hebräische Leichenlied*, BZAW 36 (Giessen: A. Töpelmann, 1923); Renate Jost, "Der Fluch der Mutter: Feministisch-sozialgeschichtliche Überlegungen zu Ri 17,1–6," in Ulrike Bail and Renate Jost (see 5.5); Channa Safrai (see 5.4.2); Marie-Theres Wacker and Erich Zenger, eds., *Der eine Gott und die Göttin* (see 4.3.1); Ina Willi-Plein, *Opfer und Kult im alttestamentlichen Israel: Textbefragungen und Zwischenergebnisse*, SBS 153 (Stuttgart: Verlag Katholisches Bibelwerk, 1993).

6.6 The One God and the Goddess

Right from the start, feminist exegesis has been preoccupied with the goddesses as much as it has with the women in the Bible. There are good reasons for this interest (see Part One). A warning is still necessary that feminist research not devote itself to these matters in a one-sided way. If we want to find out what happened in history and theology, why goddesses were attacked, suppressed, silenced, and finally eliminated from our religious tradition, it is indispensable to search again and again for the subjects, for example, of the cult of Asherah, under what conditions they lived, and so forth. The religious symbol system cannot be reconstructed independently of the lives of women and men at that time and independently of their world; otherwise the danger arises of projecting our ideas and needs today without reflection into the reality of those women and men (Schroer 1994).

Silvia Schroer, "Die Aschera: Kein abgeschlossenes Kapitel," *Schlangenbrut* 12, no. 44 (1994): 17–22.

6.6.1 Feminist Critique of Monotheism

The development of the religion of YHWH into an exclusive and patriarchal monotheism is a complex process that has consistently been the subject of exegetical and theological research. On its own, the Bible itself provides an insufficiently clear picture of this process. Hence extrabiblical sources are of great value. One of the difficulties for research and related discussion resides in the area of conceptuality. The Bible does not know the concept of theoretical monotheism; when Deutero-Isaiah denies the existence of other deities next to YHWH, it is not a matter of the pure being of divine existences, as conceived by Greek philosophical tradition, but rather of their agency. Israel's God *is* only inasmuch as S/He acts, is being experienced, or exercises power over and against other powers. In the conversations of specialists, monotheism is juxtaposed to polytheism. But religious symbol systems cannot be described as unambiguously as these terms would have one believe; they locate themselves on a variety of levels, such as rites performed in homes or by clans, worship in important sanctuaries, religious teachings of specific groups. Thus, there continue to be different groups in Israel after the Exile who hold quite different views of what the authentic faith of YHWH is. Exclusive concepts stand side by side with inclusive ones; monotheism is not yet thoroughly patriarchalized. That is, monotheism is not indissolubly tied to the only language of God that is allowed, namely language of a male God, the worship of whom can only be administered and presided over by men (see 5.4.2 on *hokhmah*). In the development of the patriarchal religion of YHWH, which after the Exile more and more carries the day, one observes processes of purification less than battles for power; one sees a power struggle between orthodoxy and heresy or syncretism.

The specific questions put by women to the history of monotheism arise exactly at this point. Suspicion is mounting that, from its inception, this monotheism has been a tale of triumph invented by men. Justifications for monotheism have been associated with war and the search for identity, often in terms of an apartheid against other people and religions. Often, the prophets' polemic does not make clear what the inhumanity of the other religions is that must be opposed. Indeed, monotheistic symbol systems may be impressive due to the advances they have achieved with their enormous efforts to concentrate on the essential and to reach clarity by abstraction. That these systems disappear, unfulfilled, so to speak, and that people in their religious practice do not persevere with them, are factors which instill doubt. No sooner has one become convinced that the principles of good and evil cannot be delegated to different powers, than Satan makes an entry on the stage of theology (compare 1 Chron. 21 to 2 Samuel 24 and the narrative frame of the Book of Job). No sooner is the confession of the one and only God clearly formulated, when the ONE receives company: in the Book of Daniel it is one called "the Son of Man," in wisdom literature it is "wisdom," the hosts of angels, and other intermediary beings (in Judaism there is, among others, the Shechinah). With its doctrine of the Trinity, Christianity looked for other ways to lessen the problematic of a purely monotheistic symbol system. The veneration of saints and Marian piety are both theologically incongruous with the system; and yet, they always manifest in the praxis of religion the very needs of people to which monotheistic religion could not respond.

What price did Israelite women pay for the worship of YHWH being turned into a monotheistic symbol system? Since this question was addressed throughout in the diachronic sections above, only a few preliminary results are to be cited now.

From the Middle Bronze Age onward (the first half of the second millennium B.C.E.), goddess worship is widely practiced in Palestine. The Goddess is associated with the cult of trees and branches, as well as with goatlike animals. As an erotic and friendly deity who was close to the people, she was said to be responsible for the growth and fruitfulness of the plant and animal world, as well as of human beings. Her partner was probably a combative, martial weather-god. The Late Bronze Age (second half of the second millennium B.C.E.), with its potential for aggressivity and its predominantly male deities, witnesses the beginning of the eradication of the marks of the Goddess. She is portrayed more and more frequently in terms of her characteristics and no longer in her gynecomorphos figure. This substitutionary tendency continues in Israelite times. The same process may be seen in biblical texts and extrabiblical sources. The goddesses' names are not often mentioned in writing. In the whole of the ancient Near East, the epiphanies of the deities were of primary importance (e.g., the tree-goddess, the martial and the erotic goddess) and not so much their names (the Egyptian tree-goddess may be called Nut, Hathor, or Isis). The Bible mentions Ashtoreth (1 Sam. 31:10; 1 Kings 11:5), Anath (Judg. 3:31; 5:6 in the personal name of Shamgar of Beth-Anath; Josh. 15:59; 19:38; 21:18; and Judg. 1:33 as part of the name of a town), and Ashera (later known as the "Queen of Heaven"). Far more important, however, were the so-called Asherah, the tall and mighty trees (in Hebrew *'elah* means tall tree and goddess) and the groves. As inscriptions from Kuntillet Adshrud and Kirbet el-Kom show, the *asherim* (wooden poles representing the Goddess) were integrated for a time into the cult of YHWH purely as representations of divine blessings; but the cult of the Goddess initially associated with them revived again and again. It had been practiced by both men and women, addressing particularly the needs of women and offering them greater participation in worship. (On Asherah, see inter alia the discussion by Braulik and Wacker in Wacker and Zenger, eds., *Der eine Gott und die Göttin;* the status of current research is summarized in Schroer, 1994.)

The profile of the God who was worshiped in the temple in Jerusalem had come about through the fusion of a combative, martial god of storms and mountains with the sun-god who had originally been worshiped in that temple (Schroer 1996: "Der israelitische Monotheismus"). The attempts to integrate aspects of the Goddess into this image of YHWH met with little success, yet her motherliness could be integrated most readily (see 6.7.2 and Schroer 1995). In times of heightened political uncertainty, Israelite people readily reverted to cults that were rooted in the country and which promised fertility, peace, bread, and blessedness. Not even the royal household could resist the cults' attraction. When Israelite people offered their sacrifice to the Goddess, it is not likely that all of them were intent on abandoning altogether the worship of YHWH.

This conflict lasted for centuries and was brought to a close only with the Exile. Those who returned from Babylon had dealt with the question of where the guilt for the Exile lay: the worship of the Goddess was above all the reason for the collapse of Israel. To a large extent, they and their successors managed to drive the cult of the Goddess out of Judah within one century and to eradicate the memory of it. It was no coincidence that the extradition of the Goddess took place in conjunction with misogynist and xenophobic legislations forbidding mixed marriages. All subsequent endeavors to integrate the Goddess at least into the language of theology (Wisdom) occurred within a system of monotheism.

It would be naive to believe that a strong cult of the Goddess always coincided with a strong position for women in the corresponding culture. The study of religion can cite examples of the opposite. The most important cult of the Goddess practiced in the world today is the cult of Maha Diva in India; its existence tells nothing about the position of women in Indian society, even though women have a strong position in that cult. When considering the Israelite period, we must keep in mind that men also worshiped the Goddess and that all of these cults existed in a patriarchal society. It would be wrong as well to assume that goddesses could not embody dimensions of aggression, war, and other perilous aspects. Nonetheless, the expulsion of the goddesses affected women in Israel in a special way. The expulsion combined with polemics against women, the defamation of their sexuality, and other patriarchal measures against them. It is true that, according to the testimony of biblical writings, there have always been women who could identify themselves with the religion of YHWH; still, this heritage of monotheism is utterly ambiguous for women of today. Within the heritage lives too much that has been dispossessed; it contains too much concrete violence. Collective remembering of such dispossession and suppression could be a road toward healing. But healing cannot advance without decisive paradigm changes in the existing symbol system of Christianity.

Susan Ackerman, *Under Every Green Tree: Popular Religion in Sixth-Century Judah* (Atlanta: Scholars Press, 1992); Helgard Balz-Cochois, *Inanna: Wesensbild und Kult einer unmütterlichen Göttin,* Studien zum Verstehen fremder Religionen 4 (Gütersloh: Gütersloher Verlagshaus Gerd Mohn, 1992); Silvia Schroer, "Die Aschera," 1994 (see 6.6); idem, "Die Göttin auf den Stempelsiegeln aus Palästina," in Othmar Keel, Hildi Keel-Leu, and Silvia Schroer, *Studien zu den Stempelsiegeln aus Palästina,* vol. 2, OBO 88 (Fribourg: Universitätsverlag; Göttingen: Vandenhoeck und Ruprecht, 1989), 89–207; idem, "Die Göttin und der Geier," *ZDPV* 111 (1995): 60–80; idem, "Der israelitische Monotheismus," 1996 (see 5.3.4); idem, "Psalm 65—Zeugnis eines integrativen JHWH-Glaubens?" *UF* 22 (1991): 285–301; idem, *Die Weisheit hat ihr Haus gebaut,* 1996 (see 4.3.2); idem, "Die Zweiggöttin in Israel und Palästina: Von der Mittelbronze IIB-Zeit bis zu Jesus Sirach," in Max Küchler and Christoph Uehlinger, eds., *Jerusalem: Texte—Bilder—Steine,* Festschrift for Hildi and Othmar Keel-Leu, NTOA 6 (Fribourg: Universitätsverlag; Göttingen: Vandenhoeck und Ruprecht, 1987), 201–25; Marie-Theres Wacker and Erich Zenger, eds., *Der eine Gott und die Göttin* (see 4.3.1), 151–82.

6.6.2 The Prohibition of Images and the Recovery of Images of God

Next to knowing how patriarchal monotheism and its hostile implications came into being historically, many Christian women are firmly committed to finding out in their praxis how the one-sided, male speech of God may be exploded. First this requires that a traditional misunderstanding be cleared up. The prohibition given to Israel against images, which in its traditional formulations belongs to the time of the Exile, forbade the veneration of cultic images, an action closely related to the prohibition of foreign cults. It did not forbid *conceptions* of God (Schroer 1996: "Der israelitische Monotheismus"). The Bible is much richer in (primarily anthropomorphous) images of God than the tradition of the church and its impoverished images of God-Father-Omnipotent (Schüngel-Straumann 1996). It would be a real gain were the images of God in the First Testament to come to life again. For here God is also a woman in labor pains, a consoling mother, a lord of the animal world or wisdom in the form of a woman who acts as a teacher, prophetess, builder of houses, counselor, or co-creator of the world. Since these images came into being within a symbol system that was already highly monotheistic, and since the language of personified wisdom was still well known to Christians of the first generation, images like these are readily integrated theologically again today. In addition, it is important to recover these dimensions of goddess worship and of the language of the Goddess that appear indispensable to us. Justice is an essential criterion that helps us not to become trapped in an esoteric consumerism of images of God. In the Bible, Wisdom personified is the advocate of the orders of justice God had ordained (*sedeqah*). If such moorings are abandoned, the resulting danger is the propagation of all too lovely images of the divinity for the well-situated middle class (Schroer 1996: *Die Weisheit hat ihr Haus gebaut*).

Helen Schüngel-Straumann (1992) has investigated the significance of *ruaḥ* in the texts of the Exile. Her studies show that *ruaḥ* was not personified to the same extent as *hokhmah* but, on the other hand, that as the creative life force of God, she was unmistakably a feminine being. This provides an exegetically grounded starting point for the further question as to whether a female third person could be contemplated in the Christian doctrine of the Trinity. Gerlinde Baumann has examined the connections between spirit and wisdom in the Bible, especially in view of this question.

Gerlinde Baumann, "Gottes Geist und Gottes Weisheit," in Hedwig Jahnow et al. (see the first bibliographical list in chap. 4), 138–48; idem, "*Wer mich findet*" (see 5.4.2); idem, "'Zukunft feministischer Spiritualität'" (see 5.4.2); Christl Maier, *Die "fremde Frau,"* 1995 (see 5.4.2);

idem, "Im Vorzimmer," 1996 (see 5.4.2); Silvia Schroer, "Du sollst dir kein Bildnis machen . . . oder: Welche Bilder verbietet das Bilderverbot?" in Gabriele Miller and Franz W. Niehl, eds., *Von Batseba—und andere Geschichten: Biblische Texte spannend ausgelegt* (Munich, 1996), 29–44; idem, *In Israel gab es Bilder,* 1987 (see 5.3.4); idem, *Die Weisheit hat ihr Haus gebaut,* 1996 (see 5.3.2); Helen Schüngel-Straumann, *Denn Gott bin ich, und kein Mann: Gottesbilder im Ersten Testament—feministisch betrachted* (Mainz: Matthias Grünewald Verlag, 1996); idem, *Ruah bewegt die Welt: Gottes schöpferische Lebenskraft in der Krisenzeit des Exils,* SBS 151 (Stuttgart: Verlag Katholisches Bibelwerk, 1992).

6.7 Biblical Foundations for an Anthropology Fair to Women and Creation

For years feminist exegesis has paid great attention to women of and women's stories in the First Testament, as well as to certain questions of Israel's history of women. At the same time, another highly rewarding area of research was left almost totally unattended, at least in the German-speaking world: the so-called biblical anthropology. For that reason, the following seeks to show by means of specific examples the need in this area for a feminist biblical theology.

The starting point of this research interest (Praetorius) is that in the dominant tradition of philosophy and theology in the West, the human condition is identified with the conditions of life pertaining to adult (white, heterosexual) men. This androcentrism renders female life invisible and locates women conceptually at the margins of "general" anthropology. In an androcentric view of the world, women or the feminine are seen only as "the other," that is, identified in terms of the male and subordinated to it. To this gender difference correspond the basic concepts of Western philosophy, in which there is a whole range of juxtapositions that were explicitly or implicitly held to reflect the ranking order of male-female: soul-body, spirit-flesh/matter, reason-desire, mind-emotion, culture-nature, transcendence-immanence, public-private, activity-passivity, acting-suffering, sublimity-beauty, substance-accident, and so forth (Klinger). The conceptual systems of Greek and Western philosophy are rigorously dualistic, so that in this way of thinking there is no third option (*tertium non datur*).

When philosophical-theological anthropology addresses what being human is in terms of being woman, it does so in tracts focused on the creation of the human being and Eve, on the sacrament of marriage, and on the ordination of priests (and why women cannot receive such ordination) (Gössmann). Since Immanuel Kant's lectures on logic, the question "what is the human being?" encompasses the three queries: "What can I know? What must I do? What may I hope for?" In this pattern resides the basic conviction of the Enlightenment, namely that "man" is a being who by "his" reason and knowledge may also reach the understanding of what proper ethical conduct is and thereby moves in faith and hope toward greater horizons. The image of the human being—of women—found in philosophical-theological anthropology is highly prescriptive. Whereas from the outset ethnological anthropology has approached the culturally different images of the human being more descriptively, it has done so without sufficiently analyzing androcentric or Eurocentric standards of value. (See the books by Moore and Rippl on feminist research into and critique of this field.)

The term *biblical anthropology* is somewhat misleading in that there is no systematic anthropology behind the biblical writings. Nonetheless, the foundations of the image of the human being and the world contained in the biblical tradition can, indeed, be ascertained and described (Walter Wolff, Crüsemann et al.). There are several reasons why feminists are interested in these biblical foundations.

1. Semitic languages offer an alternative to categorically dualistic thought and orientations rooted in formal conceptualizations. Semitic thought is stereometric, that is, it operates in terms of parallelisms that seek mutual supplementation rather than delimitation or differentiation. At the center of this way of dealing with reality, characterized by emphatic amassing of concrete aspects, there stand at all times the dynamics, effect, and relation of what is being observed and never outwardness, form, or abstract being. Hebrew language does not know the separation of concrete and abstract. This means that everything concrete points beyond itself in ever new signs, and everything abstract is forever referred back to the concrete. (For example, the word *yad* means the power and might of hand/arm, and might is always depicted in the image of a hand intervening with might.)

2. Important anthropological concepts of the Hebrew language (such as *nefesh, leb*) are hardly congruent in their meaning with the concepts of Western tradition (soul, heart); the tensions that arise here are potentially very creative for a woman-centered anthropology (Schroer and

Staubli). Standard studies on "biblical anthropology" neglect important concepts such as *rehem* (womb) which play a key role in the biblical image of the human being and of God (Trible).

3. There are biblical traditions, especially in the wisdom literature (Job 38–39, Psalm 104), which—other than Genesis 1–11—do not regard the human being as center or crown of the whole creation, but rather as a creature besides which there is also a world of animals with its own right to exist (Schroer). In relation to ecofeminist theology (Halkes, Radford Ruether, and Janowski et al.) the Bible has yet many treasures to reveal. On the whole, the substance of what the Bible has to say about human life is much less triumphalistic than what is evoked by the idea of being in the image of God (Genesis 1; Psalm 8). Above all, human life is seen in its dependencies, needs, and transitoriness. (Christine Forster is preparing a study on the understandings of transitoriness in the Psalms.) When I look at biblical and feminist images of the human being, I see a convergence in certain notions of value, to the degree to which they may be discerned in ethical discussions on so-called overpopulation, prenatal diagnostics, and the like. Two examples from biblical anthropology will be employed to illumine the significance of the preceding.

6.7.1 From Throat to Soul

In the Greek image of the human being the word *soul,* the psyche, is centrally important. It is found in every translation of the Bible. But the Hebrew word which is translated by "soul"—*nefesh*—actually means "throat." When the Israelites spoke of throat, they did not have so much the anatomical form of the larynx in mind as that the throat calls out, croaks, yodels, eagerly inhales air, hungrily and thirstily swallows nourishment and water. This concrete organ of the body was at the same time a symbol for a particular aspect of human life, namely the human being who has needs and desires and who thirsts for life.

> YHWH God formed the human being from the earth of the field
> as a being of dust and blew breath of life into the nostrils, and so
> the human being became a living throat (*nefesh*). (Gen. 2:7)

From their experiences of being strangers in Egypt, the Israelites knew only too well how susceptible people can be, precisely in their dependency and need. That is why there is the repeated admonition:

> Do not oppress the stranger. You know the throat (*nefesh*) of the
> one who is the stranger, for you were strangers yourselves in the
> land of Egypt. (Exod. 23:9)

In the relationship between God and humans, *nefesh*, the power of desiring, of yearning, craving, plays an important role. In the Shema, the prayer offered to God by Jewish women and men to this day, the innermost capacity of a human being to have feelings and to yearn for something is at issue.

> You are to love YHWH, your God, with all your heart, with all your
> *nefesh*, and with all your might. (Deut. 6:5 and elsewhere)

The examples suffice to show how little the Hebrew idea of throat-soul has in common with the Greek and our notion of souls. For in following the pre-Socratics, Plato, Aristotle, and others, we associate soul with something that has eternal being beyond the bodiliness, the audibility, visibility, and tangibility of human existence, whereas *nefesh* is bound from its most basic meaning to an organ of the body. The Septuagint translation of *nefesh* with *psyche* had fateful consequences. For Greek thinkers and, even more, their successors, the soul was a noble, nearly divine entity that was buried in the human body as in a tomb, a prison from which it can liberate itself step by step only by the cleansing process of soul migration. Opposite this more valuable soul there stands the despised body over which the soul must, for that very reason, exercise domination.

It is not only this contempt for the body that our culture has inherited from the Greek philosophers. The current craving of Christians for reincarnation finds its deeper roots in this Greek image of the human being rather than in the fascination with Oriental spirituality. The Greek *psyche* must migrate, whereas the Hebrew *nefesh* cannot do so at all. This is because by nature it finds its demise when breathing halts, upon death. The human being is a *nefesh*, living and hungering for life, as long as she and he lives, but only as long as that.

This biblical understanding takes the bodiliness and needs of human life just as seriously as the "physical" or "spiritual" dimension. It does not set them apart. Our body is a temple of God, as Paul formulated it from his Semitic tradition (1 Cor. 3:16f. and 6:19), that is to say, the body is a place of divine revelation and worship and, therefore, holy.

6.7.2 The Womb and Compassion

Biblical thought locates different feelings in the different organs of the belly. In Hebrew, there is a group of words that goes back to the same root as the Arabic *rahman* or *rahmat,* "mercy." *Raḥam* in Hebrew means "to have mercy," *raḥamîm* means "compassion" or "pity." In all of these words there is *reḥem,* the word for the female, the mother's womb, the uterus. Next to heart, *reḥem* is the most frequently mentioned inner organ in the First Testament. But even though this concept occupies so central a place in the biblical image of the human being, Hans Walter Wolff, for example, has completely ignored it. The woman's womb, the uterus, belongs to God according to the imagination and faith of the Israelites. God has not only created it but also has the power to seal or open it. In Jer. 1:5 YHWH says,

> before I formed you in your mother's womb, I have known you, and before you came forth from your mother's body I consecrated you.

For those who pray the Psalms, this mystery-filled creation of humans in the mother's body is a miracle that evokes awe and gratitude (Ps. 139:15ff.). Ultimately it is God who to their mind, like a midwife, receives the human being at birth from the mother's womb (Ps. 22:10f.). The fruitful womb and the milk-giving breasts of the woman were an image of blessing in Israel (Gen. 49:25). Such a blessing was not the work of human hands but could only be received from God's hands as a gift. Small figurines of goddesses with full breasts were put into the graves of the dead in order to provide a final blessing for them. During times when people were laid to rest on stone benches, the head of the deceased was laid into a large, omega-shaped, embossed symbol that may well have represented the uterus. Thus, at the end of life, a human being returns to the safety of the womb of the earth (Job 1:21a).

Reḥem, the womb, is also the seat of powerful emotion. The First Book of Kings recounts the well-known story of the two sex-trade workers who live together, each giving birth to a child at the same time. One suffocates her child while she is asleep. When she finds out, she switches the living and the dead child. The real mother seeks justice at the royal court. It is a difficult case since there are no witnesses, but King Solomon renders a wise judgment. Seeing that both women claim the child as their own, he orders that the living child be cut in half with a sword. The different reaction of the two women to this judgment reveals the truth (1 Kings 3:26).

> The woman, whose was the living child, spoke to the king, her compassion (*raḥamîm*) having been aroused because of her son, "My Lord, give her the living child, do not kill him!" But the other one said: "Let him be neither mine nor yours; cut him in two."

Raḥamîm is here the love of the mother that is ready to let justice go. Compassion boils in the womb of this mother, pity for a living being. *Raḥamîm*, this capacity for empathy, to feel for another, to enter into another's situation, is something that belongs in a special way to women. However, men may also be overcome by *raḥamîm*—Joseph, for example, when for the first time he sets eyes on his brother Benjamin and is so deeply moved that he cannot hold back tears (Gen. 43:30).

How much more remarkable than the application of an emotion so specific to women to the emotional life of man is that the God of Israel is again and again overcome by *raḥamîm*, by powerful impulses of compassion and mercy. The stirring of these emotions in God is associated not only with motherliness but also with fatherliness. But the Israelites never forgot where this metaphor, this image language of God's *raḥamîm*, came from (Isa. 49:15). God's demeanor toward Israel, this obstinate and yet beloved people, is compared to that of a mother toward her child. Often different souls in the breast of YHWH are in conflict. Wrath and the sense of justice urge God to punish Israel. But then compassion flares up in the belly of YHWH and the people are spared yet again. This image—like conceptions of God's motherly feelings—has been developed the furthest in the Book of Hosea. In Hosea 11, YHWH speaks of herself as the mother of the child Israel, bringing up the baby and now being prevented by her motherly womb from expelling the son (Schüngel-Straumann: "Gott als Mutter in Hosea 11"). What maintains the perduring relation of God with Israel and gives it solidity, according to Hosea, are not typically male but much more the motherly properties of YHWH, who is God and not a man. If mercy and justice conflict, Israel's God gives precedence to mercy. Even the oldest version of the biblical narrative of the flood attributes the salvation of humankind to the fact that YHWH is suddenly overcome with pity for the creatures who, a moment ago, were to be utterly destroyed. God's vow never again to destroy humankind arises from the same emotions that, in the even older Near Eastern precursors of the story of the flood, overcome the mother-goddesses when they have to witness how their human children perish (Keel 1989, 89–92; Schüngel-Straumann 1991). In innumerable phrases, the whole First Testament reminds us that the God of Israel is a God of compassion and mercy (Ps. 116:5)

Beginning with the womb, the seat of life and of compassion, we therefore arrive at a biblical image of God (worked out in detail by Trible). According to the first account of creation, man and woman are in God's image; it is really only consistent when we say that a woman's organ reveals much not only about the biblical image of being but also about God's being. But above all, the core symbolism of a woman's organ reveals a counterargument against the tabooing of menstruation that is widespread still today (to which other biblical traditions did much to contribute) and against the functionalizing of the uterus by new technologies.

Literature on philosophical-theological anthropology:

Elisabeth Gössmann, "Anthropology," in *WbfTh*, 16–22; Cornelia Klinger, "Was ist und zu welchem Ende betreibt man feministische Philosophie?" in Lynn Blattmann et al., eds., *Feministische Perspektiven in der Wissenschaft*, Zürcher Hochschulforum 21 (Zurich, 1993), 7–22; Ina Praetorius, "Androzentrismus," in *WbfTh*, 14–15; idem, *Anthropologie und Frauenbild in der deutschsprachigen protestantischen Ethik seit 1949* (Gütersloh: Gütersloher Verlagshaus Gerd Mohn, 1993).

Literature on ethnological anthropology:

Henrietta L. Moore, *Feminism and Anthropology* (Cambridge: Polity Press, 1988); Donate Pahnke, "Feministische Aspekte einer religionswissenschaftlichen Anthropologie," in Donate Pahnke, ed., *Blickwechsel: Frauen in Religion und Wissenschaft* (Marburg: Diagonal Verlag, 1993), 13–41; Gabriele Rippl, ed., *Unbeschreiblich weiblich: Texte zur feministischen Anthropologie* (Frankfurt: Fischer Verlag, 1993).

Literature on biblical anthropology:

Thorleif Bomann, *Das hebräische Denken im Vergleich mit dem griechischen* (Göttingen: Vandenhoeck und Ruprecht, 1952); Frank Crüsemann, Christof Hardmeier, and Rainer Kessler, eds., *Was ist der Mensch? Beiträge zur Anthropologie des Alten Testaments. H. W. Wolff zum 80. Geburtstag* (Munich: Chr. Kaiser Verlag, 1992); Christine Forster, "Vergänglichkeitsvorstellungen in den Psalmen" (working title of her dissertation at the Protestant Faculty of Theology, University of Zurich); Jutta Hausmann, *Studien zum Menschenbild der älteren Weisheit (Spr10ff)*, FzAT 7 (Tübingen: Mohr und Siebeck, 1995); Othmar Keel, "Jahwe in der Rolle der Muttergottheit," *Orientierung* 53 (1989): 89–92; Helen Schüngel-Straumann, "Gott als Mutter in Hosea 11," *ThQ* 166 (1986): 119–134; idem, "Weibliche Dimensionen in mesopotamischen und alttestamentlichen Schöpfungsaussagen und ihre feministische Kritik," in Marie-Theres Wacker and Erich Zenger, eds., *Der eine Gott und die Göttin*, 1991 (see 4.3.1), 49–81; Silvia Schroer and Thomas Staubli, *Das biblische Menschenbild* (working title) (forthcoming); Phyllis Trible, *God and the Rhetoric of Sexuality* (see 6.4); Hans Walter Wolff, *Anthropology of the Old Testament* (Philadelphia: Fortress Press, 1974).

Literature in relation to ecology:

Evelyn Fox Keller, *Reflections on Gender and Science* (New Haven: Yale University Press, 1985); Catharina Halkes, *Das Antlitz der Erde erneuern: Mensch, Kultur, Schöpfung* (Gütersloh: Gütersloher Verlagshaus Gerd Mohn, 1990); Bernd Janowski, Ute Neumann-Gorsolke, and Uwe Glessmer, eds., *Gefährten und Feinde des Menschen: Das Tier in der Lebenswelt des alten Israel* (Neukirchen-Vluyn: Neukirchener Verlag, 1993); Rosemary Radford Ruether, *Gaia and God: An Ecofeminist Theology of Earth Healing* (San Francisco: Harper and Row, 1992); Silvia Schroer, "Die Eselin sah den Engel JHWHs: Eine biblische Theologie der Tiere—für Menschen," in Dorothee Sölle, ed., *Für Gerechtigkeit streiten* (see 5.3.4), 83–87; Dorothee Sölle and Shirley Cloyes, *To Work and to Love* (Philadelphia: Fortress Press 1984).

Part Three

TOWARD A FEMINIST RECONSTRUCTION OF THE HISTORY OF EARLY CHRISTIANITY

Luise Schottroff

Chapter Seven

The New Testament as Source of Women's History

In what follows, I want to examine the New Testament concerning the history of women and to do so from the position of feminists. I have pragmatic grounds for limiting myself to the New Testament as my primary resource. First, from the perspective of feminism, the creation of the New Testament is an act of patriarchal domination. Second, in terms of their historical and often theological significance, noncanonical writings have the same claim to our attention as the New Testament. I restrict myself to the New Testament; in connection with noncanonical early Christian literature, I refer to publications already available and to existing research projects. Nor do I myself make a systematic examination of non-Christian sources, even though the project of a history of women in early Christianity needs the study of such sources. Only as the task of this chapter requires it do I draw on sources from outside the New Testament (Christian as well as non-Christian).

After some reflection on method (7.1), I shall address selected aspects of the history of women to which the New Testament gives witness (7.2).

Ruth Albrecht, *Das Leben der heiligen Makrina auf dem Hintergrund der Thekla-Traditionen* (Göttingen: Vandenhoeck und Ruprecht, 1986); Virginia Burrus, *Chastity as Autonomy: Women in the Stories of Apocryphal Acts* (Lewiston, N.Y., and Queenstown, Ontario: Edwin Mellen Press, 1987); Stevan L. Davies, *The Revolt of the Widows: The Social World of the Apocryphal Acts* (Carbondale, Ill., and London: Southern Illinois University Press, 1980); Anne Jensen, *Gottes selbstbewusste Töchter: Frauenemanzipation im frühen Christentum* (Freiburg, Basel,

179

and Vienna: Herder, 1992); Ross S. Kraemer, "Bibliography: Women in the Religions of the Graeco-Roman World," *Religious Studies Review* 9 (1983): 127–39; idem, *Her Share of the Blessings: Women's Religions among Pagans, Jews, and Christians in the Greco-Roman World* (New York and Oxford: Oxford University Press, 1992); idem, *Maenads, Martyrs, Matrons, Monastics: A Sourcebook on Women's Religions in the Greco-Roman World* (Philadelphia: Fortress Press, 1988); Bärbel Mayer-Schartel, *Das Frauenbild des Josephus: Eine sozialgeschichtliche und kulturanthropologische Untersuchung* (Stuttgart: Verlag W. Kohlhammer, 1995); Elaine Pagels, *The Gnostic Gospels* (New York: Random House, 1979); Griet Petersen-Szemeredy, *Zwischen Weltstadt und Wüste: Römische Asketinnen in der Spätantike* (Göttingen: Vandenhoeck und Ruprecht, 1993); Sarah B. Pomeroy, *Goddesses, Whores, Wives, and Slaves: Women in Classical Antiquity* (New York: Schocken Books, 1975); Carola Reinsberg, *Ehe, Hetärentum und Knabenliebe im antiken Griechenland* (Munich: C. H. Beck, 1989).

7.1 "Women Are Searching for Their History"

Searching for the history of women behind the writings of early Christianity necessitates asking what such historical study is seeking to accomplish.

Traditional or dominant historiography of early Christianity operates in terms of an androcentric conception of how history is to be written. In her seminal article of 1983, what Gisela Bock had to say about the traditional, androcentric science of history in general applies in particular to that conception. "Women are not merely forgotten; the feminine is understood as a special instance of the male species of 'mankind,' whereas the history of men is defined as normative history" (27). And this androcentric conception of how history is to be written claims universality for itself. As a result of recent women's studies and feminist historical scholarship, it has become quite clear that this universality is not incomplete but wrong (see Bock 1987). For example, in the androcentric histories of early Christianity, Prisca is briefly mentioned as Aquila's marriage partner, but the history of the first Christian women comes nowhere into view. Women and children remain invisible or are appendages of men.

Recent feminist historical scholarship has subjected androcentric historiography to a fundamental critique. To produce a complementary
and compensatory women's historiography next to the androcentric
one, or to lift up the forgotten contribution of women to history in general, is not enough. A depiction of Prisca as a significant woman in the
male world of history in general obscures the history of Christian
women. It leaves untouched androcentric historiography's false claim to
universality. Nonetheless, feminist writing of history can build on studies, such as Harnack's study of Prisca, that are governed by this androcentric conception. Feminist writing of history has to break through the
silence of androcentric sources and their androcentric interpretation.
Carla Ricci calls this process "the exegesis of silence."

Feminist historical scholarship demands that gender must take its place
next to the category of class as a social category at the center of historical research.

> Not only is the historiographical hierarchy of relevance turned up-
> side down, the dominant social hierarchy of value of the commu-
> nity under study (or one's own) is also subjected to examination.
> What women do, what they are supposed to do, and what they did
> is seen and assessed historiographically and socially in a new light.
> In addition, there is the basic assumption that sexual differentia-
> tion as well as sexual hierarchy are sociopolitical-cultural produc-
> tions that are not to be traced back to biological determinism or
> other (existential, transcendent) essences beyond historical pro-
> cesses. (Bock, 38)

This makes it necessary to ascertain anew, for every historical situation,
the form in which patriarchy manifests itself therein. Hence, one needs
to avoid working with a concept that, like oppression of women, economic exploitation, femininity, and so forth, transcends history.

New Testament scholarship has made successful use of a broad-based
and inclusive understanding of *patriarchy;* Elisabeth Schüssler Fiorenza
was the first to do so. Such an understanding is attentive to the differentiated interconnection between the sexist oppression of women and children. It attends as well to the different kind of oppression of men perpetrated by the elites on the one hand, and by economic exploitation,
militarism, ethnocentrism, and other means of domination on the other.
This understanding of patriarchy requires that concrete situations of relationships are established so that the interconnections may be discerned. For example, life without marriage means something fundamen-

tally different for a woman than for a man. For a woman from the poverty-stricken majority of the population, it is hardly possible to live a life without marriage if she is not economically incorporated into a mutually supportive group of women, or women and men. This is so even though she, like many other women, may long for such a life as her liberation from the risks to which pregnancy and birth expose her.

An encompassing conception of patriarchy also calls for *an examination of the limitations of one's perspective.* In the German context this means, above all, to examine critically the anti-Judaism, Eurocentrism, and other postures of domination found in existing histories of early Christianity and to enter into dialogue with feminist historians from other contexts, such as Latin America, and so forth.

According to Bock, it is useful "to look for women whose lives and work differ not only from the existing norm but also from the reality of the majority of women. Women who love women, and women in the sex trade are important examples here" (50). It is in such women that the shape of *the oppression of women and the resistance by women* first comes into view. No effort is spared to make it easy for women who accommodate themselves to the norms of patriarchy not to discover their oppression and to look on resistance as something unwomanly. The more intensively women break down patriarchal norms, the more clearly they and others are able to see the reality of oppression and the possibility of resistance. This insight of feminist historical scholarship is of extraordinary theological significance. In Jewish and early Christian tradition, the theological conception of justice is oriented by the lives of "the least" of the people, that is, by those among whom the justice that God desires must take its beginning (see Matt. 21:31f.; Luke 7:36-50).

Having a broadly inclusive understanding of patriarchy does not relieve one of the obligation to ascertain what patriarchy looks like concretely in specific historical situations. Feminist historical scholarship understands itself to be an open process that intentionally does not operate in terms of fixed concepts. This has led to astonishing and often surprising discoveries, including that patriarchy, in all its changing manifestations, could never really impose itself fully. "Putting women at the center in the context of a male-dominated society does not mean . . . that in place of a men-centered landscape there is now to be a women-centered one. The issue is not reverse discrimination . . . , rather, it is to bring the voiceless into speech" (Brooten 1985, 79). On principle, feminist historical scholarship has to keep all aspects of history in view (even those in which women do not appear) and place women at the center of historical reporting. This alone opens the way to seeing *all* of history differently.

With a critique that goes to its very foundations, feminist historical scholarship confronts the claim that androcentric historical science is universal, value-free, and objective. For that claim covers up the actual bias in favor of patriarchal elites and conditions of domination. From the point of view of feminist historical scholarship, it is imperative that one's own way of seeing things be examined and stated, that one's own bias be understood before one reconstructs anything in history.

The bias or partiality of feminist historical scholarship is determined by its rootedness in the women's movement and its toil for liberation in an all-embracing sense. My historical work arises from the analysis of my own experience and that of many other women. (See especially the work of Maria Mies on the concepts of *experience* and *partiality*.) In my context, the well-nigh grotesque inability of patriarchal institutions like the churches or universities to reorient themselves toward a more just society in the One World has historical roots as well. And the resistance of women against the inability to change has historical roots. Every piece of feminist-historical work on the roots of present structures contributes a building block for the future of a life worthy of human beings.

Its all-encompassing claim notwithstanding, the task of historical reconstruction from a feminist perspective has to be seen as piecework. The goal of a comprehensive, general history is very difficult to reach precisely because most sources have an androcentric language and outlook and serve the interests of patriarchal domination. Many an aspect of the history of women and children will remain in obscurity. "Those who acknowledge historical work to be a labor of reconstruction, also signal a new kind of modesty: they can more readily admit to the exploratory nature of their work and more openly discuss the influence of personal interests" (Brooten, 65).

As described here, I understand the historiography of women as *feminist social history*. As already indicated, this term implies that the first question to be asked is: who are "the least" in society? It also means that the everyday conditions of women of the poverty-stricken majority of the population must be established. I understand social history to be an encompassing concept which researches every aspect of life, including religion. Social historiography, therefore, includes the history of religion.

Gisela Bock, "Historische Frauenforschung: Fragestellungen und Perspektiven (1983)," in Karin Hausen, ed., *Frauen suchen ihre Ge-*

schichte, 2d ed. (Munich: C. H. Beck, 1987), 24–62; Bernadette Brooten, "Frühchristliche Frauen und ihr kultureller Kontext: Überlegungen zur Methode historischer Rekonstruktion," in *Einwürfe*, vol. 2, ed. Friedrich-Wilhelm Marquardt et al. (Munich: Chr. Kaiser Verlag, 1985), 62–93; Adolf von Harnack, "Über die beiden Recensionen der Geschichte der Prisca und des Aquila in Act. Apost. 18, 1–12," in *Sitzungsberichte der Königlich-Preussischen Akademie der Wiss. zu Berlin* (1900); Karin Hausen, ed., *Frauen suchen ihre Geschichte;* Annette Kuhn, "Frauengeschichte," in Anneliese Lissner et al., eds., *Frauenlexikon* (Freiburg, Basel, and Vienna: Herder, 1988), 338–46; Ingrid Maisch, *Maria Magdalena: Zwischen Verachtung und Verehrung. Das Bild einer Frau im Spiegel der Jahrhunderte* (Freiburg, Basel, and Vienna: Herder, 1996); Maria Mies, "Methodische Postulate zur Frauenforschung (1978)" and "Frauenforschung oder feministische Forschung?" in *Beiträge zur feministischen Theorie und Praxis*, no. 11 (1984; 4th ed., 1989): 7–25 and 40–60; Carla Ricci, *Mary Magdalene and Many Others: Women Who Followed Jesus* (Minneapolis: Fortress Press, 1994); Elisabeth Schüssler Fiorenza, "Das Schweigen brechen—sichtbar werden," *Concilium* 21 (1985): 387–98.

7.2 "And She Called All Her Friends Together" (Luke 15:9): The Places of Women's Solidarity in the New Testament

The New Testament is an excellent source of women's history. It contains texts that try to lay down rules by which women are to govern their lives but that show, indirectly and unwittingly, how women live and want to live. There are other texts that want to speak explicitly about women but always from the perspective and in the language of androcentrism. And then there are texts that seemingly do not speak of women but from which women's history can be elicited by means of critical questions.

The New Testament shows that in quite diverse contexts there was a common life of women in early Christianity. In antiquity, there may have been cases of an individual woman's isolation in the single-family household, a condition that so often impacts the experience of women today. As a rule, women worked together in common spaces both inside and outside of the larger household. In Tobit 2:11-14 and in Origen's *Contra*

Celsum (III.55) there are references to such places where women performed manual labor together (see W. Schottroff on women's work in the harem). Whether there was a room in the houses set aside for women remains to be seen. In his *De special. legibus* (III.169ff.), Philo calls most emphatically for young women to be restricted in their movements to the women's section of the house, and married women to the whole house. It is doubtful whether this custom was actually followed, seeing that it was an innovation in relation to the First Testament, and given the limited living space available to the majority of the population. The banning of women from the public sphere, which Philo seeks to bring about, was certainly not the rule in early Christianity and in Judaism. Like Philo, the First Epistle of Timothy is upset about women who move about freely in the open (1 Tim. 5:13); we hear about individual women and groups of women in public gatherings, on the streets and in marketplaces, or going on trips, such as the woman philosopher Hipparchia (Diogenes Laertius VI.96ff.) or the Christian apostle Thecla (*The Acts of Thecla*, Schneemelcher).

The view provided by the New Testament of the common life of women represents every area of life: work (Matt. 24:41 par.), women's neighborhood of solidarity (Luke 15:9), life in the streets (1 Tim. 5:13; Luke 8:1-3; Mark 15:40f. par.), in Jewish (Acts 16:13) and Christian (1 Cor. 11:5; 14:34) worship. It is to be assumed that family life in the patriarchal family took its usual course to a large extent in the company of women. Entering the life of discipleship, that is, the life of communities that revered Jesus as the Messiah, extended these companies of women; in the tradition of Jewish companies of women, they were formed into companies of solidarity. Such formations may be seen in the following texts: women gather to read the Torah and to celebrate a Jewish worship like many other Jewish companies of women (Acts 16:13; see Richter Reimer). As missionaries of the gospel of Christ, women go out two by two into the countryside; for example, this appears to be the case for Tryphaena and Tryphosa (Rom. 16:12; see D'Angelo). According to Josephus (*bell. iud.* II.560f.), the women of Damascus, with very few exceptions, voluntarily practice the Jewish religion. When the non-Jewish men of the city want to kill the Jewish population, most likely in the desire to appear supportive of Rome, they have to conceal this plan from their women. What we see here, among other things, is that there existed forms of women's organization. This permitted them, independently of their men, to embrace the Jewish religion and, on their own authority, to present themselves as a political factor. Such organizations of women, which allowed them to offer resistance publicly, must have existed also in Antioch (of Syria, most likely) at the time of Thecla or the *Acts of Thecla*. The women who openly intervene on behalf of Thecla's life (*Acts of Thecla* 27–28, 32, 34–35; see Schneemelcher) were not yet Christians when they mounted that protest. It is not known whether they were Jewish or not.

First Timothy 5:16 and Acts 9:36-43 indicate that women's groups are formed also in order to assist economically weaker women in securing their livelihood. Included in the good works of Tabitha and her deeds of mercy is sewing dresses for a group of widows. However, these "widows" are not recipients of *charity*. On their own authority they are active members of a Christian group (see also Acts 6:1; Schüssler Fiorenza). Acts 9:36 shows explicitly how the practice of solidarity within a group of women is integrated into the Jewish religious praxis. "Tabitha is a Christian woman. She lives her life in Jewish practice. . . . Thus, a Jewish-Christian woman does not have to deny her roots" (Richter Reimer, 89). In Acts 13:50, and very likely also in 17:4, 12, we are told of women's groups being active in the upper classes of Pisidian Antioch or Thessalonica and Beroea. In Acts 13:50 we see them helping the Jewish congregations in chasing Paul and Barnabas out of town; in 17:4, 12, they become adherents of the Christian message. In all these cases, the women are not Jewish by birth but they practice the Jewish religion and go together to the synagogue.

With the help of this material, the New Testament's meager information about the women of Galilee, who followed Jesus on his way from Galilee to Jerusalem, may be supplemented.

Luke 8:2 says that the Galilean women had been healed from illness or demon possession by Jesus or by disciples of Jesus (see Luke 9:2; 10:9). Like the Twelve, they travel with Jesus through the countryside and preach the reign of God; Luke 8:1-2 is to be read this way. As Luke 9:2 and 10:9 indicate, this included the healing of the sick. "The women served [*diakonein*] them [others read: him] according to what was possible for them" (Luke 8:3). Linguistically, this may mean that they supported the men's group around Jesus with financial gifts; but it may also mean, as the study of *ta hyparchonta* in any larger-sized Greek dictionary will show, that the women supported them according to their abilities, according to what was within their power. I want to question the firmly rooted tradition of interpretation according to which the women were affluent, or that Luke believed them to be such. Here are my reasons: (1) Having tied the Greek phrase to financial assets, the reading "according to what was possible for them," though linguistically highly feasible, has never been appropriated, revealing the interpreters' interest in affluent women in the New Testament. This interest may be shown to exist elsewhere (see especially Richter Reimer in relation to Acts). (2) Assuming that Joanna, the marriage partner of one of Herod's stewards, had come from the affluent classes does not demonstrate that the many other women, of whose "serving out of their resources" the text speaks, were also wealthy. (3) In the historical reality of the Jewish people in the first century, the poverty of the majority of the population is unambiguously apparent; that poverty is shown in the Gospels, including Luke's Gospel. Like the description of the Galilean women's discipleship of Jesus in Mark (15:41) and Matthew (27:55), this phrase, "out of their own resources," needs to be read against the background of the praxis of "service" in discipleship and in the Christian communities. These texts constitute a direct attempt to break down the gender-hierarchical division of labor according to which only women and slaves do the work of providing for people (see Mark 10:42-45 par.). In the context of early Christianity, to serve meant the service of proclaiming *and* providing, by men and women, and had an explicitly antihierarchical aspect. That the women served him or them "out of their own resources" is a statement parallel to that of Mark 14:8: "She has done what lay within her power."

Already, this case shows that a feminist reading of the New Testament has to fight for access to the meaning of the texts, against a solidly established tradition of interpretation that sought to place early Christianity into the affluent strata of society and, of course, sees women occupied with providing for others. (That tradition of interpretation reads Mark 15:41 in opposition to Mark 10:42-45.)

The Galilean group of women who are disciples of Jesus clearly belongs to the tradition of Jewish groups of women, or groups of women living their lives in Jewish practice (but not Jewish by birth), to whom we referred earlier. That means that we may presume that this Galilean group of women practiced solidarity within its ranks. It developed a self-awareness that enabled it also to represent the interests of women at the political level and to put forth their ideas about how Christian practice ought to be shaped.

The Galilean group of women and similar women's communities are the historical ground of the uncommon narratives of women told in the Jesus tradition. We hear of women offering resistance, like the hemorrhaging woman and the Syrophoenician woman. We hear of the women in the sex trade whom one finds in both the Baptist's movement (Matt.

21:32) and the Jesus movement (as Matt. 21:31 and Luke 7:36-50 ought to be read). This is why the important theme in feminist theology, of "Jesus and the women," is already raised in this section (and will be addressed again in 9.1).

Because of Luke 8:2, the church's tradition of interpretation has often depicted Mary Magdalene as a woman in the sex trade and identified her with the nameless woman of Luke 7:36-50. It has called her a *former* sex-trade worker who has repented of her life in that line of work. The texts provide no basis for identifying Mary Magdalene as one working in the sex trade and even less for the idea of the repentance of such workers, or of prostitution as *morally* defective. Rather, the texts show that women provide for themselves by means of the sex trade, since that is the only way open to them to survive, and that they look for structures of solidarity in the movements of John the Baptist and Jesus. The question of the relationship of Mary Magdalene and other Galilean women to these sex-trade workers may now be raised in a new way. Was there solidarity in the Jesus movement between women in the sex trade and women not engaged in that trade, and between women sex-trade workers and women who practiced asceticism, as seems to have been the case in the Christian community of Corinth? The answer is yes but requires, above all, that today's moral disqualification of women in the sex trade be overcome, as Renate Kirchhoff has demonstrated. "Women in the sex trade were not excluded as such from society but shared their reputation with the other members of the lower class, that comprised about 90 percent of the population." "Moral judgements about how sex-trade workers used their bodies . . . are too limited in perspective since they fail to take into consideration that sexual contacts (that were far more obvious in the first century c.e. than today) were an element of economic relations and were regarded as such" (Kirchhoff, 65f.). We have to reckon with the presence of women sex-trade workers in the Jesus movement and in all Christian congregations. With a very few individual exceptions, the congregations all recruited their membership from the poverty-stricken majority of the population. This segment is estimated, correctly, it would seem, to have comprised 99 percent of the population (see Alföldy, 124). For sex-trade workers, the sexual asceticism that was an attraction for women (see 7.3) was attainable only when they could integrate themselves into a small community of solidarity in which women, or men and women, could secure for them a livelihood without prostitution.

In this section I have gathered all the information about women's groups that I can discern in the New Testament; I have let them complement one another and have provided information from extra-Christian and noncanonical sources. As far as my method is concerned, this means that in this question I work in terms of relatively homogeneous structures in Judaism and Christianity within the Roman Empire. In questions of Rome's social history, this sort of homogeneity is apparent in many areas of life, including the life of women. When in the literature "the Roman woman" is set over and against "the Jewish woman," it is usually a matter of unreflective juxtaposition of women of the Roman upper class with women of the Jewish (and Christian) lower class. The one aspect of the company of women that I cannot treat in terms of homogeneity is the rigid restriction of women to the home and within it to the women's quarter. Overall, however, the cultural permeation of everyday life by Rome's culture of domination is a relevant factor in every area of Roman rule. For that reason one has to begin from a structural homogeneity even though one must be attentive nonetheless to cultural peculiarities, especially in this context, to those of Jewish existence.

Géza Alföldy, *Römische Sozialgeschichte*, 3d ed. (Wiesbaden: Wissenschaftliche Buchgesellschaft, 1984); Virginia Burrus (see first bibliographical list in this chapter); Kathleen E. Corley, *Private Women— Public Meals* (Peabody, Mass.: Hendrickson Publishers, 1993); Mary Rose D'Angelo, "Women Partners in the New Testament," *JFSR* 6 (1990): 65–86; Renate Kirchhoff, *Die Sünde gegen den eigenen Leib: Studien zu "porne" und "porneia" in 1 Kor 6, 12–20 und dem soziokulturellen Kontext der paulinischen Adressaten* (Göttingen: Vandenhoeck und Ruprecht, 1994); Carla Ricci (see 7.1); Ivoni Richter Reimer, *Women in the Acts of the Apostles: A Feminist Liberation Perspective* (Minneapolis: Fortress Press, 1995); Wilhelm Schneemelcher, ed., *New Testament Apocrypha*, vol. 2 (Louisville: Westminster/John Knox Press, 1991), 239ff.; Luise Schottroff, *Befreiungserfahrungen: Studien zur Sozialgeschichte des Neuen Testaments* (Munich: Chr. Kaiser Verlag, 1990), esp. 291ff. and 310ff. (see idem, *Let the Oppressed Go Free*, 1993, 60–79 and 138–57); idem, "DienerInnen der Heiligen: Der Diakonat der Frauen im Neuen Testament," in Gerhard K. Schäfer and Theodor Strohm, eds., *Diakonie—biblische Grundlagen und Orientierungen*, 2d ed. (Heidelberg: Heidelberger Verlagsanstalt, 1994),

222–42; Willy Schottroff, "Der Zugriff des Königs auf die Töchter: Zur Fronarbeit von Frauen im alten Israel," *EvTh* 49 (1989): 268–85; Elisabeth Schüssler Fiorenza, *In Memory of Her: A Feminist Theological Reconstruction of Christian Origins* (New York: Crossroad, 1983).

7.3 "Holy in Body and Spirit" (1 Cor. 7:34): The Forms of Women's Lives in Early Christianity

Patriarchal law and consciousness define women in terms of who owns their sexuality. The father is the master of the virgin, the husband the master of the wife. In this system, the widow is "master"-less, that is, free (see Rom. 7:2; 1 Cor. 7:39; see also Wegner on the law of the Mishnah). The divorced and the unmarried woman, the woman freed of the *patria potestas*, is also free because no man has power of disposition over her sexuality. (See Wegner in relation to the Mishnah, and Kaser, sec. 14.III and 60.IV, in relation to Roman law.) In order to understand the history of women in early Christianity, it is necessary to consider the social and economic as well as the legal and ideological dimensions of patriarchal conditions. The emancipated, unmarried woman is an obvious fact in that system but the "normal" thing for her is to get married— before puberty—and to give birth to sons as soon as physically possible. The social pressure on women to bear sons is the basic theme of biblical traditions concerning barren women. The social pressure that forces women into marriage becomes most apparent in the sources, especially whenever women refuse to marry—a basic theme of the Christian Acts of the Apostles. In section 7.4, I shall speak about materials that deal with the options for autonomous women to earn a living.

Even a cursory look at the New Testament shows that it speaks much more often of what in patriarchy is viewed as "abnormal," namely the autonomous women, than of wives and virgins. The personal identifiers of women are difficult to assess because they reflect not only kinship-relations (daughter of . . . , e.g., Luke 2:36) but also familiarity within the community ("mother of the sons of Zebedee," Matt. 20:20, instead of "the wife of Zebedee"). With the exception of Mary and Martha (Luke 10:38f.; John 11:1), the name added to assist in identifying a woman is a man's name (that of husband, son, father, brother). Identifying a woman in terms of her relationship to a man is normal for the applicable biblical and extrabiblical materials (see Köhler; Bauckham, 235f.). The number of women to whose name no identifying relationship to a man has been added is actually astounding: Mary Magdalene (Mark 15:40 and elsewhere), Salome (Mark 15:40, 16:1), Tabitha (Acts 9:36), Lydia (Acts 16:14), Mary (Rom. 16:6), Tryphaena and Tryphosa (Rom. 16:12), Persis (Rom. 16:12), Chloe (1 Cor. 1:11), Euodia and Syntyche (Phil.. 4:2), "Jezebel" (most likely an invective rather than a name, Rev. 2:20), Phoebe (Rom. 16:1), Apphia (Philemon 2). There are women who are neither named nor identified in terms of a relationship to a man; they are the Syrophoenician woman (Mark 7:26, clearly a single mother), the hemorrhaging woman (Mark 5:25), the bent-over woman (Luke 13:11), the "sinful woman" (Luke 7:36), the woman who anoints Jesus (Mark 14:3), and the Samaritan woman (John 4:9, 18).

There are a number of personally identifiable women marriage partners (with and without names). They are: Elizabeth (Luke 1:5), Mary (Luke 1:27 and elsewhere), the marriage partner of Peter (1 Cor. 9:5), Sapphira (Acts 5:1), Prisca (Acts 18:2 and elsewhere), Junia (Rom. 16:7, although it does not say there that she is a marriage partner), Julia (Rom. 16:15; she, too, may not be a marriage partner), the wife of Zebedee (Matt. 20:20 and elsewhere). The number of women that are named without any reference to their relationship to a man is greater than the number of identifiable wives (20 to 8). It may be difficult to prove in individual cases whether a woman is unmarried or divorced when there is no reference to a relationship to a man. At times it may be a woman whose marriage partner is not a Christian or who for unknown reasons is not mentioned. But the overall evidence is telling: in early Christianity, an important role is played by women who are not to be defined in terms of men. As a rule, they are not to be regarded as unmarried or divorced.

This finding is confirmed by the great number of widows. The word *chera* refers, as a rule, to the marriage partner of a deceased husband, although it may refer in a more general sense to women who are not part of any patriarchal relationship of control. We read about individual widows and of groups of them (Acts 6:1, 9:39, 41; see the rules governing widows in 1 Corinthians 7 and 1 Timothy 5). Undoubtedly, a number of women who are referred to as "the mother of . . ." have to be counted among widows. This survey challenges the image formed by the patriarchal heads (of then and now), namely, that the "normal situation" of a woman, be it in early Christianity or in societies in general of that time, was to be married, to be cared for in a marriage, and to be raising children.

Romans 16 provides an additional opportunity to test this finding. Here Paul speaks of women on account of their work and importance for the community and not because of the status their life had acquired. Without intending to do so, the chapter gives us the following information about the status of women in early Christianity: there are five women without a relationship to a man, three women who have a marriage partner (if one counts Junia and Julia among them), and two women identified as a man's mother or sister, whom one can hardly count as married women. First Corinthians 7 also shows that measured by the norms of patriarchy, unmarried, divorced, and widowed women play an unusually important role.

Moreover, the large number of widows in the New Testament must be regarded as unusual in view of the social reality. As far as the life expectancy of women and men is concerned, all we have are "demographic speculations" (Pomeroy, 68f.); they indicate 45 years for men and 36.2 years for women. Then there is the significant surplus of men; the reason for this difference in numbers between men and women is that female infants were often killed and that a large number of mothers lost their lives during pregnancy or childbirth. It was much more likely that in the course of his life a man consecutively married several quite young women, each after the death of the former wife, than that a woman outlived her marriage partner. The role of widows in the New Testament is noticeably important and, obviously, numerically significant. Given the social reality, their role represents something quite specific. The word *widow* ought not be automatically associated with "elderly woman," for there are references to young widows (1 Tim. 5:11). Also, the notion of passive dependency in terms of needing care is not relevant for understanding this phenomenon. Even though they may be poor, widows are members of the community, caring for it and giving it shape.

The history of Christian interpretation of the New Testament is an additional indicator of the unusual picture of the status of women in that work. The interpreters took their patriarchal consciousness for granted; as a rule, they declared after the fact that the women in the New Testament who were not in a relationship with a man were married or widowed. It appeared to the interpreters that the status of an unmarried or divorced woman, living alone, was not something appropriate to the New Testament or the Christian church (e.g., Tabitha or Apphia).

The reasons for the great attraction of early Christianity for women, particularly for women who were not married or did not want to live in a marriage, are the early church's preaching and practice of abstinence and the development of nonhierarchical forms of community.

Preaching and practicing abstinence took place not only in Hellenistic Corinth but also in the Jesus movement of Jewish Palestine. The repudiation of a second marriage after a divorce, found at every level of the Synoptic tradition (Mark 10:10-12 par.), supports this clearly, as does the negative stance toward sexuality and the patriarchal family in certain parts of that tradition (Matt. 24:37-44 par.; Mark 12:18-27 par.; and others). In addition to sexually ascetic ways of life, there was also the integration of married couples into the community (see the list of women marriage partners above) and the vision of great bliss found in the intimate companionship of a heterosexual marriage (Mark 10:1-10 par.). Today, the vision of that text (see 10.5) needs to be related also to same-sex companionships; the history of its suppressive interpretation has to be subjected to criticism. There are no indications at all that married women are played off against autonomous women, or vice versa, whereas in Luke 10:38-42, it is the woman who wants to learn who is played off against the housewife.

Some texts show that pressure is exerted on women in relation to how they want to lead their lives. Married women, who within their marriages abstain from sexual relations, are prevailed on by Paul to give up their abstinence in order to prevent extramarital *porneia* with women in the sex trade (1 Cor. 7:1-7; see Wire). For widows who want to marry again, obstacles are erected (1 Tim. 5:11; in rudimentary form also 1 Cor. 7:40). Widows who do not want to enter another marriage are urged to do so (1 Tim. 5:14). Christian women in marriages, who wish to separate from their non-Christian partners, are pressured to stay in their marriages (see 1 Cor. 7:15 where Paul presupposes this counsel while not favoring the use of pressure; see Justin Martyr, *Second Apology* 2). In the pressure on women to embrace lifestyles other than the ones they have chosen, disparate social practices and interests become apparent. For one, there is the interest in keeping women under control and in binding them firmly into a strictly patriarchal marriage (1 Timothy); then there is the practice of abstinence that Paul judges to be the better way, compared to which marriage is a solution of necessity. This internal contradiction within the praxis of early Christianity, which at the same time also mirrors the disparate situation of women who resist being suppressed, cannot be resolved. Neither a "before-and-after schema" (first the liberating praxis and then the suppression), nor the attributing of suppression and liberation to different groups (e.g., Paul, the oppressor, versus the liberating praxis of the Corinthian community), will work here. These questions are to be explicitly addressed in sections 8.1 and 8.4.

The diverse Christian "acts of apostles" give ample evidence that women were attracted to ways of life that called for sexual abstinence. In this context a tract by Cyprian is of interest. In his misogynist composition of 249 C.E., *De habitu virginium,* he puts into words what could otherwise only be surmised. "Virgins"—that is, women who abstain from sexual relations—are "the flower of the ecclesiastical seed," they are the "more illustrious portion of Christ's flock" (3). They obviously comprise the decisive element of the church's attraction. Cyprian is not at all worried that a sexually abstinent way of life would mean that no more children were to be born. There are enough human beings as it is. ("Now, when the world is filled and the earth supplied, they who can receive continence, living after the manner of eunuchs, are made eunuchs unto the kingdom" [23].) From the perspective of women, this route offers great advantages, as Cyprian's critical undertone itself notes: "You do not fear the sorrows and groans of women. You have no fear of child-bearing; nor is your husband lord over you; but your Lord and Head is Christ, after the likeness and in the place of the man" (22). This text further shows that the "virgins" lead a merry life and not one that is unadorned and secluded, as the bishop would have it. These women go to feasts, to the baths, they speak out in public, and put on attractive dresses. They just do not fit into the patriarchal system and play the role which, in Cyprian's view, that system prescribes for an unmarried woman. But he cannot deny that they live in sexual abstinence. He even concedes that the resurrection has already begun for them. "That which we shall be, you have already begun to be. You possess already in this world the glory of the resurrection. You pass through the world without the contagion of the world" (22). Paul expresses the same ideas as follows: "[T]he unmarried woman and virgin is anxious about the affairs of the Lord so that she may be holy in body and spirit" (1 Cor. 7:34). The *egkrateia,* the practice of abstinence of women that Paul, and two hundred years later, Cyprian, bring to our attention was not something dualistically hostile to the body. The body was not understood as a prison (as it was in dualistic thought) but as a place of sanctification. And this sanctification was not interpreted individualistically; rather, it was lived out as the sanctification of bodies *in relationships* one with another. For women, this presupposed that the power of patriarchy to dispose over their sexuality, as sketched out above, had come to an end.

No longer did any man have the power to rule over a woman's body. Even in existing marriages women fought so that the male marriage partner no longer had power over their bodies (1 Cor. 7:4; Wire). The nonhierarchical organization of common life in the communities was the second reason why women were attracted to early Christianity. Every one of the experiments of communal living brought advantages to women and disadvantages to men. Men had to relinquish privileges, for example, the free man's privilege not to do any work in the house or to provide for the meals, or the privilege to have disposition over a woman (or the woman marriage partner). Women also derived greater benefit than men from the organization of economic and social justice in the wider church, within the individual congregation, and even with the companionships that were part of the congregation (see 7.2). The benefit was greater for women, because survival in the world of poverty was much more difficult for them than for men. I shall cite only a few texts in which such experiments of solidarity are apparent: Mark 10:42-45 par.; John 13; Acts 2:42-47; 1 Cor. 12. In addition, I refer to the word *koinonia*/community as a word that signals such forms of organization of solidarity. The notion of the *familia dei* (Mark 3:31-34) and the use of the terms *brother* and *sister* point to nonhierarchical relationships, as is made plain again and again, for example, in Matt. 23:9: "Call no one on earth 'father.'" Historically it is entirely appropriate to regard the communities of early Christianity as particularly places of women and to designate the vision that was lived out in them with the albeit ambiguous words *women church*. It was the vision of a community of women and men worthy of this name, because it had made the first steps at least to break with the domination of men over women and with many other things patriarchy takes for granted.

The methodological procedure of this section is based in the homogeneity of the legality, consciousness, and practice of patriarchal power over women throughout the Roman Empire and the subjugated cultures within it, such as the Jewish culture. It is undoubtedly necessary in every individual case to be attentive to differences in law (e.g., laws governing dowry or divorce) or in the concrete praxis of women's oppression. Still, the basic structures are uniform. For an assessment of the New Testament as a source of women's history, this means that one should not adhere to that tradition of scholarship that endeavors to differentiate between individual writings and layers of tradition (i.e., Matthew has a different theology than Mark, Mark a different one than the pre-Markan tradition, and so on). The reason for not following such a tradition is that it separates what historically belongs together. Differences need to be attended to here as well, but in doing so one should not lose sight of the homogeneity of the early Christian movement.

Richard Bauckham, "Mary of Clopas (John 19:25)," in George J. Brooke, ed., *Women in the Biblical Traditions*, Studies in Women and Religion 31 (Lewiston, N.Y.: Edwin Mellen Press, 1992), 231–55; Cyprian, *De habitu virginum*, in *The Ante-Nicene Fathers*, vol. 5, Alexander Roberts and James Donaldson, eds. (Buffalo: The Christian Literature Company, 1886), 430–36; Mary Rose D'Angelo (see 7.2); Max Kaser, *Römisches Privatrecht: Ein Studienbuch*, 2d ed. (Munich and Berlin: Beck, 1962); Ludwig Köhler, "Die Personalien des Oktateuchs," *ZAW* 40 (1922): 20–36; Martin Leutzsch, "Apphia, Schwester!" in Dorothee Sölle, ed., *Für Gerechtigkeit streiten: Theologie im Alltag einer bedrohten Welt* (Gütersloh: Gütersloher Verlagshaus Gerd Mohn, 1994), 76–82; Sarah Pomeroy (see first bibliographical list in this chapter); Luise Schottroff, 1990 (see 7.2); idem, "Die Samariterin am Brunnen (Joh 4)," in Renate Jost, Rainer Kessler, and Christoph M. Raisig, eds., *Auf Israel hören: Sozial-geschichtliche Bibelauslegungen* (Lucerne: Edition Exodus, 1992), 115–32; Willy Schottroff, "Die Armut der Witwen," in Marlene Crüsemann and Willy Schottroff, eds., *Schuld und Schulden* (Munich: Chr. Kaiser Verlag, 1992), 54–89; Elisabeth Schüssler Fiorenza, *But She Said: Feminist Practices of Biblical Interpretation* (Boston: Beacon Press, 1992); Luzia Sutter Rehmann, "'Und ihr werdet ohne Sorge sein . . .': Gedanken zum Phänomen der Ehefreiheit im frühen Christentum," in Dorothee Sölle, *Für Gerechtigkeit streiten*, 88–95; Judith Romney Wegner, *Chattel or Person? The Status of Women in the Mishnah* (New York and Oxford: Oxford University Press, 1988); Antoinette Clark Wire, *The Corinthian Women Prophets: A Reconstruction through Paul's Rhetoric* (Minneapolis: Fortress Press, 1990).

7.4 "She Toiled Much and Hard for You" (Rom. 16:6): Women's Work

The title is a citation from Romans 16, a letter of commendation and list of greetings by Paul, honoring the value and work of ten women and seventeen men from a number of Christian congregations. In speaking of their work, he uses the Greek verb *kopian* three times when speaking of the toil of women (Mary, v. 6; Tryphaena and Tryphosa, v. 12; Persis, v. 12). Paul often uses this verb to describe his own work and that of other coworkers of God. (This expression is taken from 1 Thess. 3:2.) *Kopian* means hard work, like heavy work with the soil. In early Christianity, *kopian* was for a time a sort of code word expressing the understanding people had of themselves as God's "fellow workers." The word fell out of use in post–New Testament times. It was "no longer fitting . . . when clergy became a rank placed above all others" (Harnack, 7). The words *kopian* and work and *diakonein* and serve, both key terms in Christianity, show the intentionality of the reflection on hierarchy in the world of work. In equal measure, they show the deliberateness of the step to undermine all manner of oppression by having everyone assume the lowest position (Mark 10:42-45 par.). But that step means something very different for women than for men. Women of the lowest class do the work of providing for others (*diakonein* means to wash, cook, serve at table, carry water . . .), and they work in the fields; the word *kopian* implies that these women are among those who work on the land, even though the ideology of patriarchy has consistently denied that women did work outside of the house. On the other hand, free men never do any domestic work even if they are daily-wage earners on the land. The world of work is steeped in hierarchy: the 99 percent of the population who belong to the lower classes, more or less living in poverty, are manual laborers. Domestic work and care of small children marks the line of dominance that runs between women or slaves (male and female) and free men. Working the land is the lowest end of the world of work next to the domestic work of "serving." "Serving" is not paid work; working the land as a daily-wage earner or as a tenant is remunerated (with money, food, or board). Women's wages are barely half of what men are paid for the same work. Women's wage-work is the rule in the life of women of the lower classes and provides only a supplementary income; it does not permit women to enjoy economic independence.

What did Mary do (Rom. 16:6), a woman about whom we know no more than that she toiled much and hard "for you"? What did that "toil" mean for her in the context of work on the land, domestic work, manual labor, and work for the congregation?

It has to be noted at the outset that to speak of her work in the language of working the land, or to call the work of women "serving," took nothing from those women. It is only for free men that a loss of prestige arises from those words; that is, for men who do not have to work on the land.

There are several texts that provide insight into labor conflicts of early Christianity.

Acts 6:1ff.: As a result of a conflict, service at table and service of the word are separated (most likely divided among men).

Luke 10:38-42: The division between the domestic work and "listening to (=learning) the word" creates conflict between Mary and Martha. (Jesus' resolution of the conflict is only half a solution, since he and Mary should have given a hand in that kitchen work.)

1 Tim. 5:13: Young women learn and move about freely in public; they teach and speak openly (see 1 Tim. 2:11f.). The text vilifies them by calling them *argai*, lazy. If read against the patriarchal ideology of the text (see 5:14), this means that those women refused to do the work of house and kitchen.

1 Cor. 14:34f.: Women speak out in the gatherings of the congregations and want to learn outside the house.

Those conflicts allow us to draw certain conclusions. *Diakonein* and to serve originally had a holistic connotation (see 9.3 on this point) in which domestic work and the service of the Word were to be held together. Free men also did the former, and it was free men (in this instance the Jerusalemite Apostles) who after a certain time refused to do that work any longer (probably because they did not wish to serve women or did not want to let them have a part in the service of the Word; see Acts 6:1).

For women such a holistic understanding of work meant that they freed themselves from housework and went about learning and teaching outside their homes and in public. This was resisted by patriarchal men. Luke 10:38-42 treats the division between housework and learning as a problem among women only; this is a retreat from Mark 10:42 and parallels, where to serve is declared to be something everyone is to do. The

Gospel of Luke confirms this view (22:26). The conflicts arose, therefore, from women refusing to do domestic work and the necessity for men to look after it and, thereby, having to serve women.

So, what did Mary do (Rom. 16:6)? She shared her housework with men and redirected the energy thus set free into learning and teaching as well as into organizing the life of congregations so that they could stay together. In addition, she worked—whenever she could find paid work—to support herself, even though it is very likely that she did not earn enough to support herself completely. The community which her congregation offered allowed her to manage financially without a male marriage partner. Therefore, "She has toiled much and hard for you" means that the holistic understanding of work allowed her to take part in shaping the life of her congregation and its community not only by cooking, but also, and more importantly, by participating in its learning, public work, and responsibilities for all of its members. She most certainly experienced Christian men who wanted to push her back into the home, men who deemed it most unseemly that she also wanted men to serve her, and that she even claimed to have the authority to teach them (1 Tim. 2:12).

In light of the poverty of the population, the difficulty of the domestic work done by women must be kept in view; it was by that hard work that they survived. They could not freely decide what kind of work they wanted to do. There would have been no freedom for learning and teaching without structures of solidarity in the economic as well as the domestic sphere. The word *learning* comes up again and again in the reports about conflicts and shows what women fought for most of all.

In this section I have deliberately tried to look at the three levels of women's work together, to attend to the triple track of providing for others, earning an income, and building up the congregation. Now I want to point out what information is available about the work of women in early Christianity, because traditional biblical scholarship does not address this subject. When it does address it, it takes for granted that *woman = housewife*. Feminist exegesis has done an excellent job in providing the information about woman's work in the congregation and in positions of authority. Elisabeth Schüssler Fiorenza's *In Memory of Her* offers a superb overall presentation of this aspect of women's work. In relation to work women did in order to earn an income, I refer particularly to the treatise "Ketubot" of the Mishnah and to the Edict of Diocletian. Recent research on women has uncovered other source materials (N. Kampen, I. Richter Reimer, W. Scheidel, S. Treggiari, et al.).

I have written on women's work in the home and on their paid work. At the time of writing, Ursula Schachl-Raber (Salzburg) is preparing a new study.

Monika Eichenauer, *Untersuchungen zur Arbeitswelt der Frau in der römischen Antike* (Frankfurt: Peter Lang, 1988); Rosmarie Günther, *Frauenarbeit—Frauenbindung: Untersuchungen zu unfreien und freigelassenen Frauen in den stadtrömischen Inschriften* (Munich: W. Fink, 1987); Adolf von Harnack, "*Kopos (Kopian, Hoi Kopiontes)* im frühchristlichen Sprachgebrauch," *ZNW* 27 (1928): 1–10; Natalie Kampen, *Roman Women Working in Ostia* (Berlin: Mann, 1981); idem, "Römische Strassenhändlerinnen," *Antike Welt: Zeitschrift für Archäologie und Kulturgeschichte* 16 (1985): 23–42; Siegfried Lauffer, ed., *Diokletans Preisedikt* (Berlin: de Gruyter, 1971); Ivoni Richter Reimer (see 7.2); Walter Scheidel, "Feldarbeit von Frauen in der antiken Landwirtschaft," *Gymnasium* 97 (1990): 405–31; Luise Schottroff, "DienerInnen der Heiligen" (see 7.2); idem, *Lydia's Impatient Sisters: A Feminist Social History of Early Christianity* (Louisville: Westminster/John Knox Press, 1995); Susan Treggiari, "Jogs in the Household of Livia," *Papers of the British School at Rome* 43 (1975): 48–77.

Chapter Eight

Conceptions of the History of Early Christianity in Feminist-Theological Perspective

Traditional New Testament scholarship works with a number of basic historical assumptions; they are to be discussed critically in this section. I identify these basic assumptions or conceptions of the history of early Christianity in terms of their key concepts: *early Catholicism;* the parallelism of *itinerant radicalism and love patriarchalism; gentile Christianity free of the law; the authors* of the texts and *the enemies* of Paul; and *delay of the parousia.* In these concepts, Christian anti-Judaism and sexism often coincide. In what follows, I do not wish to claim that all exegetes (and many women exegetes, including feminist exegetes) use these concepts at all times and do so uncritically. But it is rare for these widely used models of interpretation to be examined critically. Nor do I wish to claim that feminist exegesis has put in place its own counterconceptions. What I do claim is only that there is now—or there certainly ought to be—a process of discussion in feminist exegesis on these questions.

8.1 Early Catholicism, or Conflicts within Patriarchy?

As a rule, New Testament scholarship works with the notion of a development that led from Jesus to *early Catholicism.* Ernst Käsemann uses that term to refer to a "contrary understanding of Spirit, church, office and tradition" within the New Testament (1964, 239–52). On one side,

Käsemann sees Jesus, Paul, and Pauline Christianity and, on the other, Luke-Acts and the Pastorals. According to him, the chief dividing line between the sides is how they answer the question whether *every* Christian partakes in charisma and spirit or do special office holders stand at the head of congregations? I have stayed here with the androcentric conceptuality, because what early Catholicism means in relation to women is of marginal consequence for that discussion. *Early Catholicism* is no negative concept there but denotes a *necessary development in history,* namely toward a church in the world (Käsemann, 249). The development is said to be historically necessary because, for example, enthusiasm and heresy among their members forced the congregations into the golden middle way of adapting to the surrounding society. (There is frequently a reference also to Judaism at this point.) For women, this line of reflection means that even 1 Tim. 2:12-15 is being justified, for example, as a necessary counterposition to gnostic heresy with its dualistic hostility to the body and rejection of having children.

The apologetic and misogynist side of this way of thinking is sharply criticized in feminist discussions. (See especially Elisabeth Schüssler Fiorenza's critique of the justification of the Pastorals in her *Bread Not Stone,* chap. 4, where she describes several models of that apologetic, and my *Lydia's Impatient Sisters,* chap. 2, and the detailed analyses provided there.) The *final point* reached by the development of early Christianity is deemed to be oppressive to women and judged *negatively* in feminist discussion. In this context Elisabeth Schüssler Fiorenza speaks of a patriarchalization process (e.g., *In Memory of Her,* 35) and describes the individual aspects of this process in a highly differentiated way. However, Christa Mulack no longer regards Paul as an ambivalent figure, as Schüssler Fiorenza does; for Mulack, Paul represents an anti-Jesuanic religion oppressive of women of which the gospel writers themselves are not entirely free either (26ff.). The question is: should this model of development not be basically rejected in feminist discussion? For, not to put too fine a point on it, it works with a paradise-fall image: in the beginning, around Jesus and in his vicinity, there was a "discipleship of equals" (Schüssler Fiorenza 1983, 97) and at the end the "patriarchal superordination has won" (334). But, at the same time, the Gospels of Mark and John *also* kept awake the view of the alternative character of the Christian community. Even more than Elisabeth Schüssler Fiorenza already does, should a feminist understanding of the history of early Christianity not bid farewell to the notion of a development from a bright beginning to a gloomy end? The struggles of women and men for liberation from the oppression of women and from the oppression resulting from hunger and resignation had an impact already on the beginnings of the Jesus movement. The domination of patriarchy is present also among its members and in their leaders, as evidenced in the quarrel about who ranks higher among the disciples (Mark 10:35-45 par.). Over and against the model of a development toward injustice, one needs to hold the notion of the fight against injustice and, therefore, of the simultaneity of the praxis of liberation and the attempts to subvert it through patriarchal oppression.

From a different point of view, Lone Fatum criticizes the feminist image of the beginning of early Christianity as the place of women's liberation and the subsequent fall into patriarchy. In her view, Christianity was fundamentally and from the outset a seamless oppression of women. The view that there are early Christian texts that are liberating for women (e.g., Gal. 3:28) and that there was a history of women's liberation within early Christianity is, in her judgment, a feminist apologetic that shuts its eyes to the reality of Christian patriarchy. According to Fatum, even in a feminist hermeneutic of suspicion the normative authority of the biblical text remains the unacknowledged presupposition. The stance from which Lone Fatum assesses feminist exegesis to be apologetic in its entirety is her acceptance that analysis can be undertaken from an objective standpoint. This leaves aside a foundational principle of feminist theory and theology, namely that such objectivity is an illusionary and inconclusive asseveration of dominant patriarchal scholarship (see 7.1). In addition to challenging Lone Fatum's understanding on the basis of principles of scientific theory, one must ask her to demonstrate historically how so many women in early Christianity could have been so mistaken. Deconstructing patriarchal texts should not render invisible the history of women's resistance and of their liberation that may lurk behind even such texts. Otherwise the image of patriarchy is raised up to the level of an invincible superpower. As I see it, the word *apologetic* itself is in need of differentiation. One must ask what in feminist exegesis is defended with apologetics: a status quo, that is, a theology and church that oppresses women, or the history of liberation and the hope of women? My own work, for example, is meant to be apologetic in the latter sense.

Even the First Epistle to Timothy gives glimpses of the fight against patriarchy, particularly the fight for women's liberation, although it is the voice of the oppressors, above all, that is heard at the level of the text. But the epistle is very clearly and against its will a document of the history of women's liberation. In the second and third century many texts were produced which, at the level of the text, are oppressive of women—an especially harsh example is the Syrian Didaskalia—but which involuntarily show a living church of women and laypeople. The conception of conflicts within patriarchy that does not reckon with a development from a good beginning to a more or less bad ending has a disadvantage. The conforming belief must be relinquished that there once was an overall successful beginning. It has the advantage that it does not let the fight for women's liberation and justice appear as well-nigh hopeless. Even small islands of liberation are and were the beginning of the *basileia tou theou*.

Hans Achelis and Johs. Flemming, *Die syrische Didaskalia übersetzt und erklärt* (Leipzig: J. C. Hinrichs, 1904); Lone Fatum, "Image of God and Glory of Man: Women in the Pauline Congregations," in Kari Børresen, ed., *Image of God and Gender Models in Judaeo-Christian Tradition* (Oslo: Solum Forlag, 1991), 56–137; Ernst Käsemann, *Exegetische Versuche und Besinnungen*, 2 vols. (Göttingen: Vandenhoeck und Ruprecht, 1960, 1964); Christa Mulack, *Jesus der Gesalbte der Frauen: Weiblichkeit als Grundlage christlicher Ethik* (Stuttgart: Kreuz Verlag, 1987); Christine Schaumberger, "Paradies—Exodus—Gerangel: Zu Mustern feministisch-theologischer Patriarchatswahrnehmung und -deutung," in *Reader der Projektbeiträge zur Sommeruniversität 1988 in Kassel* (Gesamthochschule and Universität Kassel: 1989), 15–35; Luise Schottroff, *Lydia's Impatient Sisters* (see 7.4); Elisabeth Schüssler Fiorenza, *Bread Not Stone: The Challenge of Feminist Biblical Interpretation* (Boston: Beacon Press, 1984); idem, *In Memory of Her*, 1983 (see 7.2); Ulrike Wagener, *Die Ordnung des "Hauses Gottes": Der Ort von Frauen in der Ekklesiologie und Ethik der Pastoralbriefe* (Tübingen: J. C. B. Mohr, 1994).

8.2 Itinerant Radicalism and Love Patriarchalism, or Work for Justice?

The sociological model of interpreting early Christianity, associated with the concepts of *itinerant radicalism* and *love patriarchalism*, works with the parallelism of two forms of society in early Christianity. There was a charismatic group of nonsedentary people who upheld a radical ethos (the renunciation of possessions and of family). Next to it were congregations or sympathizers who led the allegedly normal and patriarchally organized life. As a consequence of being Christian, this patriarchal organization practices patriarchal rule from the top down with a more loving manner than found in the surrounding patriarchal society, but without questioning the structures of domination (e.g., that men rule over women). The survival of the church was made possible by the success of love patriarchalism. In certain respects, this sociological model overlaps with the model described in 8.1, namely, the replacement of the democratic structure of congregations with early Catholicism. They overlap most noticeably in their androcentrism and in their legitimation of patriarchal rule in church and society. The model dominates in the social histories of early Christianity found in Western exegesis. It is the version proposed by Gerd Theissen that is discussed most regularly in Germany and North America.

Feminists critique this model (1) because it legitimates patriarchy and (2) because of the androcentrism of the notion of itinerant radicals (see especially Schüssler Fiorenza). Whether women were also among those itinerant radicals is still a matter of controversy in feminist discussion. Monika Fander and Amy-Jill Levine accept Theissen's model to a large extent; they believe that the female partners of the itinerant radicals did not move about the countryside and carried on with the patriarchally organized life of the housewife and mother. The point of departure for my fundamental objections to the sociological model of itinerant radicalism–love patriarchalism is not a concern for whether or not I can demonstrate that women were among these radicals. (I believe that there were women among them; see D'Angelo.) Basically, what I question is the purpose that this model attributes to itinerant radicalism. In the model I criticize, how these radicals lived and what they proclaimed is seen in analogy to the itinerant philosophers of Cynicism. Individual (young) men—and perhaps one or more exceptional women—leave the well-to-do home (of their parents) and enter a life of ascetical critique of culture. Their poverty results from the renunciation of poverty. Their ethos is elitist; it is not intended to be imitated. On every discernible historical level, the Gospels and the source Q make it quite plain that the Jesus movement and Jesus himself wanted to live their lives for the sake of and together with the whole people. Jesus' praxis of life is imitated in discipleship of him and this includes the healings, the exorcisms, the multiplication of loaves and bread, and the proclamation of the nearness of God's reign. This is not an elitist ethos of a self-aware minority; here the issue is the healing and the hope of an oppressed and hungry people. At first, the women that take part in the toil of the harvest, in the work of the beginnings of God's reign, gain new spaces and possibilities in their lives. Where the battle is one against hunger and disease, there the struggles for survival of women and children take center stage. This is where God's reign begins. It is not as objects of charity that women and children are present in the Jesus movement; they are there also as those made whole and as those who act. So they are present in the movement also as itinerant women prophets. The Gospels do not paint a picture of women at home fighting the real battles for bread and life while, out on the street, an elitist group dispenses big words and then lets itself be served by the women. In its component dimension of itinerant radicalism, which is all too often considered in isolation, the model of itinerant radicalism–love patriarchalism is both androcentric *and elitist*. My basic objection proceeds from the social-historical situation of the population as a whole and from feminist-liberationist theology's question about the relevance, for that population, of Jesus and his followers.

Mary Rose D'Angelo (see 7.2); Monika Fander, "Frauen im Urchristentum am Beispiel Palästinas," *Jahrbuch für biblische Theologie* 7 (1992): 165–85; idem, *Die Stellung der Frau im Markusevangelium: Unter besonderer Berücksichtigung kultur- und religionsgeschichtlicher Hintergründe* (Altenberge: Telos Verlag, 1989); Hans-Peter Kuhnen, ed., *Mit Thora und Todesmut: Judäa im Widerstand gegen die Römer von Herodes bis Bar-Kochba* (Stuttgart: Württembergisches Landesmuseum, 1994); Amy-Jill Levine, "Who's Catering the Q Affair? Feminist Observations on Q Paraenesis," *Semeia* 50 (1990): 145–61; Luise Schottroff and Wolfgang Stegemann, *Jesus and the Hope of the Poor* (Maryknoll, N.Y.: Orbis Books, 1986); Luise Schottroff, "Wanderprophetinnen: Eine feministische Analyse der Logienquelle," *EvTh* 51 (1991): 332–44; Elisabeth Schüssler Fiorenza, *In Memory of Her* (see 7.2); Gerd Theissen, *Studien zur Soziologie des Urchristentums* (Tübingen: J. C. B. Mohr, 1979), Eng. trans. (selections): *Social Reality and the Early Christians: Theology, Ethics, and the World of the New Testament* (Minneapolis: Fortress Press, 1992).

8.3 Gentile Christianity Free of the Law, or Option for the God of Israel and Jesus the Messiah?

The notion of the *gentile Christianity free of the Law* determines almost without exception the Christian exegesis of Paul and the self-definition of Christians in relation to Judaism. Exceptions to this rule may be found in the circle of those engaged in Jewish-Christian dialogue. But the exegetical resources on which theological education and practice rely (lexica, commentaries, textbooks) work with this notion. I shall sketch in outline the currently dominant notion of gentile Christianity free of the Law. The Pauline gospel denies that the Law, that is, the Scriptures in the perspective of Jewish people, has the ability to lead to salvation. On the contrary, the Law leads into sin and into death before God if people try to find salvation in fulfilling the Law. God justifies the believers without the Law and only by faith in Christ. Paul's texts are read in light of this notion and may, indeed, be fitted into it (e.g., Gal. 2:16 and Rom. 3:20-21). Paul's sharp repudiation of circumcision of Christians who are Gentiles (that is, non-Jewish) by birth shows the gospel free of the Law in uncompromising clarity. The self-definition of Christians in terms of delimitation from Judaism is comprised by the repudiation of circumcision of non-Jewish men who believe in Christ.

This understanding has pervaded exegesis and gained a firmly fixed place in its tradition. On a variety of levels, critical questions must be put to this view of Christianity as "free of the Law" and as being gentile-Christian in its identity: (1) Do the texts of Paul (and the others from the New Testament, including words of Jesus, drawn on to substantiate this notion) really say what they are supposed to say according to this notion? (2) In this notion, what understanding of the Law is attributed to Judaism? (3) What consequences does this notion have for the identity of Christian women?

In relation to the first question (it is treated more fully in my work in *Schuld und Macht*), I note that Paul repeats unambiguously that it is unreservedly necessary for those who believe in Jesus to live also according to the Law, the Torah (see 1 Cor. 7:19; Rom. 3:31; 7:12). But it is the gloomy fate of sin imposed on all humankind that all human beings, Jewish and non-Jewish alike, do *not* live according to the Torah (Romans 1–3). Paul's lament about the murderous reality of the world of humans, uttered particularly in Rom. 3:9-20, can still be directly understood today. Through the death and resurrection of Christ God has intervened in the worldwide dominance of sin and death. God declares humans to be righteous and sets them free from sin's structures of violence. By God's will, that is, the Torah, humans have been liberated for life. Paul rejects circumcision for non-Jewish men because, in his view, it infringes on the salvation-creating power of God's action in Christ. The Epistle to the Galatians shows more than other sources that it was very much a matter of controversy among the followers of Jesus whether or not men of non-Jewish origin needed to be circumcised when they converted. Pauline texts also mirror the lively process of discussion among Christians as to what consequences were now to be drawn from God's will, the Torah, for their practice of life (Rom. 12:2, "to discern the will of God"). It is not true to history that the first generations of believers in Christ set themselves apart from Judaism. Gentile Christians, too, believed themselves to have become Jewish and that is how non-Jewish society classified them. The step into the divorce of Christianity and Judaism was taken most likely after the defeat of Bar Kokhba.

In relation to the second question I note that the picture of Jewish piety and manner of life drawn by the notion of gentile Christianity free of the Law imputes legalism and *hybris* before God to Judaism (by fulfilling the Torah, Jews "want to earn their own salvation"). Jesus is said to have fundamentally challenged Jewish legalism in his critique of Pharisaism and of the Torah. Mark 2:27 is said to pronounce that Judaism places the law above human beings. The use alone of the word *law* in this context creates the image of a formalistic, misanthropic, and petrified Jewish faith ("late Judaism"). As a result of such imputation, Jewish tradition has always been perceived in a distorted way and misinterpreted by Christians; the Jewish protest against this view of Judaism has not been heard in the domain of Christian theology. The great work of Paul Billerbeck (and Hermann L. Strack, *Kommentar zum Neuen Testament aus Talmud und Midrasch*, 4 vols. [Munich, 1924–28]) rests on that kind of Christian understanding of Judaism as "legalistic." Because that work is still an important tool for exegesis, it fosters the Christian incrimination of the Jewish religion. The notion of gentile Christianity free of the Law prevents early Christianity from being seen as a part of the history of the Jewish people. Paul's view that circumcision for non-Jewish men has to be rejected must also be understood within the context of contemporary conceptions of non-Jewish males converting to Judaism. Circumcision was the hallmark of being Jewish and the most unambiguous step of becoming Jewish. Clearly, there were discussions whether men could not become Jewish without circumcision (see Josephus, *Antiquities* 20:17ff.; Jubilees 15:25-34; Philo, *De migr. Abraham,* 89–93). To separate Paul from the context of Judaism is historically absurd and theologically disastrous. At that time there was no perception of Christian identity *based on delimitation from Judaism.*

In relation to the third question I note that when Christian identity over and against Judaism is defined in terms of the repudiation of circumcision and the Law, one has to ask what that would have meant for the women of Jewish or non-Jewish origin who joined Christian communities. Elisabeth Schüssler Fiorenza interprets the Pauline view of circumcision as being liberating for both Jewish Christians and gentile Christian women. "If it was no longer circumcision but baptism that was the primary rite of initiation, then women became full members of the people of God with the same rights and duties" (*In Memory of Her*, 210). Judith M. Lieu objects to this view by saying that in Judaism women were held to be full members without restrictions—and were thus as "uncircumcised." Continuing her objection, she says that in the context of Gal. 3:28, Paul makes it clear that he understands God's people to be a people of men. Even in the negative determination of Christian identity (no circumcision), Paul is concerned only with men. Both Elisabeth Schussler Fiorenza and Judith M. Lieu presuppose that the Pauline statements regarding circumcision are meant to depict Christian identity over and against and in contrast to Judaism. I want to issue a fundamental challenge to that presupposition. Paul does indeed understand God's people to be a people of men and he does reject circumcision for men of non-Jewish origin (see only his Epistle to the Galatians). But he does not as yet know of a Christianity in opposition to Judaism. He depicts the identity of those who believe in Jesus within the context of internal Jewish discussion and life. The life of Christian women both of non-Jewish and of Jewish origin is part of Jewish women's history until far into the second century. They are Jewish women and Christian women (*Jüdinnen und Christinnen*). The study of the history of Jewish women, of female proselytes and sympathizers of Judaism, and of the differences in their religious practices, will create access for Christian women to their early Christian mothers and sisters. There are already some foundational studies of the history of Jewish women on which Christian women exegetes of the New Testament can build. I have in mind the work of Bernadette Brooten, Judith Plaskow, Ross Kraemer, Barbara Geller-Nathanson, and Judith M. Lieu; all of them exemplify the historical research done primarily by Jewish women. The issue for feminist exegetes is not only to become cognizant of the achievements of their sisters who work in the Jewish history of women but also to raise questions about the history of early Christianity and the equally well-rehearsed theological conceptions as to what constitutes Christian identity. The notion of a gentile Christianity free of the Law is anti-Judaistic, hostile to women, and historically questionable.

It was Jewish women who were the bearers of early Christianity as well as women of non-Jewish origin who, like Lydia (Acts 16:13ff.), voluntarily embraced the Jewish religion and its practice of life. It is grotesque that through the concept of gentile Christianity these women are displaced from the center to the margins, since it puts the issue of men's circumcision at the core of things even more massively than Paul had done.

I have shown above (see 7.4) that Christian women fought hard to be able to learn and to teach publicly. There can be no doubt that the focal point of this embattled learning and teaching by women was the Torah, the will of God, the "law" (*nomos*). The women wanted to be teachers of the law—just like the Jewish woman of whom Juvenal tells (Sat. 6:542ff.)—and they loved the sabbath like the women whom Martial derides in his epigram (IV.4, 7). Women mutually taught one another what it means to live according to the Torah and to believe in Jesus as Israel's Messiah. In the Midrash on the Book of Ruth (Billerbeck, 1:25), we learn that Naomi told Ruth the precepts for proselyte women and men: "'My daughter, it is not the custom of the daughters of Israel to go to the theatre and circus of the gentiles.' Ruth replied (1:16) 'Wherever you go, I will go.'" Without intending it to be exhaustive, Naomi adds another list of precepts for proselytes. I am not concerned here with this list but with the fact that the text reveals traces of traditions of Jewish women's teaching on which Christian women could build. That this text belongs to a later time than early Christianity may in this instance be left aside. Even Juvenal, the hater of women and Jews, knew of such a tradition of teaching, and he lived much earlier (Sat 6:542ff.). The refusal to attend the Gentiles' theater and circus (see Schäfke) cost many a Jewish and Christian woman her life, since Rome demanded attendance there as a demonstration of loyalty to the state. Naomi's instruction reveals a politically responsible Judaism of women that in terms of the practice of life is closely related to the early Christian history of women. That Christian and Jewish women together practiced Jewish rituals, thereby drawing further the wrath of the church father Chrysostom, is documented in tradition (*Adv. Judaeos* II.3ff. and elsewhere; Eng. trans., see Kraemer 1988, no. 31). As far as I know, tradition does not document that Christian women were interested in distancing themselves on the level of ideology or conduct of life from Jewish women. From the perspective of feminism, the definition of Christian identity at the level of ideology is fundamentally problematic.

Judith R. Baskin, ed., *Jewish Women in Historical Perspective* (Detroit: Wayne State University Press, 1991); Bernadette Brooten, *Women Leaders in the Ancient Synagogue* (Chico, Calif.: Scholars Press, 1982); Shaye J. D. Cohen, "Crossing the Boundary and Becoming a Jew," *Harvard Theological Review* 82 (1989): 13–33; idem, "The Rabbinic Conversion Ceremony," *Journal of Jewish Studies* 41 (1990): 177–203; Barbara H. Geller-Nathanson, "Toward a Multicultural Ecumenical History of Women in the First Century/ies C.E.," in Elisabeth Schüssler Fiorenza, ed., *Searching the Scriptures*, vol. 1: *A Feminist Introduction* (New York: Crossroad, 1993), 272–89; Ross S. Kraemer, 1988 and 1992 (see first bibliographical list in chap. 7); Sally O. Langford, "On Being a Religious Woman: Women Proselytes in the Greco-Roman World," in Peter J. Haas, ed., *Recovering the Role of Women: Power and Authority in Rabbinic Jewish Society* (Atlanta: Scholars Press, 1992); Amy-Jill Levine, ed., *"Women Like This": New Perspectives on Jewish Women in the Greco-Roman World* (Atlanta: Scholars Press, 1991); Judith M. Lieu, "Circumcision, Women, and Salvation," *NTS* 40 (1994): 358–70; Judith Plaskow, *Standing Again at Sinai: Judaism from a Feminist Perspective* (San Francisco: Harper and Row, 1990); Lilian Portefaix, *Sisters Rejoice: Paul's Letter to the Philippians and Luke-Acts as Seen by First-Century Philippian Women*, Coniectanea Biblica, NT Series 20 (Stockholm: Almquist and Wiksell International, 1988); Ivoni Richter Reimer (see 7.2); Werner Schäfke, "Frühchristlicher Widerstand," in *ANRW* II Principat, vol. 23.1 (Berlin: de Gruyter, 1979); Christine Schaumberger and Luise Schottroff, *Schuld und Macht: Studien zu einer feministischen Befreiungstheologie* (Munich: Chr. Kaiser Verlag, 1988); "'Gesetzesfreies Heidenchristentum'—und die Frauen?" in Luise Schottroff and Marie-Theres Wacker, eds., *Von der Wurzel getragen: Christlich-feministische Exegese in Auseinandersetzung mit Antijudaismus* (Leiden: E. J. Brill, 1996), 227–45; Elisabeth Schüssler Fiorenza (see 8.1); Eveline Valtink, "Feministisch-christliche Identität und Antijudaismus," in Luise Schottroff and Marie-Theres Wacker, eds., *Von der Wurzel getragen*, 1–26; Marie-Theres Wacker, "Der und Dem anderen Raum geben: Feministisch-christliche Identität ohne Antijudaismus," in Luise Schottroff and Marie-Theres Wacker, eds., *Von der Wurzel getragen*, 247–69.

8.4 "The Author" of the Texts and "the Enemies" of Paul, or Common Preparation of the Way and the Hymns?

In its introductions to the Bible, traditional scholarship has always asked about the identity of the author of New Testament texts (the Gospels and Epistles), where he [*sic*] is to be located geographically and in which period of time. I would like to problematize these questions fundamentally and to do so from the perspective of feminist liberation theology. To be able in the end to assign this or that text to a female author—in the manner of Harnack who determined that the Epistle to the Hebrews had been written by Prisca—is not my concern. Rather, I seek to submit the concept of *author* to an encompassing analysis that is critical of patriarchy. To caricature the point by overstating it: the "author," as traditional scholarly introductions envisage him, is a white man, seated at his desk in his book-lined study, where now and then he has a cup of tea brought in by his wife or his housekeeper (if he is Catholic). Of course, this is a caricature, yet it is easily verifiable when one studies, for example, the commentaries on and introductions to the Gospels and what they say about Matthew, Mark, Luke, and John. Listen to a random example: "It is an attractive supposition that the author had a function in his community, e.g., was a teacher, but it cannot be proved. He possessed a Jewish-influenced feeling for style, good Greek linguistic feeling, and a synagogue education" (Luz, 94).

The Gospels have a complex prehistory, both oral and written, an understanding which this tradition of scholarship also accepts.

Therefore, the model of "the author" may already be criticized from the perspective of that prehistory. In relation to Paul, the situation is very different. As far as the putatively genuine Pauline letters are concerned, Paul is understood to be an author who is well educated and authoritative, in the sense of exercising predominance. He writes down fundamental truths of theology and responses to actual problems in the congregations, or he has his "amanuensis" (see Betz on Gal. 6:11) write them down. I am a Protestant. In my Protestant tradition of scholarship, Paul has unmistakably the features of a German *Pfarrherr* (the current German *Pfarrer*, minister, is derived from this older term *Herr* of the *Pfarrei*, translated "lord of the parish"), or of a German professor. For example, the German word *Amt* (office) as the translation of *diakonia* (of the Apostle) has this connotation.

I wish to suggest a counterproposal to such images, in which the scholars' position flows unreflectively into their historical object of study. The texts of the New Testament are not the products of individual men's (or women's) writing. They are, rather, the outcome of a long and common struggle of women and men for the life that God has given and that God desires. The texts stem from the treasures of the *koinonia,* from the sharing in and of fear, hope, and bread, from the common exploration as to what steps to take next in everyday life. Paul, too, does not understand himself as an educated individual being, but as a link in a chain. It is the chain of those who taught him hope and of those who, together with him and at times also in critical distance from him and his kind, give form to the new life before God (1 Cor. 15:3; 1:1; and the notations in the letters concerning their sender). The idea of an "author" manifests its insufficiency very clearly in connection with the Epistle to the Colossians, which is and is not from Paul. Paul's letters are filled with hymns, words of consolation and blessing. These epistles are in large parts much more a hymnbook of the poor than the product of an individual man's theological labor.

I concede that my use of the term "hymnbook of the poor" is open to challenge. Yet it appears suitable to me for depicting the *subjects* who speak there and their language (the genres of speech). In the Gospel of Luke, I do not encounter an educated Hellenist who portrays his Christianity in political-apologetic form. Rather, I come face to face with the speaking, storytelling, consoling, and singing of women and men who are not so fundamentally different from those in the communities that are behind Mark or Matthew. Profiling the Synoptic Gospels in contrast one to the other, which had such an important place in research to date, should be reconsidered once again. There are indeed differences among them. But when I discern that all the Gospels have a comparable eschatology ("an expectation of the nearness of God"; see 8.5), these differences need to be assessed anew. The individual input of a so-called author is small and ought to be minimized even in the case of Paul. He is not the ingenious inventor of a theology, but one follower of Jesus among many who together reflect on and talk about theology and the conduct of life.

As far as feminist analysis is concerned, texts that originated in collectivities and in relation to which the question of individual authorship is inappropriate place us before new questions. In her feminist analysis of the Gospel of Matthew, Elaine Wainwright has shown that this Gospel is not the work of one man; nor is it that of a community, the tone of which is set by men. Women were part of the writing of the Gospels. The Gospels are contradictory in themselves in that they contain traditions of women, traditions that are critical of patriarchy and that show the suppression of women carried out by patriarchy.

The notion of *the enemies* of Paul or *the enemies* of Jesus is similarly indicated by a hermeneutic of domination. On the one side, there stands the teacher of the truth (Jesus or Paul) and, on the other, the "enemies" who teach a false doctrine and who are depicted in terms of every possible attribute of enmity. They are the hypocritical Pharisees, libertine Corinthians, emancipated women, Judaizers, and so forth. This notion adheres to the basic conviction that Paul is always right and that Jesus has declared war against the Jewish religion. It is a notion that is very deeply rooted in the history of exegesis. As an example, I point only to the genre of "dispute" or to the thesis of the parables' location in the apologetics and polemics of Jesus against the Pharisees. Today, in dominant exegesis, there are also critical reconsiderations of this notion of "enemies." In my view, the question is rightly raised as to whether those disputes are not really a manifestation of the Jewish culture of disputation, and whether Paul is not at times wrong.

Antoinette Wire's book on First Corinthians offers a new feminist point of departure for this question. She portrays a living and contentious congregation in Corinth, in which women fought for and achieved particular rights. This congregation is made visible in and through Paul's rhetoric, and it becomes clear what his position means for Christian women there. My critique of her book is directed only at the exegesis of Paul, that is to say, the establishment of what it is that Paul himself *wants* to say. The criticism of the notion of Paul's "enemies" ought to be carried further and combined with a feminist-critical exegesis of Paul (see 8.3). I plead for a new feminist point of departure, not only in relation to the question about who the people in the Corinthian congregations were, but also in relation to what Paul wanted to say. His theology also has to be rewritten from a feminist-liberation theology perspective (see especially Tamez).

Hans Dieter Betz, *Galatians: A Commentary on Paul's Letter to the Churches in Galatia* (Philadelphia: Fortress Press, 1979); Irene Dannemann, *Aus dem Rahmen fallen: Frauen im Markusevangelium. Eine feministische Revision* (Berlin: Alektor Verlag, 1996); Ulrich Luz, *Matthew: A Continental Commentary* (Minneapolis: Fortress Press, 1992); Elsa Tamez, *The Amnesty of Grace: Justification by Faith from a*

Latin American Perspective (Nashville: Abingdon Press, 1993); Elaine Mary Wainwright, *Toward a Feminist-Critical Reading of the Gospel according to Matthew*, BZNW 60 (Berlin and New York: de Gruyter, 1991); Antoinette Clark Wire, *The Corinthian Women Prophets: A Reconstruction through Paul's Rhetoric* (Minneapolis: Fortress Press, 1990).

8.5 Delayed Parousia, or Hope in the Nearness of God?

Traditional New Testament scholarship perceives the eschatology of early Christianity in terms of linear time: the first generation's expectation of an imminent second coming was soon understood to be a mistake, the "delayed parousia" became a matter of course, and eschatology itself turned into the doctrine of the last things. In depicting the early church's expectation of an imminent parousia, for example, through the statements that the reign of God is "at hand," this "nearness" is interpreted—without substantiation—as a span of time in the chronological procession. Because a particular concept of time (the linear procession of time) is taken for granted, no question is raised as to what understanding of time and, therefore, of God, is in the texts. This unexamined notion of nearness has determined the discussion about the expectation of an imminent parousia since the discovery of that matter at the end of the nineteenth century. The governing conception of the interpretation of early Christian eschatology, which came to the fore at that time and which determines Western exegesis today, correctly associates early Christian eschatology with contemporary Jewish apocalyptic. But their differences are emphasized: other than early Christian eschatology, Jewish apocalyptic is calculating, for it is typical for it to try to determine what time still remains. Rudolf Bultmann's program of demythologization sets an existential interpretation of eschatology, said to be given by the New Testament, over and against Jewish apocalyptic and its calculations and mythological view of the world. For that interpretation, this view of the world is merely a Jewish shell that has no substantive impact on the eschatology of Christianity. A distinction is made here between Jewish *apocalyptic* and Christian *eschatology*. (See Luzia Sutter Rehmann for a critique of the traditional interpretation of New Testament eschatology and that interpretation's anti-Judaism.)

What must be questioned today is the manner in which scholarly conceptions of *interpreting* early Christian eschatology take the issue of the linear understanding of time for granted. It must be questioned because the linear understanding of time belongs to the winners in history, in whose interest it is that things keep on going as they are. In other words, linear understandings of time are an aspect of society's patriarchal ruling class.

Critical analysis of linear understandings of time can be found in the feminist critique of traditional Christian theology (Rosemary Radford Ruether) as well as in the philosophical critique of the idea of progress (Walter Benjamin) and in recent studies in apocalyptic (Jürgen Ebach, Luise Schottroff, and Luzia Sutter Rehmann). To characterize the linear understanding of time that is unjustly applied to the interpretation of early Christianity, I appropriate a well-known and eloquent remark by Rosemary Radford Ruether: "endless flight into an unrealized future" (1983, 254). That same understanding of time is also at work in the conception of eschatology as *expectation of an imminent parousia*. The scholars' understanding of the expectation of an imminent parousia is preoccupied with the span of time until the end, a span which, when measured against the flight into the endless, is qualified as "imminent." It then also had to prove itself to be a "mistake." And while this interpretive concept of the expectation of an imminent parousia has some foundation in the texts (such as Luke 10:9 par.), even though the sense of nearness still requires examination, "the delayed parousia" as an interpretive concept is a pure invention of scholarship.

Luzia Sutter Rehmann has provided us with a new feminist point of departure in the understanding of early Christian eschatology. By means of all texts that speak of women's childbearing, she shows that early Christian eschatology speaks the language of hope in the nearness of God, a language that understands women and the earth giving birth as an act of resistance against death. A new perception of early Christian eschatology yields wholly different designations of time than does a linear expectation of an imminent parousia. The language of eschatology is the designation of the present time (Schottroff). It interprets the present as a time of fright about the collapse of the security proffered by patriarchy (Matt. 24:37-39 par.), a time of growing and ripening (Matt. 13:33-34 par.) or of staying awake in the night.

It is often helpful to understand the nearness of God promised in the texts as nearness to a divine space or a divine power. God's nearness strengthens women and men and empowers them for actions in relationships of solidarity. Early Christian eschatology has often been misunderstood, particularly in relation to its connection with Christian praxis and ethics. The notion of an interim ethics arose, suggesting that, on account of nearness of the end, people considered the practical formation of life irrelevant and did not want to bring about changes in their condition. This misunderstanding of Christian apocalyptic eschatology went hand in hand with a repudiation of the legalism of the Jewish orientation of conduct (see 8.3). Yet the texts of the New Testament clearly declare that those who wait are spurred into action by their wakefulness. For example, Jesus' words when sending out the twelve (Matt. 10:5-15 par.). provide a concise articulation of the connection between anticipating the coming of God's reign and human acting (esp. vv. 7–8 par.). A new feminist point of departure for the understanding of early Christian eschatology emerges, on the one hand, from the critique of an ideology of dominance in the absolutizing of the linear conception of time. On the other hand, that point of departure is rooted in a feminist spirituality that grows from the experience of God's nearness.

Such a new point of departure in the interpretation of early Christian eschatology has an impact on the reading of all early Christian texts, since the eschatology in them cannot be regarded as a partial dimension only. Rather, it is the foundation of faith and praxis.

Walter Benjamin, "Zentralpark," in *Illuminationen: Ausgewählte Schriften* (Frankfurt: Suhrkamp Verlag, 1969); Rudolf Bultmann, "New Testament and Mythology: The Problem of Demythologizing the New Testament Proclamation," in Rudolf Bultmann, *New Testament Mythology and Other Basic Writings*, ed. Schubert M. Ogden (Philadelphia: Fortress Press, 1984); Jürgen Ebach, "Apokalypse: Zum Ursprung einer Stimmung," in *Einwürfe* 2 (Munich: Chr. Kaiser Verlag, 1985), 5–61; Rosemary Radford Ruether, *Sexism and God-Talk* (Boston: Beacon Press, 1983); Luise Schottroff, *Lydia's Impatient Sisters* (See 7.4); Luzia Sutter Rehmann (see 7.3).

Chapter Nine

The Feminist Adoption and Critique of New Testament Theology

Feminist theology has not only taken on the task of writing anew the history of women in early Christianity. Right from the start, in both critical rejection and new reflection, it has also addressed itself to the theological substance of the New Testament. I cite some of the theological themes that are discussed with particular intensity: the cross as a theme of Christology, sacrifice, the concept of God, serving and holding office, sexuality and the image of woman, and sin. The way early Christian understandings were incorporated into systematic theology and its concepts cannot be discussed in what follows here. I restrict myself to the discussion in feminist theology of the contents of New Testament theology that presents its arguments in exegesis and seeks to develop a *historical* analysis. Here, too, I can present only a brief consideration of what is still an open process of discussion, as well as first indications of research and lines of engagement.

9.1 Cross—Sacrifice—The Concept of God—Christology

The primal anger of feminist Christian women at Christian theology was and is aroused repeatedly by dominant theologies of the cross and their understanding of God. The idea of a god who sacrifices his son is criticized for being bloodthirsty. Because the sacrifice that is demanded of women is provided with additional christological legitimation, a Christ who sacrifices himself is experienced as oppressive of women. I want to refer especially to an article by Sheila Briggs, who radically applies this critique to a New Testament text—and not, as is usually the case, to the history of doctrine or to the history of interpretation of the New Testament. Sheila Briggs examines the Philippians hymn (Phil. 2:6-11) from the perspective of a black female liberation theologian in the United States. She distinguishes among three categories of texts in the New Testament. First, there are texts in which the voice of the oppressed may still be heard. Second, there are texts that reflect the interests of the dominant elite in the ancient church, in the process of hanging on and canonizing the texts of the New Testament. Finally, there are the ambiguous texts in which it is not clear whether their *effect* was to conserve oppression or produce criticism of the oppression. According to Briggs, Phil. 2:6-11 belongs to the third category. In that text, slavery is idealized. It is idealized in that Christ is said willingly to have become a slave—but since when does a slave have the option to choose? It is further idealized through the christological differentiation that softens the analogy between the enslavement of Christ and the enslavement of human beings. The text "does not challenge the interests or beliefs of slave-masters. Yet, there is an irreducible tension in the idea of a God who becomes a slave" (149). That is why she counts the Christ hymn among the ambiguous texts.

Regula Strobel summarizes the feminist critique of theologies of the cross as follows: "The virtues mediated by the theology of the cross, from humble obedience and giving up the self, to serving and sacrificing love, have a stabilizing effect on the existing distribution of power in society and intensify the oppression of women in a patriarchal society" (60). Sheila Briggs's article firmly establishes that the Philippian hymn, and with it the whole Christology of early Christianity, has an oppressive effect, in spite of the condescending God. Thus, it is of no avail here to argue that the history of interpretation of the New Testament and its effect are oppressive, but not the New Testament itself.

This raises a number of tasks for research and the need for extensive discussion. I cannot consent to Sheila Briggs's analysis. My counterarguments are these: (1) If this text has an oppressive effect, whence the need in Western interpretation to defuse it? In Western interpretation, Christ's being a *slave* and his *poverty* are said to represent his *humanity*. But this humanity was and is thereby deconcretized: Christ's becoming human has nothing to do with poverty and slavery in human reality. (2) These texts originate in Christian congregations composed in the majority of poor people and in which there were many female and male slaves. In our anger with the history and current reality of the church, a feminist critique of these texts must beware of not taking something away from those people. They sang their hymns that a messenger of God freely shared their fate, and in that way beheld in the face of sister slaves the face of Christ. Marli Lutz writes: "In the Philippian congregation, poor and oppressed people hailed in hymn and celebrated the victory of the crucified Christ, in the very midst of the suppressive powers of the Roman Empire. Women and men, without great and visible power, came to know that they were participants in a project that went far beyond their own immediate interests. They stuck to that project; their dreams are made of it" (74).

Undoubtedly, the androcentrism of the Philippian hymn deserves critique, but the text is a hymn of those who hunger for bread, life, and justice. They come together to do the work of liberation. Thus, my counterarguments arise from a critique of the dominant interpretation, and from social-historical analysis. Thus far, both of these areas of work are studied in rudimentary ways only. As far as substance is concerned, other aspects of the New Testament's image of God, such as the understanding of God as father, also need to be subjected to critique and studied anew.

Regula Strobel's challenge to Christologies of the cross of feminist and other liberation theologies is radical in the most profound sense of the word. On the basis of the feminist critique of the Christology of the cross sketched above, she concludes that a theological linking of the cross and salvation has to be rejected. The life and action of Jesus "becomes liberating and redeeming for me, because I have learned from others . . . in a fragmentary manner, the meaning of liberation given as a gift, forgiveness of guilt readily granted, and engaging oneself so that another may obtain justice" (189). The validity of faith does not depend on the fact that, even in the face of death, Jesus held fast to this pattern of action. Nor does it depend on the resurrection. "This does not mean that there is no suffering and no crosses. . . . But, I think that cross and salvation and redemption should no longer be tied one to the other as a theological system" (189). I do not wish to gather counterarguments in response to this critique but, rather, state two reasons for my support of a feminist theology of the cross. For me, believing also contains an emotional and historical link to the dead. Salvation and redemption are something I cannot experience without the remembrance of the dead and their labors for justice, of Jesus, of the dead in the wars that I have lived through and live through now, and of the dead whom I have loved.

The second reason comes from a text from the Jewish tradition of martyrdom. It has taught me a social-historical understanding of Jesus' death as an aspect of Jewish liberation history (see Kuhnen in particular). This text helped me to understand historically such peculiar statements as "died for our sins" (1 Cor. 15:3) or "means of expiation" (Rom. 3:25). The Fourth Book of Maccabees (the dating of which is placed anywhere from 35 to 118 C.E.) reflects on the Jewish men and women in the resistance against Rome. In 17:20-22 we read:

> These, then, who have been consecrated for the sake of God, are honored, not only with this heavenly honor, but also by the fact that because of them our enemies do not rule over our nation, the tyrant was punished, and the homeland purified—they having become, as it were, a ransom for the sin of our nation. And through the blood of these devout ones and their death as an atoning sacrifice, divine Providence preserved Israel that previously had been mistreated.

The remembrance of those martyrs and the liberating power of their death apparent in this text must not be confused with interpretations of the reconciling death of Jesus that are tools of oppression.

What also needs to be raised in this context is the discussion about a *wisdom Christology* as an *alternative* to a Christology of the cross.

Theologically, the feminist critique of traditional Christologies of the cross has its positive flip side in the feminist search for a spirituality that draws on wisdom traditions for its language of God, as well as its Christology. There is a basis for wisdom Christology in a number of New Testament texts that connect Christ and Sophia: Matt. 11:16-19 par.; 11:25-27 par.; 11:28-30; 23:34-39 par.; 1 Cor. 1:24. Connecting with a discussion in the history of religion going back to the 1920s, feminist Christian women have interpreted Jesus as Wisdom and have discovered dimensions in this Christology that are liberating for women (Schüssler Fiorenza, Schroer, Cady, Ronan, and Taussig et al.). My critical questions focus on two issues: (1) Does seeing Jesus as Wisdom *in opposition* to Jesus crucified do justice to the New Testament's Christologies of the cross? Or is it not, rather, that a justified repudiation of later oppressive Christologies is here projected back into the New Testament? (2) Can a wisdom Christology do justice to the gospel of the poor who have embraced the Jesus tradition? The wisdom literature, such as the Wisdom of Solomon, Proverbs, or Sirach, has different concerns. In relation to the gospel of the poor and its importance for an option for women that goes back to Jesus (and was still upheld in early Christianity), the tradition of the prophets, especially Trito-Isaiah, is a more direct point of reference than the wisdom tradition.

The subject of "Jesus and women" has taken a prominent place in the women's movement of recent years. It continues to be important for women and women's groups who seek to develop an independent way as Christian women. Christology flows, often implicitly, into the representation of the liberating history of women drawn, above all, from the four Gospels (see 7.2). Under the title "Jesus and women" it is the historical uniqueness of Jesus that is frequently presented. This means that a good deal of energy is expended in presenting Jesus in opposition to Judaism. Unfortunately, this subject has a pertinacious anti-Judaistic history (see 9.2 on anti-Judaism in feminist exegesis). In addition, the historical endeavor to establish the uniqueness of Jesus is theologically problematic, because here the interest in his uniqueness is dealt with on a false level. It is in the confession of Jesus, or in the prayers to him, and in the reflection on these, where his uniqueness belongs and not in the historical discussion. There is an anti-Judaism that is related to the subject "Jesus and women." This means that when the history of women and Jesus in early Christianity is studied in the Christian women's movement, it should be studied as part of the Jewish history of women.

Sheila Briggs, "Can an Enslaved God Liberate? Hermeneutical Reflections on Philippians 2:6-11," *Semeia* 47 (1989): 137–53; Susan Cady, Marian Ronan, and Hal Taussig, *Sophia: The Future of Feminist Spirituality* (San Francisco: Harper and Row, 1986); Mary Rose D'Angelo, "Abba and 'Father': Imperial Theology and the Jesus Tradition," *JBL* 111, no. 4 (1992): 611–30; Cain Hope Felder, ed., *Stony the Road We Trod: African American Biblical Interpretation* (Minneapolis: Fortress Press, 1991); Martina Gnadt, "'Abba Isn't Daddy': Aspekte einer feministisch-befreiungstheologischen Revision des Abba Jesu," in Luise Schottroff and Marie-Theres Wacker, eds., *Von der Wurzel getragen*, 115–31; Julie Hopkins, *Toward a Feminist Christology: Jesus of Nazareth, European Women, and the Christological Crisis* (London: SPCK, 1994); Emil Kautzsch, *Die Apokryphen und Pseudepigraphen des Alten Testaments* (1900), 2 vols. (Darmstadt: Wissenschaftliche Buchgesellschaft, 1975); Hans-Peter Kuhnen, ed., *Mit Thora und Todesmut* (see 8.2); Marli Lutz, "Filipenses: A Comunidade ainda canta," in Frank Veldin, Regene Lamb, and Marli Lutz, *Aspectos Liturgicos nas cartas de Paulo*, Estudos Biblicos 35 (1992), 68–75; Elisabeth

Moltmann-Wendel, Luise Schottroff, and Dorothee Sölle, "Kreuz," in *WbfTh*, 1991, 225–36; Luise Schottroff, "Wanderprophetinnen" (see 8.2); Silvia Schroer, "Jesus Sophia: Erträge der feministischen Forschung zu einer frühchristlichen Deutung der Praxis und des Schicksals von Jesus von Nazaret," in Doris Strahm and Regula Strobel, eds., *Vom Verlangen nach Heilwerden: Christologie in feministisch-theologischer Sicht* (Fribourg and Lucerne: Edition Exodus, 1991), 112–28; Elisabeth Schüssler Fiorenza (see 7.2); idem, "Auf den Spuren der Weisheit—Weisheitstheologisches Urgestein," in Verena Wodtke, ed., *Auf den Spuren der Weisheit* (Freiburg, Basel, and Vienna: Herder, 1991), 24–40; Dorothee Sölle, *Thinking about God: An Introduction to Theology* (Philadelphia: Trinity Press International, 1990); idem, "Warum brauchen wir eine feministische Christologie?" *EvTh* 53 (1993): 86–92; Regula Strobel, "Feministische Kritik an traditionellen Kreuzestheologien," in Doris Strahm and Regula Strobel, eds., *Vom Verlangen nach Heilwerden*, 52–64; Angelika Strotmann, "Weisheitschristologie ohne Antijudaismus? Gedanken zu einem bisher vernachlässigten Aspekt in der Diskussion um die Weisheitschristologie im Neuen Testament," in Luise Schottroff and Marie-Theres Wacker, eds., *Von der Wurzel getragen*, 153–75.

9.2 The Image of Woman—Sexuality—Sin

The following is not about the *history* of women but about the *image* of woman in early Christianity. This image has to be examined in terms of its function with regard to the place of women in society. The conception of femininity and masculinity and sexuality is closely related to the image of women. In this context the topic of *sin* should also be discussed, even though the New Testament itself only partially connects this topic with the woman and sexuality theme. Yet it is that connection that governs the definition of what "the woman" is both in the history of theology and of the interpretation of the New Testament.

The history of theology is dominated, indeed, by the virgin birth, by the virginal Mary as the *counterimage* of sinful Eve—the mythic embodiment of all women. Such is not the case in the portrayal of Mary in the opening narratives of the Gospels according to Matthew and Luke. Whereas the traditional discussion of virgin births in the history of religion and the customary interpretation of the texts function in terms of the idea of *conception by a divinity*, feminist discussion is critical of such a reading. In a seminal work, Jane Schaberg has shown that like Mary, the "ancestral women" of Jesus in Matthew 1 are outside the patriarchal family structure. These women suffer injustice, and with their sexual activity they threaten to destroy the social order. According to Schaberg, in the New Testament legends of Mary (Matthew 1; Luke 1, 2) the understanding of how Mary conceived the child is not that of a miraculous virginal conception. Schaberg maintains that a very different view appears here, namely, that during her engagement Mary was seduced or sexually assaulted. "In Matthew 1, God 'acts' in a radically new way, outside the patriarchal norm but within the natural event of human conception. The story of the illegitimacy of Jesus supports the claim that Luke makes, that Mary represents the oppressed who have been liberated" (1989, 119).

A detailed discussion is not possible here, but I will present my own thesis, which, even though it contradicts Schaberg's central thesis, does not wish to distract from the significance of her book for feminist exegesis. On the level of what the texts want to say, I see a narrative about the miracle of a fatherless birth. Contrary to the understanding that the text itself presupposes, namely that a woman becomes pregnant only through sexual intercourse with a man (see only Luke 1:34), the legend of Mary tells that Mary brought a child into the world through the creative power of the *pneuma* (the *ruaḥ*) without the procreation of a man or a male divinity. In light of the pivotal veneration of men's procreative prowess in patriarchal ideology and biology (including those of the ancient world), the legend of a fatherless pregnancy is critical of patriarchy at a decisive point. I do not fundamentally reject that the *historical* Mary may have experienced sexual violation; what I do see in these *legends* of Mary is the intent to tell of a wondrous event, namely that of a pregnancy without procreation.

While both of these interpretations (see Brigitte Kahl on the Lukan legends) demonstrate aspects of women's liberation, it must be noted that, next to such liberative aspects, these legends also show their very opposite, namely massive oppression of women, for example in the misogynist form of Matthew's legend of Joseph (see Wainwright).

This makes apparent a structure that pervades the whole New Testament. Next to texts that put women at the center and show them on the road toward liberation (e.g., the legends of Mary in Luke 1; see also John 4), there are found in the New Testament—as in other texts of early Christianity—texts that massively and openly insult and oppress women. The "household codes," the Pastorals (esp. 1 Tim. 2:12-16), 1

Cor. 11, and 14:33-36 are texts within the New Testament that must be cited for their *explicit* oppression of women. But there are many texts in addition to these which, when submitted to more precise feminist analysis, are oppressive of women *in actual fact.* As a result of their androcentrism, even texts critical of patriarchy, such as Phil. 2:6-11, are oppressive of women. There exist encompassing analyses of the portrayal of women in individual New Testament writings, especially of Matthew (Wainwright), Mark (Fander, Vogt, Dannemann), and Acts (Richter Reimer). *The Woman's Bible Commentary* provides information about the already available research findings concerning other writings of the New Testament. Feminist research will need to continue its study of the images of women in early Christian texts and how those images functioned for women themselves; it must also clarify further the struggles that are at the bottom of this contradictory structure (see 8.4).

The misogynist image of women or the misogynist parenesis of the New Testament is one of the aspects of early Christianity on which a specific anti-Judaism has fastened its attention, with the claim that it is oppressive to women. This misogyny is accounted for in terms of its rootedness in Judaism. Another instance of Christian anti-Judaism originates specifically among women; it focuses attention on passages of the New Testament that are liberating for women (e.g., individual traditions of Jesus or Gal. 3:28). Here an early Christianity that is liberating for women is seen in *contrast* to a Judaism that is oppressive of women. The significant and lively anti-Judaism debate within feminist theology, which is by no means concluded (see 2.4), focused to a very large extent on these images of women in the New Testament. A survey of this debate has been provided by Katharina von Kellenbach, Leonore Siegele-Wenschkewitz, and Christine Schaumberger. Without a doubt there are misogynist traditions in Judaism (Plaskow, Küchler), but they cannot legitimate Christian anti-Judaism.

I name only those aspects of the problem that are important for the interpretation of early Christian texts. (1) Since the whole history of Christian interpretation of the New Testament, up to and including the present, has worked with anti-Judaistic presuppositions, feminist exegesis must analyze critically every thought that is appropriated from the tradition of interpretation. In this context, it is particularly what the tradition of Christian scholarship has had to say concerning women in Judaism (in Hellenism) and in Christianity that must be subjected to the critical scrutiny of the analysis of patriarchy. What image of Judaism and of women and what understanding of class is it working with? The history of anti-Judaism in Christian feminist theology was set in motion through the unexamined acceptance of anti-Judaism from the so-called recognized traditional scholarship. (2) The conception of a Christian religion and institution that have historically cut themselves off from their Jewish matrix and are something "new" on the level of teaching and proclamation is historically false (see 8.3). What is depicted in that conception as "new" substance is historically erroneous as well as permeated with a denigration of the Jewish tradition. (3) The self-perception of Christianity, namely, that in comparison to Judaism it is actively liberating for women (e.g., in the person of Jesus), is based in an ahistorical thinking about the liberation of women in Christianity past and present.

What early Christianity thought about sexuality and femaleness and maleness has not yet been examined comprehensively. An article by Bernadette Brooten has set the trend and continues to do so. She demonstrates that in 1 Cor. 11:2-16, for theological reasons, Paul calls for a clear differentiation of the sexes. "The boundaries between femaleness and maleness must not be erased on account of the fact that women have short and men long hair. But even when women have long hair, the differentiation is not made sufficiently clear thereby" (132). And that is why Paul demands that women wear veils in worship services. According to him, even though Christian life supports women's autonomy (see 7.3), the order that puts men higher than women *must* be rigorously kept by Christians. The female must be passive, for which reason lesbian love is a confusion (Rom. 1:26f.) that endangers the hierarchy of gender.

Even though early Christianity fosters women's autonomy and independence from patriarchal domination within the family, the misogynous tradition of Aristotle's definition of femaleness and maleness is apparent in the texts such as Rom. 1:26f. "If the male, therefore, is that which gives origin to the movement and the active, and the female as such the passive, then the woman cannot add semen to the man's semen, but only matter" (Aristotle, *Gen. an.* 1.20f; 29a). Another basis for the understanding of sexuality is the idea that it is a dangerous force which, when left uncontrolled, can destroy life and health (Matt. 5:28-30; 1 Cor. 7:29ff.). Men's sexuality is seen here not only as the active force but also as very hard to keep in check so that, according to Paul, married women need to renounce asceticism in order to keep their men's sexuality under control (1 Cor. 7; see 7.3). Judith Plaskow has charted the "road toward a new theology of sexuality." From her one may learn to make sexuality a subject of theology, as it had been in Judaism and early Christianity.

One may also learn from her to look for positive points of connection in tradition that release a theology of sexuality from the misogynist heritage of Aristotle or Jean-Jacques Rousseau. Finally, one may learn from her to understand sexuality as a gift of God, in just relationship, free of a gender dualism polluted with domination.

In the age of imperial Rome, the conceptions of women that in many cultures and religions were already misogynist became in a particular way even harsher. For now, the myth of woman being the cause of the fall made its way. Evil and suffering came into being through the sexual activity of a mythical woman (whether it was Eve in Judaism and Christianity or Sophia in Gnosticism). Eve is the seducible seductress and became involved with Satan. For that reason women are generally defined in terms of their sexuality, and female sexuality is seen as guilt-ridden, dangerous and destructive. Traces of that myth are already present in the New Testament (2 Cor. 11:3; 1 Tim. 2:14-15). Later on, this mythology and misogyny spreads abroad also in early Christianity of all places. Eve becomes the embodiment of sin (Pagels, Küchler, Schüngel-Straumann); sin and sexuality are identified with each other. Subsequently, this Christian interpretation of Genesis 1–3 had its impact on the Christian interpretation of the New Testament, especially in the form of a hostility toward women and the body that most of the time lurks below the surface.

Another form of Christian hostility toward women is to be found in the tradition of interpretation of Paul's doctrine of sin. In both the history of Christian doctrine and the interpretation of the Epistle to the Romans, the understanding of sin as human autonomy plays a very important role. Sinful human beings are they who are determined to attain salvation through their own means. The exemplary sinner is "the Jew." For example, one finds this expressed by Ernst Käsemann and Rudolf Bultmann. In mentioning this fact, I do not wish to make a general attack on their interpretations of Paul. In biblical tradition, however, autonomy before God is something associated with those who rule (see only Luke 1:51), all of whom in actual fact misuse their power. But by regarding sin as the demeanor of domination on the part of *all* human beings, men's practice of domination is generalized and legitimated as a consequence. Furthermore, the reality of women, their "complicity" (Thürmer-Rohr) and self-sacrifice (Plaskow), is ignored, and the analysis of the sin of women is blocked. Complicity, a sin of women, is declared, instead, to be a virtue of the Christian woman. The discriminatory declaration of emancipation (of women or of liberation movements in the Two-Thirds World) as sin is yet another aspect of how the Christian interpretation of Paul's doctrine of sin is applied in a manner oppressive of women.

The history of interpretation of the Epistle to the Romans, indeed, of the whole New Testament in relation to the question of sin, is misogynist in many ways and must be unambiguously resisted by feminism. But it is also necessary to ask anew what is actually said about sin in Paul's Romans. I find in Paul a discerning and liberating analysis of the resignation and powerlessness of the lowly, who know well what God's will is but who have allowed the praxis of God's will to be taken from them (Rom. 7:14ff.). In this text, and from his androcentric perspective, Paul laments the estrangement of humans. On the one hand, people clearly know that God's will, that is, the Torah, is the path in life for them. But, "I do not what I wish to do but what I detest" (v. 15; cf. vv. 18 and 19). What humans do is estranged from God's will. Paul uses a striking image. The human being is like a cocoon that is incapable of acting; in it sits the demon sin making the human, like a puppet, do what is detestable (see esp. vv. 17 and 20). Paul understood this analysis of the estrangement of humanity to be universally applicable; it is actually spoken from the perspective of an adult Jewish male. There is a similar view of human estrangement in 2 Esdras. Paul laments the estrangement and, in doing so, analyzes the structure of death made by humans. But the basis of his lament and analysis is the experience of liberation: "Thanks be to God through Jesus Christ our Lord" (v. 25). From the point of view of social history, Paul speaks from the perspective of Jewish men who, within the structure of violence of the Roman Empire, experience themselves as fettered slaves who want to live by the Torah but cannot. Despite its androcentrism, this analysis offers fresh energies for the analysis of the acquiescence ever and again expected for women and given by them, in their own powerlessness, in their "complicity" (Thürmer-Rohr). Paul cannot deliver the feminist analysis of the specific entanglement of women in patriarchy's structures of death. Instead, what one may learn from him is how a paralyzing analysis that results in no action may become a liberating lament, since his analysis is part of a liberating process.

Bernadette Brooten, "Darum lieferte Gott sie entehrenden Leidenschaften aus: Die weibliche Homoerotik bei Paulus," in Monika Barz, Herta Leistner, and Ute Wild, *Hättest du gedacht, dass wir so viele sind? Lesbische Frauen in der Kirche* (Stuttgart: Kreuz Verlag, 1987), 113–38;

Irene Dannemann, *Aus dem Rahmen fallen* (see 8.4); Monika Fander, 1989 (see 8.2); Tal Ilan, *Jewish Women in Greco-Roman Palestine, Texte und Studien zum Antiken Judentum* 44 (Tübingen: J. C. B. Mohr, 1995); Brigitte Kahl, *Armenevangelium und Heidenevangelium: "Sola scriptura" und die ökumenische Traditionsproblematik im Lichte von Väterkonflikt und Väterkonsens bei Lukas* (Berlin: Evangelische Verlagsanstalt, 1987); idem, "Jairus und die verlorenen Töchter Israels: Sozioliterarische Überlegungen zum Problem der Grenzüberschreitung in Mark 5,21–43," in Luise Schottroff and Marie-Theres Wacker, eds., *Von der Wurzel getragen*, 61–78; Katharina von Kellenbach, "Anti-Judaism in Christian-Rooted Feminist Writings: An Analysis of Major American and West German Feminist Theologians" (diss., Philadelphia, 1990); Max Küchler, *Schweigen, Schmuck und Schleier: Drei neutestamentliche Vorschriften zur Verdrängung der Frauen auf dem Hintergrund einer frauenfeindlichen Exegese des Alten Testaments im antiken Judentum* (Fribourg: Universitätsverlag; Göttingen: Vandenhoeck und Ruprecht, 1986); Carol A. Newsom and Sharon H. Ringe, eds., *The Women's Bible Commentary* (Louisville: Westminster/John Knox Press, 1992); Elaine Pagels, *Gnostic Gospels* (see the first bibliographical list in chap. 7); Judith Plaskow, *Sex, Sin, and Grace* (Washington: University Press of America, 1980); idem, *Standing Again at Sinai* (see 8.3); Ivoni Richter Reimer (see 7.2); Jane Schaberg, "The Foremothers and the Mother of Jesus," in Anne Carr and Elisabeth Schüssler Fiorenza, eds., *Motherhood: Experience, Institution, Theology* (Edinburgh: T. & T. Clark, 1989), 112–19; idem, *The Illegitimacy of Jesus: A Feminist Theological Interpretation of the Infancy Narratives* (New York: Crossroad, 1987); Christine Schaumberger, ed., *Weil wir nicht vergessen wollen . . . Zu einer feministischen Theologie im deutschen Kontext*, Anfragen 1 (Münster, 1987); Christine Schaumberger and Luise Schottroff, 1988 (see 8.3); Luise Schottroff, *Lydia's Impatient Sisters* (see 7.4); Helen Schüngel-Straumann, *Die Frau am Anfang: Eva und die Folgen* (Freiburg, Basel, and Vienna: Herder, 1989); Leonore Siegele-Wenschkewitz, ed., *Verdrängte Vergangenheit, die uns bedrängt: Feministische Theologie in der Verantwortung für die Geschichte* (Munich: Chr. Kaiser Verlag, 1988); Elsa Tamez, *The Amnesty of Grace* (see 8.4); Christina Thürmer-Rohr, *Vagabonding: Feminist Thinking Cut Loose* (Boston: Beacon Press, 1991); Thea Vogt, *Angst und Identität im Markusevangelium: Ein textpsychologischer und sozialgeschichtlicher Beitrag* (Fribourg: Universitätsverlag; Göttingen: Vandenhoeck und Ruprecht, 1993); Elaine Mary Wainwright (see 8.4).

9.3 Serving and Holding Office

One of the foci of feminist theological exegesis was and is the new interpretation of New Testament texts that inform us about the work of
women who were in positions of authority in early Christian congregations.

Rom. 16:7 speaks of "Andronicus and Junia. . . . They are eminent
among the *apostoloi*." Bernadette Brooten has studied the history of this
text's interpretation from the ancient church onwards. She has demonstrated that in the ancient church, the name of Junia was known to be
the name of a woman and that Junia herself was regarded as an apostle.
The view that the one Paul mentions was a male apostle called Junias,
emerged first with Aegidius of Rome (1245–1316 c.e.) and has been on
a victory parade since the Reformation. The interest that is being pursued here is utterly clear: a female apostle called Junia in early Christianity would seriously question the biblical legitimation of the gender hierarchy established in the great church. In dominant theology, Paul the
Apostle embodies above all men's claim on office and leadership, a claim
that excludes women. I name a number of propositions in connection
with Rom. 16:7 that were meant to rule out that Junia was a woman.
The Greek circumflex accent on the accusative ending Junian is to make
it clear that it is the man's name Junias and not the woman's name Junia.
Even the most recent edition of Nestle's *Greek New Testament* (27th ed.,
1993) and the newest edition of Walter Bauer's *Lexicon of the New Testament* (the sixth "completely revised" German edition of 1988) make use
of that accent, even though it goes against the tradition of the handwrit-
ten documents—whenever they made use of accents at all—as well as
against the philological fact that there is no evidence of a man's name
Junias. Another move to deny the actuality of a woman apostle called
Junia is the emphatic assertion that Junia is Andronicus's marriage partner and not an apostle, but that she was "renowned among the apostles."

The Lutheran translation of Scripture (German: revised in 1984) still
speaks of Junias. The newest translation of Scripture prepared in North
America (NRSV, 1989) has "Junia." Feminist discussion on that conti-
nent is less repressed than in Germany. A shortened version of Bernadette Brooten's study first appeared in German in 1978, exemplifying
what interests of power, or better, of domination, are encountered in the
field of exegesis and how they are asserted even against ancient texts.
One comes across similar findings again and again, such as the interpre-

tations and translations of *diakonein* and *prostasis* as descriptions of Phoebe's function in the congregation (Rom. 16:1).

The interpretation of the word *diakonein* (and the group of words associated with it) is much disputed. (See 7.4.) Traditional exegesis distinguishes between men's serving (= the office held by men; service of the Word) and women's serving (= housework, caring for small children). A *diakonia* specific to women, such as visiting other sick women, was within the range of conceivability.

Feminist exegesis has often concentrated on the question of the work of women in positions of authority. This has resulted in new interpretations which will be difficult to contest. In this connection the work of Elisabeth Schüssler Fiorenza above all is highly creative. I shall sketch some of the results of the feminist discussion in this area.

In early Christianity, *diakonia* does not refer to an "office" in the sense of hierarchy of offices. Because of the associations of the word *office* (German *Amt*) with domination or "ruling over" (German *Herrschaftsamt*), it is incorrect to translate *diakonia* as "office." Early Christianity tried in many of its congregations to do away with divisions of labor based on the hierarchy of gender. I think of the division of labor that assigns women to unpaid or poorly paid work while assigning men to work that is better paid and embodies ruling power. I use *racist* when speaking of division of labor between slaves and free people. I am fully aware, of course, that the enslavement of people in antiquity is not based in racial theories like those of the nineteenth and twentieth centuries. Still, the legitimation of slavery and the actual treatment of female and male slaves is to a large extent congruent with modern racism. Ancient societies openly lived out their hierarchies; at every turn, ordinary life made them very apparent (e.g., in the way people dressed). Hierarchy assured that a man born free would never do any work associated with the household. The hierarchy of the household was clear: beginning at the bottom, there was the female slave, the male slave, the unmarried woman born free, the married woman born free, and so forth. The adult man and father, born free, is master over the rest of the household.

Every attempt to break free from this hierarchy and to do away with it altogether in the early Christian congregations always had to meet resistance from both without and within (see the household codes). Conflicts in connection with the abrogation of this hierarchy are visible, for example, in Luke 10:38-42 and parallels, depicting the conflict over who is higher in rank (Mark 10:35-40 par.). (See 7.4.) The First Epistle to

Timothy is an excellent but most involuntary witness to the fact that women took part on their own authority in teaching and the work of public leadership, including that of teaching men. The Syrian *Didaskalia* (from the beginning of the third century C.E. in northern Syria) is, like 1 Timothy, clearly a document about the oppression of women on the one hand, but also a document about a militant church of women and laypeople on the other. (For an interpretation, see Schottroff, *Lydia's Impatient Sisters*, 143ff.) It is part of the program of every gospel to abrogate hierarchies (Mark 10:42-45 par. and John 13); the texts all speak an androcentric language as if the hierarchies to be done away with were only those between men. However, the context of early Christianity shows that the domination of women by men and of slaves by free people was also noted with critique and changed in practical life. For that reason, it is only consistent that Jesus calls on his disciples (male and female) to wash the feet of the other disciples (both male and female!). It was quite customary that women washed the feet of men. But that free men washed the feet of women and of slaves—even female slaves—was an act of revolutionary dimension. At that time washing feet was an act observed punctiliously and with utter deference to existing hierarchies. (See 10.5, the citation from Joseph and Asenath.)

Hans Achelis and Johs. Flemming (see 8.1); Bernadette Brooten, "'Junia . . . hervorragend unter den Aposteln' (Rom. 16,7)," in Elisabeth Moltmann-Wendel, ed., *Frauenbefreiung: Biblische und theologische Argumente*, 3d ed. (Munich: Chr. Kaiser Verlag, 1982), 148–51; Marlene Crüsemann, "Unrettbar frauenfeindlich: Der Kampf um das Wort von Frauen in 1 Kor 14,33b–35 im Spiegel antijudaistischer Elemente der Auslegung," in Luise Schottroff and Marie-Theres Wacker, eds., *Von der Wurzel getragen*, 199–223; Ross S. Kraemer, 1992 (see 8.3); U.-K. Plisch, "Die Apostelin Junia: Das exegetische Problem in Rom. 17,7 im Licht von Nestle-Aland 27 und der sahidischen Überlieferung," *NTS* 42 (1996): 477–78; Luise Schottroff, "DienerInnen der Heiligen" (see 7.2); idem, *Lydia's Impatient Sisters;* Elisabeth Schüssler Fiorenza, *In Memory of Her;* Caroline Vander Stichele, "Is Silence Golden? Paul and Women's Speech in Corinth," *Louvain Studies* 20 (1995): 241–53.

Chapter Ten

Feminist Praxis of Interpreting the New Testament

Diverse traditions have become part of the feminist praxis of interpreting texts of early Christianity: the ruling biblical scholarship of the academy, the reading of Scripture practiced in liberation movements of the Two-Thirds World, the discussion of feminist social science, dimensions of psychological theory and therapy, and, above all, the creative rage and enthusiasm of women who have recognized the Bible as an instrument of women's oppression while, at the same time, seeking the history of their foresisters as a source of their power. I shall try once again, from my perspective, to summarize briefly this diversity that merges in feminist reading of the Bible. (See Part One by Marie-Theres Wacker.)

10.1 The Location of Bible Reading: Women's Movement and Feminist Science

In the recent women's movement, insofar as there was and is an interest at all in Christianity, an autonomous reading of the Bible has emerged. It is autonomous in that both the tradition of exegetical scholarship and the prevailing practice of interpretation in the churches were experienced as instruments of domination hostile to women. What women say in relation to membership in the church varies most widely at this point. For many, the liberation of women within the Christian tradition and church is a contradiction in itself; others—among whom I count myself—work for a fundamental transformation of the churches. However wide the difference on this issue, in the women's movement within the churches or at its edges, there is unanimity about the great need for a critical reassessment of the Christian history of oppressing women and of the misogynist texts of the Bible. At the same time, there is agreement that in the Bible there are to be found traditions and traces of women's history with which women today can connect. Regardless of the proximity or distance to ecclesial institutions, both sides of the autonomous reading of the Bible are experienced by women as acts of liberation and are heeded with intense interest. Discarded are the old reading glasses of the academy's scholarship and its domination, and of the church's dogmatics. This allows new and fascinating discoveries to be made in communal readings of the Bible. Unfortunately, such readings are difficult to document since so much of it is recorded in "informal" literature. Some texts published in anthologies by established publishing houses allow us nonetheless to appropriate indirectly this reading of Scripture, for example, the anthology by Schmidt, Korenhof, and Jost.

The women who are moved by women and who were and are at the margins of biblical scholarship in German-speaking countries endeavor to pursue in a new way the work of New Testament scholarship (or of Scripture as a whole). The difficulties they face are enormous. I can cite them here only for the German context since the development particularly in North America took such a different course. While a feminist scholarship could establish itself there within the academic institutions, it is still out of the question in Germany. As a rule, it is neither possible to write a dissertation in the area of New Testament from the perspective of feminist theology, nor even to get an appropriate education in feminist theology. The pressure on women to conform is horrendous. Very rarely do women obtain positions in which they can do feminist scholarly work. Discourse between dominant biblical scholarship and feminist science exists only in most narrow forms (see the study by Hübener and Meesmann). And yet, despite these difficulties, there is today a wide circle of German-speaking women theologians engaged in scholarly work who both do and advance feminist exegesis. For these women scholars, the living bond to the movement of "lay" women is a normal dimension of their self-awareness. The initial protest of women, who regarded themselves as "barefoot theologians" (feminist Christian women whose orientation is intentionally that of the base communities as contrasted to the academy), against the developments of feminist theological science are pointless now, since divisions of that kind are counterproductive for the women's movement. Part of the collaborative energy is directed today more to institutionalizing feminist theology at universities and other places.

Britta Hübener and Hartmut Meesmann, eds., *Streitfall Feministische Theologie* (Düsseldorf: Patmos, 1993); Eva Renate Schmidt, Mieke Korenhof, and Renate Jost, eds., *Feministisch gelesen,* 2 vols. (Stuttgart: Kreuz Verlag, 1988, 1989).

10.2 "From Life to Scripture— From Scripture to Life"

The title for this section is a citation from a book by liberation theologian Carlos Mesters. In a short formula it expresses the method of how Scripture is read in liberation theology. But it may also clarify feminist reading of the Bible and how it and liberation theologies are connected. The women's movement is in sisterly relationship with the peace movement, the ecological, and the One-World movements. Today these relationships have enabled women in initially androcentric liberation movements to actualize their interests more decisively—in the German-speaking context as well as in other countries. One model of reading Scripture has become quite prominent in the women's movement; it draws on the tradition of reading the Bible in North American liberation theology and women's movements. It is the model developed by Elisabeth Schüssler Fiorenza in her four hermeneutical steps (see 2.1.5). Many women also work with an ecumenical three-step method (Schroer 1993). In the context of describing the feminist practice of interpreting the New Testament, it is important to reiterate that scholarly feminist exegesis of the New Testament, given its point of departure, is also drawn into the process of reading "from life to Scripture—from Scripture to life." The questions put to history and traditions arise from reflections on women's experiences and struggles. For that very reason, they remain in a fundamental tension with a New Testament scholarship that implicitly or explicitly, and unjustly so, claims neutrality and objectivity for itself (see 7.1).

Regene Lamb and Claudia Janssen, "Die Herausforderung feministischer Bibelauslegung: Zur Gratwanderung zwischen akademischen Idealen und alltäglicher Erfahrung," *Junge Kirche* 54 (1993): 609–13; Carlos

Mesters, *Vom Leben zur Bibel, von der Bibel zum Leben*, 2 vols. (Mainz: Grünewald; Munich: Chr. Kaiser Verlag, 1983); Luise Schottroff, *Lydia's Impatient Sisters*; Silvia Schroer, "Feministische Bibelforschung: Anliegen, Methoden und Inhalte," in L. Blattmann et al., eds., *Feministische Perspektiven in der Wissenschaft*, Zürcher Hochschulforum 21 (1993), 41–52; Dorothee Sölle, *On Earth as in Heaven: A Liberation Spirituality of Sharing* (Louisville: Westminster/John Knox Press, 1993), ix–xi.

10.3 The So-called Different Approaches to the Bible

In conferences and books, one frequently finds listings of newer ways of interpreting Scripture in which "different approaches" are placed one next to the other: feminist interpretation, materialist reading, bibliodrama, depth-psychological interpretation, and others. Such a way of looking at and listing how Scripture is accessed is problematic, since it fails to indicate that these approaches—disregarding for the moment that they overlap—are not on the same level. This becomes quite plain when one asks the following two questions: (1) What aim does this interpretation of Scripture pursue? (2) What is the history that is to be written with a specific interpretation of the Bible, or on which historiography does that interpretation rely? A reigning interpretation of Scripture, such as that of the historical criticism in the universities, writes an androcentric history that is uncritical of patriarchal structures. This assertion is easy to verify, for example, by an analysis of the image presented there of Paul. Even an androcentric history of the lowly does *not* tell half the truth as long as women remain invisible (see 7.1). An approach to Scripture that does not wish to work with the tools of history must—consciously or unconsciously—depend on existing historiography. And when a biblio-drama reading of Scripture, for example, makes use of the interpretation of historical criticism, there will be androcentrism and incorporation into patriarchal structures. Such critical observations seek to make it plain that a pluralistic apposition of approaches to Scripture feigns an openness that is justified only after the elements of historiography and the purposes have been critically examined in terms of feminism or feminist liberation theology. Of course, feminist liberation theology works with the tools of historical criticism, but it does so with a historiographical orientation and a hermeneutic that differ from those of dominant historical criticism.

10.4   The Tools

A presentation of a methodical reflection on the historical toil of feminist exegesis is not my purpose here; for that discussion Part One of this book can be consulted. Elsewhere I have discussed these questions in connection with the procedures of feminist social history (Schottroff 1995). My present concern is to pass on practical experiences in relation to the tools to be used.

In the field of biblical studies, the torrent of androcentric and patriarchal publications that pours from the established institutions is an often suffocating and discouraging impediment for a feminist exegete. She faces a mountain of books. She knows that they are androcentric, while presenting themselves nonetheless as scholarly. And then she is often constrained to legitimate herself within that scholarship which, in Germany at least, is very difficult. In this situation I suggest the following: demystification is the only thing that will help here. Methodologically, demystification means to subject the reigning biblical scholarship to an analysis of patriarchy. In terms of practice, the following procedure will suffice for the demystification. I will restrict my analysis to one verse of Scripture. At the outset it is useful to choose a verse that is about a woman, such as John 4:18. Then I gather as many interpretations of that verse as I like from scholarly commentaries, monographs, articles, and so forth and analyze them in terms of one or two feminist questions. What image of women is transmitted in these interpretations? Are any questions raised by them about the life and world of women, their oppression, and their struggles? What is at the heart of the interests pursued by these interpretations?

Such a procedure can be carried out relatively easily and leads to demystification and clear perception of traditional and institutionalized interpretation of the Bible—not only of the one verse, for the pattern is the same. This procedure also awakens curiosity about what the text actually says. Does John 4:18 really say that the Samaritan woman was a hussy, as traditional interpretation wants us to believe?

In order to gain one's own historical insights after having demystified the giants, a number of old-fashioned tools can be very handy. Prepare an accurate arrangement of the contents of the text and determine its genre. The latter requires that existing classification of the genre be looked at critically and, if need be, demystified. Furthermore, it is helpful to divide one's procedure into several working steps: What literary, social-historical and religio-historical context am I working in? What is my understanding of the history of early Christianity? (See chap. 7.)

Another practical phenomenon to be named is the widely experienced initial intimidation by extrabiblical sources referred to in scholarly literature, often in an obscure system of abbreviations that is hard to comprehend. It is truly an experience of liberation to read a tract about women by Tertullian in translation; it is liberating because freedom is served when one knows who the enemies are. The impression created by the giants that consecrations of a higher order are required in order to read extrabiblical sources is without substance. The only requirement is to do the detective work to find the translation and, for a more precise study, the sources in the original languages. I name proven resources that assist in accessing extrabiblical sources.

For Talmud and Midrash: H. L. Strack and Günter Stemberger, *Introduction to the Talmud and Midrash,* 2d ed. (Edinburgh: T. & T. Clark, 1996); *for First Testament Apocrypha and Pseudepigrapha:* Leonhard Rost, *Judaism outside the Hebrew Canon: An Introduction to the Documents* (Nashville: Abingdon, 1976); *for Jewish writings of the time of the Second Temple:* Michael E. Stone, ed., *Jewish Writings of the Second Temple Period* (Philadelphia: Fortress Press, 1984); *for ancient authors:* Paul Kroh, *Lexikon der antiken Autoren* (Stuttgart, 1972); *for New Testament Apocrypha:* Wilhelm Schneemelcher, ed., *New Testament Apocrypha,* 2 vols. (Louisville: Westminster/John Knox Press, 1991); *for literature of the ancient church:* Bertold Altaner, *Patrology* (New York: Herder and Herder, 1960).

It is useful for the historical work of feminist exegesis to get an understanding of the context of the patriarchy of antiquity through the witness of patriarchy itself. Aristotle (384–322 B.C.E.) and, after him, Cicero (106–43 B.C.E.) have described patriarchy as a social system and ideology, as have all philosophers of antiquity who wrote about the economy and the household. Since Cicero's description of patriarchy was made with a view to Rome's world domination, it is particularly close historically to the world of early Christianity. All these theoreticians of patriarchy presuppose a similar and encompassing concept of patriarchy, as

described in section 7.1. I would like to cite a number of key ideas from these self-portraits of patriarchy as resources for the exegesis of the New Testament.
Aristotle on the genesis of the creatures, bk. 1, chap. 20:

> [A]nd a woman is as it were an infertile male; the female, in fact, is female on account of inability of a sort, namely, it lacks the power to concoct semen out of the final state of the nourishment.
>
> [W]hat happens is what one would expect to happen. The male provides the "form" and the "principle of the movement," the female provides the body, in other words, the material. Compare the coagulation of milk. Here the milk is the body, and the . . . rennet contains the principle which causes it to set.
>
> Thus, if the male is the active partner, the one which originates the movement, and the female *qua* female is the passive one, surely what the female contributes to the semen of the male will not be semen but material. (*Generation of Animals*, trans. A. L. Peck [Cambridge: Harvard University Press, 1943], 103, 109, 111)

From Aristotle's *Politics:*

> Thus by nature most things are ruling and ruled. For the free person rules the slave, the male the female, and the man the child in different ways. The parts of the soul are present in all, but they are present in a different way. The slave is wholly lacking the deliberative element; the female has it but lacks authority; the child has it but it is incomplete. (Trans. Carnes Lord [Chicago and London: University of Chicago Press, 1984], 53)

Cicero, on the *res publica:*

> But we must distinguish between different kinds of domination and subjection. For the mind is said to rule over the body, and also over lust; but it rules the body as a king governs his subjects or a father his children, whereas it rules over lust as a master rules his slaves, restraining it and breaking its power.
>
> But if a free people chooses the men to whom it is to entrust its fortunes . . . then certainly the safety of the state depends on the wisdom of its best men, especially since Nature has provided not only that those men who are superior in virtue and spirit should rule the weaker, but also that the weaker should be willing to obey the stronger. (*De republica,* trans. C. W. Keyes [Cambridge: Harvard University Press, 1951], III-37, I-51)

Cicero on dutiful action:

> We may assume that it is naturally common to living things to have the desire to procreate [*libido procreandi*]. The first stage of society, then, is in the basic man-wife relationship [*prima societas in ipso coniugo est*]; a second stage is in the children of that union; and a third stage is in the single household [*una domus*] where all the members share everything [*communia omnia*]. The household is the foundation of the city, what we might call the "seed-bed" of the state. (*De officiis*, trans. Harry G. Edinger [Indianapolis and New York: Bobbs-Merrill Co., 1974], I-54)

Columella, a Roman writer on rural life, who lived during the first century C.E., summarizes the discussion in the economics of antiquity about marriage as the primal cell of the state (bk. 13 of *On Agriculture and Trees*, preface):

> Xenophon, the Athenian, in the book, Publius Silvinus, which is entitled *Economicus*, declared that the married state was instituted by nature so that man might enter what was not only the most pleasant but also the most profitable partnership in life. For in the first place, as Cicero also says, man and woman were associated to prevent the human race from perishing in the passage of time; and, second, in order that, as a result of the same association, mortals might be provided with help and likewise with defense in their old age. Furthermore, since man's food and clothing had to be prepared for him, not in the open air and in woods and forests, as for the wild animals, but at home and beneath a roof, it became necessary that one of the two sexes should lead an outdoor life in the open air, in order that by his toil and industry he might procure provisions which might be stored indoors, since indeed it was necessary to till the soil or to sail the sea or carry on some other form of business in order that we acquire some worldly substance. When, however, the goods thus secured had been stored under cover, there had to be someone else to guard them after they had been brought in and to carry on the operations which ought to be performed at home. For corn and other forms of food provided by the earth needed a roof over them, and the young of sheep and of the other kinds of cattle, and fruits, and also all else that is useful for the sustenance and tending of mankind had to be safely kept in security. Wherefore, as the duties which we have described call for both labor and diligence, and as the acquisition of those things which have to be safeguarded at home calls for no small amount of

attention out of doors, it is only right, as I have said, that the female sex has been provided for the care of the home, the male for out-of-doors and open-air activities. God, therefore, has assigned to man the endurance of heat and cold and the journeys and toils of peace and war, that is, of agriculture and military service, while has handed over to woman, since he has made her unsuited to all these functions, the care of domestic affairs. And since he has assigned to the female sex the duties of guardianship and care, he made woman on this account more timid than man, since fear conduces very greatly to careful guardianship. On the other hand, since it was necessary for those who sought for food out of doors in the open air sometimes to repel attacks, God made man bolder than woman. But seeing that, after they had acquired substance, memory and attention were equally necessary for both sexes, God granted no smaller a share of these qualities to women than to men. Then, too, because nature in her simplicity did not wish either sex to enjoy the possession of every advantage, she desired that each should have need of the other, since what one lacks is generally present in the other.

These were the views not unprofitably expressed by Xenophon in the *Economicus* and by Cicero, who translated his work into the Latin language. For both amongst the Greeks and afterwards amongst the Romans down to the time which our fathers can remember domestic labor was practically the sphere of the married woman, the fathers of the family betaking themselves to the family fireside, all care laid aside, only to rest from their public activities. For the utmost reverence for them ruled in the home in an atmosphere of harmony and diligence, and the most beauteous of women was fired with emulation, being zealous by her care to increase and improve her husband's business. No separate ownership was to be seen in the house, nothing which either the husband or the wife claimed by right as one's own, but both conspired for the common advantage, so that the wife's diligence at home vied with the husband's public activities. (Lucius Junius Moderatus Columella, *De re rustica*, trans. E. S. Forster and E. H. Heffner [Cambridge: Harvard University Press, 1955], 175–79)

This patriarchal ideology and the patriarchal reality to which it gave shape are present throughout the New Testament, meeting there both agreement and critique.

It is very important for feminist exegesis that it establish for itself a context of linkages within feminist discussion, both in life and in scholarship. There is by now such wealth of feminist and feminist theological scholarship, as evidenced in the bibliographical listings of this book, that help can in fact be found in answering many a question. As far as the New Testament is concerned, Christian women may learn significantly from Jewish feminist discussion. For a first introduction to feminist exegesis I recommend, therefore, a book by Judith Plaskow. It does not have the New Testament at all for its subject, but it is nevertheless of great help in feminist New Testament exegesis. A rich source for the history of Jewish women is Samuel Krauss's often overlooked work on Talmudic archaeology.

A good, first entry into the riches of North American feminist biblical scholarship is provided by Shelley D. Finson's bibliographic resource and *The Women's Bible Commentary*, edited by Carol A. Newsom and Sharon A. Ringe.

The wealth of feminist exegetical discussion in contexts the languages of which are less well known is more difficult to access. Yet, the further development of feminist exegesis in the German-speaking context—or even in the Western European one—requires the dialogue with women exegetes of the Two-Thirds World. Access to the Latin American discussion is provided by a special number of *RIBLA* (1993), which includes summaries in English, as well as by Milton Schwantes (1992).

The context of linkages within feminist discussion permits feminist exegetes to learn from and mutually critique one another. Still, this context frequently leaves something to be desired. Women often find themselves in the position of having to reinvent the wheel because there is no information about where other women have already done advance work. That is why participation in women's networks, such as the European Society for Women's Theological Research, is an essential component in feminist research.

Shelley D. Finson, *Women and Religion: A Bibliographic Guide to Christian Feminist Liberation Theology* (Toronto: University of Toronto Press, 1991); Samuel Krauss, *Talmudische Archäologie*, 3 vols. (Leipzig, 1911–19; reprint Hildesheim, 1966); Carol A. Newsom and Sharon H. Ringe, eds., *The Women's Bible Commentary* (Louisville: Westminster/John Knox Press, 1992); Judith Plaskow, *Standing Again at Sinai; RIBLA—Revista de Interpretación Bíblica Latino-Americana* 15 (1992/3), "Por Maos de Mulher"; Luise Schottroff, *Lydia's Impatient Sisters*, 1995; Milton Schwantes, ed., *Bibliografia Bíblica Latino-Americana*, vol. 5 (1992) (São Bernardo do Campo, 1993).

10.5 A Proven Model of Exegetical Working Steps and an Example of Interpretation: "What God Has Joined Together . . ." (Mark 10:2-12)

First I shall introduce a schema or model of working steps in exegesis that has proven its worth over the years in diverse contexts—such as women's groups, women's conferences, exegetical work by students preparing to teach at every level in the school system, and students preparing for ordination to ministry. I do not wish to enter into the theory of this model (I refer the reader to my book *Lydia's Impatient Sisters*) but, instead, present it through the interpretation of a text.

A Model for Exegetical Working Steps

	In relation to parables
1. First text analysis through	1. First text analysis through
• determining the text's basis	• determining the text's basis
• arranging the parts	• arranging the parts
• assessing linguistic weight and peculiarities	• assessing linguistic weight and peculiarities
• determining the genre	• determining the genre
2. Classification in terms of intellectual history and the history of religion (First Testament, postbiblical Judaism, Hellenism)	2. Classification in terms of intellectual history and the history of religion (First Testament, postbiblical Judaism, Hellenism)
	• clarification of the metaphorical tradition wherein the parable is located (attention particularly to the First Testament and rabbinic parables)
	• clarification of the relation between narrative and God's reign, that is, how the two levels in the parable are related

3. Social-historical analysis in terms of
   - the concept *critique of patriarchy*
   - details in the text

   - the overall situation of the Jesus movement or early Christian communities

3. Social-historical analysis in terms of
   - the concept *critique of patriarchy*
   - details in the narrative ("image")

   - the overall situation of the Jesus movement or early Christian communities
   - the relation between social reality and the narrative ("image")

4. The literary context
5. Coordination of the text with Jesus' message and praxis or that of his followers in early Christianity

4. The literary context
5. Coordination of the text with Jesus' message and praxis or that of his followers in early Christianity

The text I have chosen for demonstrating the model is Mark 10:2-12. The questions I want to put to the context of this passage derive from the experiences of women within the context of my life. (1) Where in the Christian tradition can I find at least initial steps toward a liberating treatment of sexuality and relationships between human beings? (Or is there no tradition at all to which I can refer?) (2) What role does this text of Mark's Gospel play in the ideology of oppression of my ecclesiastical tradition?

By even thinking it worth considering that in the tradition of Christianity there are not only traditions hostile and suppressive to sexuality, I apply in a somewhat pointed form the hermeneutic of suspicion that Elisabeth Schüssler Fiorenza describes. It is my suspicion that the patriarchal theology in the tradition of Christianity suppresses not only women, children, sexuality, and other religions, but also the texts of Scripture itself and, for that reason, the people who speak in them.

Judith Plaskow has demonstrated that the Jewish tradition concerning sexuality is shaped decisively by the belief that sexuality is a powerful source of energy and, for that reason, needs to be placed within the control of society. Historically speaking, this control was oriented by patriarchy and its domination, which meant the oppression of women. Yet, within this "model of energy and control" there also are Jewish traditions that a feminist vision of sexuality can connect with. For example, according to these traditions, women have a right to sexuality (the so-called Onah laws; see Plaskow, 180). Sexuality is understood as a good gift of God and the sexual relationship (within patriarchal marriage) as a place of sanctification (185).

A feminist vision of sexuality does not understand it narrowly as genital sexuality and limited to a legitimated (that is, a patriarchal) marriage. Openness to diverse forms of living is an essential element of feminist ethics. In it, liberated sexuality is a creative life force within human relationships that are built on mutuality and not on subordination. The creative power of sexuality within human relationships is all-encompassing. It can create relationships between women and women, women and men, young and old; it can liberate from the prison of social structures and make for relationships without suppression.

Before I can look for the answer to the two questions to Mark 10:2-12 cited above, I must try to understand the text historically. I have to structure my historical work in such a way that I may be able to judge whether the existing Christian tradition is justified or not. That tradition asserts that this text declares Jesus' prohibition of divorce and presents patriarchal marriage as the norm for Christian life—priestly celibacy in Roman Catholic ethics excepting. It is my experience that the domination-oriented Christian traditions of interpretation and ethical norms have a longer life span than the Christian faith itself. In the extensively secularized society of my context, it is this tradition that still negatively or positively determines behavior: either patriarchal marriage as the norm or everything is permitted. While the reversal of an oppressive Christian norm into laissez-faire (I refer again to Plaskow) may grant adultery to women as it has done for men for a long time, it still confronts women as yet another form of exploitation.

I will now study historically the text of Mark 10:2-12 against the background of these experiences and this vision, using the model of exegetical working steps introduced earlier.

Determining the text's basis (step 1) is particularly relevant in relation to verse 7. There are ancient manuscripts that at this point shorten the citation from Gen. 2:24. They leave out "and he shall cleave to his wife." Such deletions are taken by traditional exegesis today as legitimation for reading the text "the modern way." The "man" who leaves father and mother may also be a woman. The word *anthropos*/human being in the citation from Gen. 2:24 must not be read androcentrically on account of the deletion; so the argument goes. In Gen. 2:24, including its Greek version, there is no ambiguity as to the maleness of the human being.

Such a deliberate correction of this androcentrism on the part of Mark, as it is widely claimed today in connection with Mark 10:7, would uncover most-unexpected treasures for the exegesis of the whole Gospel of Mark. The "human being," within whom Jesus helps fight an evil spirit in the synagogue of Capernaum (Mark 1:23), could be a woman, as could the "human being" with the withered hand (Mark 3:1). But the very same exegetes who read Mark 10:7 inclusively read these healing narratives, and the word *anthropos* elsewhere in Mark, in androcentric form. The alleged parity of the sexes claimed for Mark 10:7 in recent traditions of interpretation (I shall name no individual examples, since this feature is so widespread) serves to conceal the exegete's own patriarchal androcentrism. I look in vain in those interpretations for a critique of patriarchal marriage. Thus, Mark 10:7 has to be read as being androcentric, as the older traditions of interpretation did. The abbreviation of the quotation from Gen. 2:24 is of no consequence to the substance of the text. The full text was very much in the minds of all affected at that time. No critical distance toward androcentrism is to be noted here.

Arranging the parts of the text (step 1) shows verses 2–9 describing a discussion between Jesus and male and female Pharisees. (That there were female Pharisees—for example, the mother of Paul, Acts 23:6—should become much more part of the exegetical consciousness than has hitherto been the case.) Verses 10–12 are the halakic teaching of Jesus to his men and women disciples, that is, the Christian community. The subject of the discussion and the halakah is the question of how divorce is to be dealt with. Within this context, verses 6–9 speak of sexuality and patriarchal marriage. Traditionally, literary criticism often assigned verses 2–9 and 10–12 to different historical levels (e.g., vv. 2–9 to Jesus and 10–12 to the Markan congregation). Such a literary-critical operation does not dispense with the necessity of understanding the text in the form in which it has been passed on. Only then may one ponder whether a hypothesis on how the text came to be adds something to the interpretation—or violates the text.

The *linguistic weight* (step 1) becomes noticeable especially in the multiplicity of formulations for sexual and social communion. The quotation from Gen. 2:24 contains such a formulation: "one flesh." In verse 8 it is reinforced through commentary and interpreted in the following verse as a bonding accomplished by God. This clear emphasis of the bonding of man and woman in marriage is the basis of the halakah in verses 10–12: marriages may be ended by divorce but the bonding continues even after the divorce. For that reason, divorce is obviously a small problem for the Christian community. The bigger problem is the second marriage after a divorce (see below).

The *genre* of the text (step 1) is widely seen to be "the disputation" in relation to verses 2–9 and "the instruction of the disciples" in relation to verses 10–12. Both these determinations of genre incorporate specific christological presuppositions within themselves, but do so without reflecting on them: Jesus is the herald of a teaching which, when compared to that of Judaism or the Pharisees, is quite new, and he is himself, beyond question, the church's teacher of authority. Historically and theologically, these determinations of the genre are questionable. Was Jesus actually seen in opposition to Judaism when this text came to exist and was passed on, until it finally found its written form? (See 8.3.) Was his teaching held to be something that had to be carried forward with institutional force? I judge both presuppositions to be historically untenable. I find the construct of a "disputation," in which the male and female participants are enticers who wish to "tempt" Jesus, theologically questionable. Both parts of this text should, instead, be seen within the frame of Jewish theological culture, as a debate among equals (as a rule, they were men) using arguments from the common tradition of Scripture. Neither side of the debate intends to produce a victim. Jesus is being tested (v. 2) as to whether he is able to hold up his side theologically; he is not being "tempted" in order to create reasons for his execution (Mark 3:6 notwithstanding—*this* text gives no indication of a "tempting"). Even Paul does not consider Jesus' halakah in verses 10–12 as an authority beyond question (see 1 Cor. 7:10-16; he also understands v. 9 as halakic). For him, a second marriage by men after a divorce is not a problematic matter (1 Cor. 7:11), and he himself sets aside an obstacle put in the way of a woman divorcing (1 Cor. 7:15; here we have a reflection in Paul of the tradition that we know from Mark 10:9-12 par.). In what the Gospels say concerning divorce and in 1 Corinthians 7 we face excerpts of a living halakic process of discussion rather than an authoritative and normative doctrine within the context of the institution "the church." I regard the genres in verses 2–12 to be a theological debate within the context of interpreting the Scriptures (vv. 2–9) and halakic teaching within a process of discussion (vv. 10–12).

The *context of intellectual history and of the history of religion* (step 2) that has to be taken into consideration when interpreting Mark 10:2-12 is, on the one hand, the biblical creation narrative and how Jews in the first century C.E. interpreted it. On the other hand, the halakic discussion among Jews and their praxis concerning divorce have to be heeded. Contrary to the still widely held belief that Jewish women did not have the right to initiate a divorce, one must now reckon with the fact that they did have this right and made use of it (Brooten; see also now P. Yadin 18, lines 57–59, in N. Lewis). In order to understand our text, it is important to be clear about what view of bonding in marriage is present in Mark 10:2-12. Verses 10-12 state clearly that after a divorce (that is to say when the first marriage partner is still living) a second marriage is adultery in the sense of the Decalogue. The man or woman who enters a second marriage breaks the bond of the first marriage. The divorce only partially dissolves the marriage; it regulates above all the economic aspect of divorce. For this understanding of marriage, Deut. 24:1-4 and Papyrus Murabaat 115 are to be consulted. Deut. 24:4 states that a woman, who after her divorce marries again, becomes unclean for her first marriage partner (but only for him). Should the first husband wish to marry his first wife again after her second marriage has been dissolved by divorce or her second marriage partner has died, he is forbidden to do so; her sexual intercourse with the second man has made her taboo for the first man. She could marry any man in a third marriage except her first partner. Sexual intercourse establishes a bond that is dissolved not by divorce but only by renewed sexual intercourse; even after that it still signals a special relationship.

Papyrus Murabaat 115 (see Koffmahn, 127ff.) addresses "the rare case of the remarriage or reconciliation of two persons who were previously married to each other" (133). "Despite the customary terminology of divorce letters that the woman is free and that she can become the marriage partner of any other Jewish man, it is to be doubted that the giving of a letter of divorce brought about the absolute dissolution of the marriage" (134). The financial aspect of this marriage contract corresponded to the regular contracts of marriage. But the division of the relationship (line 5: "to unite himself anew and take back the same Salome . . .") indicates that there is no new beginning of marriage for the man. In any case, the woman had not entered into a new marriage in the meantime.

Mark 10:11 presupposes that the bonding continues beyond a divorce also for a man. But one must at least ask whether men in the Jewish and early Christian context might not as a matter of course have several sexual relationships simultaneously or consecutively without one relationship touching the other. Paul judges the relationship of a Christian man (married or not) with a female sex-trade worker to be *porneia* and not adultery. His repudiation of *porneia* in this sense is directed against a praxis that men in the Christian congregation (in Corinth) took for granted. He has to muster a solid argument (1 Cor. 6:12-7:7; see Wire) in order to question the sense of Christian men that buying sex was quite alright. We know from the papyri in the Babatha archive that Babatha, a Jewish woman who died at a relatively young age at the time of Bar Kokhba, was married (after the death of her first partner) in a second marriage to a man who was married (see Lewis). But men's polygyny was morally suspect in Judaism of that time (see Billerbeck, 3:650).

Mark 10:2-12 moves within the context of the Jewish discussion on marriage and divorce. The exclusivity of the married relationship and the continuity of the sexual bond beyond divorce is presupposed for men here, as it is, for example, in Qumran, CD 4:20–5:6.

A social-historical analysis critical of patriarchy (step 3) of Mark 10:2-12 has to establish what the social consequences were and are of the praxis the text presupposes and propagates.

There is an assertion made, especially in older exegesis, that Jesus taught the absolute prohibition of divorce because he sought to protect women from men arbitrarily wanting a divorce. This misses the reality of women altogether. Women guarded carefully their letters of divorce because those letters assured them certain rights and clarified their financial situation. Letters of divorce served the protection of women. To do away with them would have meant the loss of important rights for women. But Mark 10:2-12 does not say at all that Jesus taught the absolute prohibition of divorce. The text does not advocate that divorce is prohibited but, rather, that the women and men who follow Jesus should not remarry after a divorce, because the former sexual bonding contin ues to be effective beyond divorce (even without further sexual contact between the former partners, would need to be added).

The text says about divorce that it was a judicial regulation, sanctioned by Moses and God, "against the hardness of your hearts" (v. 5). This is addressed to the Pharisees mentioned in verse 2. The "your" is most likely spoken especially to the men who lay claim to the possibility of divorce (the Pharisees' question in v. 2 is about them). Jesus does not dispute the judicial legitimacy of men practicing divorce; he judges that practice to be "hardness of heart."

The widespread anti-Judaistic interpretation of this passage is inappropriate to the text. What Jesus judges to be an expression of "hardness of heart" toward God, namely the particular practice of divorce, is said in this interpretation to be *Jewish* law or statutes of *humans* contrary to *God's* original creative will. *God's* original creative will is said to be the foundation of the *Christian* understanding and practice of marriage. The

Christian condemnation of divorce, based on the assumption of an absolute prohibition of divorce by Jesus, is anti-Judaistic in its roots. This anti-Judaistic pattern of interpretation shapes the whole tradition of interpretation of Mark 10:2-12 and parallels known to me, even where the rootedness of the text's conceptions in the Jewish context is explicitly discussed. The anti-Judaism remains even when interpreters try to defuse the supposed "prohibition of divorce" by Jesus with a construction from dogmatics, to the effect that Jesus reckoned with the "hardness of heart" also of Christian women and men and that, like the Sermon on the Mount, his prohibition of divorce is the radical claim of God that indicts humans and before which they prove themselves to be sinners. (Here God stands against the Torah of Moses.)

The text does not issue a prohibition of divorce as long as it is read in the context of Mark 10:2-12. Only the literary-critical isolation of Mark 10:9 from Mark 10:10-12 permits the assumption of a prohibition of divorce. But it is not only the literary context that needs to be taken seriously; so must the social-historical one. As indicated, a prohibition of divorce would in the light of the social praxis of the Jewish people be hostile to women. Part of the social-historical context to be studied is the early Christian praxis of divorce. Neither in Paul nor elsewhere in early Christianity does an absolute prohibition of divorce by Jesus play any role; what one does find is pressure on women seeking divorce to make divorce more difficult (Justin, *Second Apology* 2, 1 Cor. 7:10f. could be read this way). Arguments against women seeking divorce are not based on a prohibition against it by Jesus; instead, a point of morality is cited ("jealousy" is the reason for the couple's estrangement) or else Gen. 2:23 is used (for example, I Clement 6:3). The ancient church did not interpret Mark 10:9 and parallels as an absolute prohibition of divorce; it did not prohibit divorce either nor even make it more difficult for men. The Christian praxis that is advocated by this text is not to prevent divorce but, rather, to make it more difficult to enter a second marriage during the lifetime of the divorce partner by defining it as adultery. However, this praxis (see 1 Cor. 7:10-12, where it applies only to women) is part of the context of early Christianity's option for a life free of marriage (see 7.3).

But if Mark 10:6-9 cannot be understood as an absolute prohibition of divorce by Jesus, what does the text say?

This question may be answered with the help of the next working step. Those who have been raised from the dead (Mark 12:25) live without marriage—that is what *the literary context* says (step 4), supporting thereby the freedom from marriage of the divorced (Mark 10:10-12). This does not mean that married people live under the verdict that marriage is the second-best solution (as Paul states in 1 Corinthians 7). The Jesus tradition, rather, draws the relationship of married folk into a larger vision. I wish to describe this vision by placing Mark 10:6-9 into the context of the Beatitudes, that is, into the larger context of *Jesus' message and praxis* (step 5).

To have one's hunger satisfied and to laugh are signs of the kingdom of God (Luke 6:21 par.). The experience of this eschatological joy may already be had in the community of Jesus' followers through sharing bread and response-ability for and to the tears of sisters and brothers. Early Christianity's praxis of freedom from marriage is not conjoined with a general denigration of sexuality and marriage. Next to the negative view of women's sexuality (1 Tim. 2:12-16) stands the vision of Mark 10:6-9. These verses talk of marriage, as the Beatitudes do, as being satisfied and laughing, in a way that is both visionary and reality-related. The activities of the Jesus movement get their wings from the movement's visions. Mark 10:6-9 describes marriage as a nonhierarchical, encompassing relationship that extends from the sexual relation to the shared household. The man's parents do not have the right to determine the young couple's life—a radical difference from the patriarchal praxis of the whole Roman Empire (including Jewish society). Not a word about the man's dominance—a remarkable fact in light of the fact that, in patriarchy, this dominance is the foundation of the entire social order (see 10.4). Marriage is not entered into for the purpose of producing offspring. Mark 10:6-9 speaks about marriage differently than later Christian or Roman-Hellenistic ethics does. The solemn opening "from the beginning, at the creation . . ." itself indicates that this is not the language of norm, but of vision.

On the basis of the Jewish understanding of sexuality as a gift of creation (see Plaskow), a vision is painted of the happiness of perfect communion between two human beings. The closest parallel in substance to Mark 10:6-9 that I know is the language of love found in the Jewish novel of conversion about Joseph and Asenath, written close to the time of the New Testament. (In terms of methodology, I once again seek to determine the context of intellectual history and of the history of religion [step 2], seeing that the reflections on Mark 10:6-9 in the context of Jesus' message and praxis [step 5] led to new questions.) After a lengthy period of longing, the lovers Asenath and Joseph find each other. Asenath expressed her love—in an unusual manner—by washing her beloved's feet. This would have been done under "normal" circumstances by a slave woman or another woman who stood lower than she did in the hierarchy of the household. For that reason, her beloved rebuffs her doing so.

> Thereupon Asenath said to him: "No, my Lord! For now you are my lord, and I your servant. Why do you choose another virgin to wash your feet? But your feet are my feet and your hands are my hands, your soul my soul. No other is to wash your feet." Thus urging him, Asenath washed his feet. (Joseph and Asenath 20.4f.)

Standhartinger, in particular, demonstrates that next to the "long version" cited above there is a "short version" that portrays a much more self-assured Asenath (106f.).

Asenath's language of humility is in tension with her self-assured action. The story goes on to tell that, having finished the foot washing, she seats herself at Joseph's right hand (or that Joseph seats himself at her right, according to some manuscripts). Sitting at the right hand indicates that one has the seat of honor and participates in power (see Mark 10:37). The text alludes to Gen. 2:24 and points up a traditional interpretation of Gen. 2:24 to which Mark 10:6-9 also belongs. I want to add Song of Songs 8:6 as a further link in the chain of this tradition of interpretation.

> Wear me as a seal upon your heart, as a seal upon your arm. For love is strong as death and passion as irresistible as the realm of the dead. Its fire is blazing, a flame of the Lord.

These texts all sing to a communion that includes the sexual relation. But the word *sexuality* in today's speech is conducive to an inappropriate genitalization of sexuality. That the man will cleave to his wife (Gen. 2:24; Mark 10:7 in one part of the manuscript tradition) and that the two shall be "one flesh" is unjustly narrowed down in the Christian tradition of interpretation today to describing sexual intercourse (see Kirchhoff on 1 Cor. 6:16). Like the two texts I have cited as being parallel in substance to Mark 10:6-9, the four verses from Mark tell of God's gift of an encompassing communion between a man and a woman. All texts clearly manifest a critical awareness of the patriarchal hierarchization of the relation of men to women customary to their societal context. What they do not manifest is the critical awareness that to narrow the sexual relation (in a holistic sense) to the heterosexual relationship (that is, the legitimated marriage) means to deprive all human beings of the creative and rebellious potential of sexual power in other human relationships. This is where the interest in social control, referred to by Judith Plaskow in her "model of energy and control," impinges on the perception of sexuality as a gift of God.

So what does it mean: ". . . let not human beings put asunder"? In the context of Mark 10:2-12, it means that every divorce that leads to a new marriage and, therefore, to the final dissolution of the first relationship, destroys a relationship which, in its origin and essence, could be "as strong as death." That sentence does not mean that broken marriages are indissoluble, that divorces contradict the will of God, and that human beings may in this question tyrannize other human beings. The consequence that the halakah of Jesus draws from this vision of love is to declare a second marriage to be adultery. In the context of early Christian praxis of freedom from marriage, that decision was plausible—and especially for women. Today it lacks plausibility. Today I advocate that the vision of Mark 10:6-9 be extended to every genuine and life-enhancing relationship between human beings. I further advocate that these texts be set free from the prison of their Christian usage as an immovable, normative given. The halakic discussion of earlier days was open to different opinions and decisions and took place in the full awareness that every decision has a limited range of meaning.

The relation of fallen creation to intact creation is addressed in this text by the juxtaposition of "hardness of heart" (v. 5) and the beginning of creation (v. 6). In its interpretation of fallen creation, traditional (and especially Lutheran) dogmatics has declared sin or hard-heartedness to be unchangeable: the world is evil, all humans are adulterers and murderers. That is why harsh laws alone can help. This is not how this text sees it—nor the New Testament (Paul included). The reality of loss and betrayal notwithstanding, there is successful love that spreads the aroma of creation and of God's reign. It is legitimate both methodologically and theologically not only to read Mark 10:6-9 in connection with texts about community in marriage, but also to place them into the context of vision of communion between women, and between God and human beings: Ruth 1:16 and Rev. 21:3-6.

Bernadette Brooten, "Konnten Frauen im alten Judentum die Scheidung betreiben? Überlegungen zu Mark 10,11–12 und 1 Kor 7,10-11," *EvTh* 42 (1982): 65–80; idem, "Zur Debatte über das Scheidungsrecht der jüdischen Frau," *EvTh* 43 (1983): 466–78; Christoph Burchard, *Joseph und Aseneth* (Gütersloh: Gütersloher Verlagshaus Gerd Mohn, 1983);

Monika Fander, 1989 (see 8.2); Renate Jost, *Freundin in der Fremde: Rut und Noomi* (Stuttgart: Kreuz Verlag, 1992); Renate Kirchhoff (see 7.2); Elisabeth Koffmahn, *Die Doppelurkunden aus der Wüste Juda* (Leiden: E. J. Brill, 1968); Napthali Lewis, ed., *The Documents from the Bar Kokhba Period in the Cave of Letters: Greek Papyri* (Jerusalem: Hebrew University of Jerusalem, 1989), with regard to Babatha; Judith Plaskow, *Standing Again at Sinai* (see 8.3); Paul Riessler, *Altjüdisches Schrifttum ausserhalb der Bibel* (1927; repr. Darmstadt: Wissenschaftliche Buchgesellschaft, 1966); Luise Schottroff, *Lydia's Impatient Sisters,* with regard to the model of exegetical working steps; Elisabeth Schüssler Fiorenza, *In Memory of Her;* Angela Standhartinger, *Das Frauenbild im Judentum der hellenistischen Zeit: Ein Beitrag anhand von "Joseph und Aseneth"* (Leiden: E. J. Brill, 1995).

Index of Ancient Sources

First Testament

255

New Testament

Extracanonical Jewish Literature

Early Christian Literature

Literature of Classical Antiquity

Index of Modern Authors